THE ESSENCE OF BUDDHISM

WITH AN INTRODUCTION

THE ESSENCE OF BUDDHISM

WITH AN INTRODUCTION

BY

ANAGARIKA H. DHARMAPALA

BY

P. LAKSHMI NARASU.

GYAN

Published by

Gyan Publishing House
5, Ansari Road
Daryaganj, New Delhi-110002
Phone: 011-47034999, 9811692060
E-mail: books@gyanbooks.com

Distribution Network
gyanbooks.com
India, USA, Canada, UK, Australia, France

ISBN : 978-81-212-2281-5 (HB)
First Published, 1907

2nd Impression 2020

Printed at: Gyan Press, Delhi.

The
Essence of Buddhism
Author: Anagarika H. Dharmapala, P. Lakshmi Narasu

THE
ESSENCE OF BUDDHISM

WITH AN INTRODUCTION

BY

ANAGARIKA H. DHARMAPALA

BY

P. LAKSHMI NARASU.

Buddham çaraṇam gacchāmi.
Dhammam çaraṇam gacchāmi.
Sangham çaraṇam gacchāmi.

Madras:
SRINIVASA VARADACHARI & CO.

1907

Namaççākyamunaye thathāgatāya, arhate, samyak sambuddhāya.

Bright shineth the sun in his splendour by day
And bright the moon's radiance by night,
Bright shineth the hero in battle array,
And the sage in his thought shineth bright
But by day and by night, none so glorious so bright
As Bhagavat, the source of all spiritual light.

—DHAMMAPADA, 387.

There is one alone unchanging,
From whose face the darkness flies,
High-born, luminously beaming,
Uncompared, beyond comprise—
Bhagavat, the far-seeing,
Bhagavat, the very wise.—PARAYAṆA SUTTA.

There is nowhere in all the world
That his reason has not been ;
Not a fact whereof the Master
Has not pierced the origin.
He will end the doubter's questions,
If they will but let him in —*Ibid*.

Dedicated

to

All whose hearts are vast like the sea
And full of compassion and love ;
Whose thoughts, like the sweet Philomel,
Soar high and lofty for ever ;
Who, regardless of consequences,
Use their reason to distinguish
What is true from what is untrue ;
Who work with zeal to share with all
The easy path of salvation
Revealed by Him who read aright
The problem of origination.

PREFACE.

THIS volume is the final form assumed by a series of essays on Buddhist subjects originally contributed to certain South Indian magazines. It has been prepared with the aim of bringing together, within a small compass, the leading ideas of Buddhism, and interpreting them in the light of modern knowledge. It lays no claim to originality. Much of the material it contains may be found in the works of well-known orientalists. Nor does it pretend to be the fruit of Pali or Sanskrit scholarship, despite the quotations it may contain from works in those languages. It professes to be nothing more than the humble offering of a disciple in the service of his Master.

In presenting the teachings of his master it is incumbent on the disciple never to lose sight of the fundamental principles on which those teachings themselves rest. For the Buddha the voice of authority is in truth itself, and wherever the truth leads, thither the disciple must follow. Accordingly, the dictum accepted in all schools of Buddhism as the sole regulative principle is that nothing can be the teaching of the Master, which is not in strict accord with reason, or with what is known to be true. In giving a conspectus of their religion all Buddhist writers of note have sought the aid of logic and psychology. Their regard for the general validity of ideas has been so great that they have not infrequently set aside the *Sutras*, which are commonly regarded as the basis of their religion. Hence, in expounding Buddhism in the light of modern knowledge, the author has in no way swerved from his position as a Buddhist, but has only followed a practice current among the Buddhists from the very earliest times. If he has succeeded in giving Buddhism the aspect of modernity, he has done so, not by seasoning modern ideas with a little Buddhistic sauce, but by getting beneath all forms of Buddhism and bringing to light the essential truths therein contained.

The attention of thoughtful men in Europe and America has been drawn to Buddhism. Already there are in those countries organizations for the spread of Buddhism. A branch of the Mahabodhi Society with its headquarters in Chicago is doing valuable work in the United States. A Japanese Buddhistic Mission, established in San Francisco, publishes a journal, called *The Light of Dharma*, which is said to be widely read in America. A Buddhistic Society, established in Leipzig, besides publishing a journal, called *Der Buddhist*, is actively at work in disseminating the teachings of the Tathāgata by means of popular lectures and cheap literature. Divested of certain mystical outgrowths, Buddhism will doubtless attract many occidentals. Nevertheless it has been asserted that Buddhism is too chaste to win adherents where marriage is not considered detrimental to high thinking. But even on this score Buddhism has nothing to fear. There have been from the earliest times schools of Buddhism that have maintained that a laic also can attain arhatship. A religion that is supple enough to include the *Vajrāchāryas* of Nepal as well as the *Sthaviras* of Ceylon has certainly room in it for puritanical ascesticism as well as the innocent pleasures of a conjugal life.

The possibility of a revival of Buddhism in India has been presaged by an eminent historian. With the spread of education and independent thought it is not unlikely that the Dharma will appeal to that growing circle of thoughtful Indians, who no longer find any charm in Rama or Rahim, Krishna or Christ, Kali or Lakshmi, Māri or Mary. Nor are signs wanting which betoken a lasting interest in the teachings of one whom all India once revered as born to take upon himself the sins of all mankind. As the true *swadeçi* spirit takes firmer root and grows, the immortal name of Sākyamuni, which now lurks in the garbled story of the Buddhāvatār, is sure to rise above the surface of oblivion, and shine in all its eternal glory and grandeur.

The marrow of civilized society, it has been truly said, is ethical and not metaphysical. The forces that underlie and maintain civilized society are not the belief in *ātman* and *brahman*, or trinity in unity, or the immanence and transcendence of God, but truthfulness, charity, justice, tolerance, fraternity—in short, all that is summed up in the word Dharma or Buddhism. Rightly did Emperor Asoka make Buddhism the basis of his government. Not till the "white light" of the Buddha has once again penetrated into the thought and life of the Indians can they hope to regain that pre-eminence among nations that they possessed in the time of Asoka. Not till the *Dharma* becomes the guiding spirit of all nations will their peace and safety be assured. It might be pretentious for the author to hope that his book will prove serviceable in hastening this consummation so devoutly wished. But he cherishes the hope that his book will in some measure be helpful in leading to a clearer understanding of the teachings of his Master.

In conclusion the author expresses his thanks to all his friends who have encouraged him in the preparation of his book, and especially to those who have rendered help in putting it through the press.

MADRAS,
367, MINT STREET,
May, 1907.

P. L. N.

INTRODUCTION.

Namo Buddhāya!

I have read with pleasure, rather rapidly, the "Essence of Buddhism" and glanced through the chapters: Historic Buddha: Rationality of Buddhism; Morality of Buddhism; Buddhism and Caste; Women in Buddhism; The Four Great Truths; Buddhism and Asceticism; Buddhism and Pessimism; The Noble Eightfold Path; The Riddle of the World; Personality; Death and After; The Summum Bonum.

The author is a scientist and as such deserves to be heard. He has made a study of Buddhism from authoritative sources, and as a scholar has analysed the comprehensive system of religion founded by the Tathagato.

India is the home of Buddhism. It is to the people of India that our Lord first proclaimed the Dhamma, 2496 years ago. His first five disciples were Brahman ascetics, and His two prominent disciples, Sariputta and Mahā Moggallana, were Brahmans; the President of the first Council, held three months after His Parinibbana, was Mahā Kasyapa, a Brahman; and the Upholder of the Faith in the time of Asoka was Tissa the "son of the Brahmani Moggali of Moggali." According to the prophetic utterance of our Lord the Dhamma, shedding lustre in its purity, lasted for full 1,000 years in India, and then began the decline following the law of disintegration five hundreds later, when it was brought into contact with the cohorts of Allah, whose fire and sword played havoc with the followers of our Blessed Tathagato. The ruins in Bamian, Central Turkestan, Afghanistan, Kandahar, Kashmir, the Gangetic Valley, and in distant Java, testify to the extirpation of the great religion by the iconoclastic Arabs, fresh in their zeal for the glorification of the 'Prophet of Arabia.'

The home of Buddhism—the Majjhima Desa—since the tenth century A. C. has been made desolate. No yellow robed Bhikkhus and white-robed Upasakas are there to greet the weary pilgrim from foreign lands as in the days of Fa Hian, Huen Chang, and Itsing. After 700 years a new race from the West has conquered India, and thanks to the antiquarian researches of European scholars, they have made it possible for the Indians to again appreciate the ancient Aryan inheritance which was preached to their forefathers under the name of Dhamma.

Professor Narasu is a product of Western culture. He is a scion of an ancient Dravidian family. He completed his education in Western lore under European masters, and he is now professor of science in a first grade college. The superstitions of religion he had abandoned for scientific truth, and his studies in the domain of comparative religion has been accentuated by his observations in the practical daily life of the yogis of Southern India. The law of progress under British Rule in India is slow; but it is manifest in every department of life. The publication of the present volume by Professor Lakshmi Narasu indicates that even from the basis of a purely rationalistic foundation Buddhism appeals to the cultivated intellect more than a theosophic pantheism. Professor Narasu has studied the life of the "Teacher of the Nirvana and the Law" from a purely human standpoint, and discusses the three characteristic aspects of the Dhamma from the standpoint of psychology and science. The "Essence of Buddhism" I recommend to the non-Buddhist and the scientific agnostic, for it will, I hope, give an impulse for a further study of the Dhamma that has given comfort to thousand millions of people within the past 25 centuries.

Anagarika H. Dharmapāla.

MAHA BODHI HEADQUARTERS
ISIPATANA, SARNATH, BENARES.
APRIL 28 $\frac{2451}{1907}$.

CONTENTS.

THE HISTORIC BUDDHA.

PAGE

What Buddhism is—Sākyamuni not a supernatural founder of Buddhism—Incidents in Sākyamuni's life non-essential—Value of Buddha's personality—Birth of Buddha—His early life and renunciation—Training under Arada and Udraka—Severe ascetic penance—The incident with the herdsman's daughter—Attainment of enlightenment—His determination to preach—Starting for Benares and meeting with Upaka—Stay at Benares and formation of the holy brotherhood—Visit to Rajagriha and conversion of Bimbisāra—Conversion of Sariputra, Maudgalyāyana, and Mahā Kāsyapa—Other disciples—Ineffectual plots of Devadatta—Patrons and benefactors of Buddha—State of India then—Calumnies against Buddha and how they were exposed—Daily life of the Blessed One—His method of exposition—His last tour and end—Disposal of the remains of the Blessed One—Historicity of Sākyamuni—His position among founders of religions—His claims to greatness 1

THE RATIONALITY OF BUDDHISM.

A system of philosophy and practical ethics—Reason the ultimate criterion of truth—Futility of authority and revelation—Rationality of all beliefs—Cultivation of faith—Schools and sects of Buddhism—Only one way, that of reason—Reverence to relics and images an act of devotion—Adaptation to pre-existing religions—Invocation of Amida by the Japanese Buddhist—The *triçaraṇas*—No transcendental superiority in Buddha—Attitude towards miracles and wonders—Freedom from fanaticism and persecution—The missionary impulse

PAGE

in Buddhism—Spread of Buddhism—Spirit of generosity and compassion—Influence on the development of arts—Development of science and knowledge—Reason and purity of heart the gist of Buddhism ... 21

THE MORALITY OF BUDDHISM.

The goal of Buddhism—The ten transgressions and ten precepts—The precept against the destruction of life—Sacrifices in ancient India—Care for animals—Partiality for vegetarian diet—Mixed diet the best food—Extreme observance of the precept—Attitude towards war—Spirit of tolerance a result of the observance of the precept—The precept against theft—Motives for such abstinence—Socialistic spirit of Buddhism—The precept against adultery—Sexual excesses denounced by religions—Attitude towards legitimate intercourse—The precept against falsehood—Lying one of the gravest offences—Hypocrisy fostered by churches—Lying under necessity—The precept against drink—Prevalence of drink in Ancient India—Buddhists first to enjoin total abstinence—Nature and effect of alcohol—The six ruinous things, and drink one of them—The precept against vain talk—The precept against evil reports—The precept against selfishness—Jealousy an intense form of selfishness—The precept against evil passions—The demands of justice and equity—Love should be healthy and wise—Duty of practising universal love—Anecdote showing the practice of love—The true import of the Jātakas—Claims of Christianity to be the only religion of love—The precept against ignorance and doubt—Scepticism a means of knowing the truth—The roots of Buddhism—Difference between the ethical teachings of Buddhism and Brahmanism—Ethics of Buddhism not egoistic—Its ethical system a study of consequences, of Karma and Vipāka—Purely autonomous—Moral ideas have nothing to do with supernatural beings—The Eternal self is not of any ethical value—Basis of morality purely subjective—Buddhism teaches that the good of humanity is the

PAGE

good of the individual—Deliverance from sorrow by following good—Morality rests on egoism and altruism is applied egoism—Morality in the Vedanta and in Buddhism—Other differences—The ideal of the future perfection of mankind 39

BUDDHISM AND CASTE.

Universality of salvation—The story of Buddha's beloved disciple and the girl of the Mātanga caste —The Brahman a specially Indian phenomenon—No support for the existence of specific differences in men—Differences only through occupation and conduct—No difference in Dharma between one caste and another—No caste for those joining the Saṅgha—Social conditions then prevailing uncertain—Only the social significance of castes, if any, recognised in Buddhism—The development of caste due to ambition and selfishness—The attitude of later Buddhists—Arguments of the *Vajrasuchi*: Brahmanhood not constituted by life principle or descent or body or learning or origin from Brahma—Attempts by Brahmans to bolster up their religion, the *Gita* one of such attempts—Caste the mainstay of Hinduism—Ethnological basis of caste a pure myth—Failure of attempts to classify mankind—Purity of blood mythical—Heredity has nothing to do with ethical culture—Unwarranted supposition of the possibility of development for superior peoples only—Caste quite noxious, and therefore disregarded by Buddhism 70

WOMAN IN BUDDHISM.

Examples of the high status of women in Buddhism —Low estimation of women in India—Buddhist revolt against this a success—Strict rules for the relations between the sexes—Theoretical equality—Treatment of women fair—Example of Burmese women—Marriage ceremony among Buddhists very simple—A religion of free individuals—That the Teaching is destructive of family life is not true 89

PAGE

THE FOUR GREAT TRUTHS.

The four truths: existence of misery, its cause, emancipation from misery, and means of emancipation—These truths not dogmas—Existence of misery: Schopenhaur's description thereof—Religion arises from the instinct of self-preservation—Attempts at a perfect life: Buddha's attitude—World-process not all perfected—Evolution in all forms of life—Final stage of self-conscious growth to co-extensiveness with all life ... 97

BUDDHISM AND ASCETICISM.

Religion of ancient India sacrificial—Rise in power of the Brahmans who knew the sacrificial arts—Human sacrifice the greatest—Strong belief in self-mortification, illustrated by Bramanism and Jainism—Gautama's trial of self-mortification and his discovery of its fruitlessness—Sermon in the Deer Park at Benares—Asceticism and luxury equally spurned by the Dharma—Wealth rarely procures ease of body and mind—Perfect freedom and sanity of life, the attainment of *bodhi*—The charge of indolence against the bhikshus false—Invaluable services by the bhikshus—Their work in Japan—Wrong allegation of failure to inculcate patriotism, the episode of Ajatāsatru and the Vajji—The greatness of King Asoka, the cause thereof—Utter eradication of egoism and the ideal 106

BUDDHISM AND PESSIMISM.

Buddhism not pessimistic—Inward discord of Schopenhaur contrasted with the inward harmonies of Buddhism—Existence of suffering recognised, but a nobler life opened out—Life is not condemned, but peace must be striven for—Resignation and means of attaining happiness taught—Buddhism not a religion of despair—Duty of furthering evolution with a view to attain perfection 119

THE NOBLE EIGHTFOLD PATH.

PAGE

The middle path, the noble path—Morality of Buddhism represented by the eightfold path—Eight essentials specified—Right belief necessary for right action—Animistic and metaphysical beliefs the sources of religious error—Right action, thought and peace safeguarded by reason and science—Attainment of bodhi directed by right views—Value of actual practice —Purification of one's acts—Observance of moral precepts the practice of morality—Nature of charity—Aim in acts of charity—Right living the outcome of right action—Means of subjective purification—Practice of self-control—Nature of the will, not a faculty determined by itself—Requisites of a rightly directed will—Attainment of the freedom of *bodhi*—Training of the will—Practice of right thought—Intellectual enlightenment essential to salvation—Practice of *Dhyana* for tranquillity—*Dhyana*, not losing consciousness—*Dhyana* and *Yoga* contrasted—*Dhyana* must be coupled with *pragna*—The ten impediments; permanent self and scepticism two of them—Efficacy of ceremonies and rites the third—The remaining seven impediments —Falsity of the accusation against the greater importance in Buddhism of intellectual powers than ethical virtues 126

THE RIDDLE OF THE WORLD.

Everything in a state of flux—Cause and effect—Causal nexus—No first cause—Idea of Iswara falsified by rational argument—Natural laws only descriptive—Argument of purpose fallacious—No connection between morality and Iswara—Morality an outcome of social limitations—General belief in Iswara not a proof of his existence—Historical proofs fallacious—Existence not a manifestation of the absolute—The nature of concepts, higher and lower concepts—Methods to reach the transcendental, three classes thereof—Nature of ecstatic intuition, no proof of a 'subliminal self'—Examina-

PAGE

tion of the claim of ecstasy to be unquestioned—Universe not a product of the individual self—Idealistic position examined—Exact position of the Blessed One, a consistent phenomenalism—One's experiences are given him only as a content of one's consciousness—Memory—Nothing external or internal as contents of consciousness—The practical origin of the distinction between 'I' and "external world." 144

PERSONALITY.

Various views of human personality—Belief in a permanent self or soul most pernicious—Wrong conception of the unity of compound things, the origin of the false belief—Existence of an *atman* categorically denied by Buddhism; permanence of personality apparent, not real—No psychological basis for the existence of an outside experiencing self, the atman—Comparison of the brain to a piano criticised—Mutual conditioning of the ego and not-ego—The ego not an eternal, immutable entity—Criticism of the theory of spontaneity—The freedom of the will examined—Division of the contents of consciousness into two classes, the origin of transcendental entities—Human personality a compound of body and mind—Dissolution of individuality the source of happiness—Denial of a separate self liberates the individual from error 163

DEATH AND AFTER.

Man a complex of skandhas—Life a union of the skandhas, their dissolution death—Consciousness not separable from the organism, proved by psychology—Existence of extra-human spirit agencies not established by the researches of the Psychical Research Society—No evidence of the continuance of the conscious person afforded by science—Individual existence a complex of karmas which, after death, are re-born in others—Transmigration of an actual entity from one birth to another not admitted by Buddha, but the content of the ego is preserved in others—Evolution of the organised animal

PAGE

from its ancestral series—Psychical interdependence of human beings, and continuance of psychic life after the individual—Immortality of humanity—Our lives incorporated and continued in a collective eternity of humanity—Person as well as society, the living embodiment of past physical and psychical activities—Criticism of the Buddhist school believing in a mystery underlying the transmigration of *karma*—Self, immanent and not transcendent—The Buddhist doctrine of *karma* extends over the whole of phenomenal existence—The difference between this doctrine and the Brahmanic theory of transmigration—Perfectability by self-culture and self-control, hence Buddhism not fatalistic—Dissolution of body and mind, but continuance of life in deeds. 179

THE SUMMUM BONUM.

Three corner-stones of Buddhism—*Anityā*, a perpetual flux—Anitya not necessarily illusory (*mithya*)—*Anatmata*, the non-existence of an absolute, transcendent entity—The ego, not unchangeable, but alterable and improvable—Unity of consciousness not explained by the unity of an underlying *atman*—Renouncement of the *atman*, rids sorrow—*Nirvana* not an absorption in the universal soul—Not also an annihilation of all activities—Negative aspect of Nirvana, the extinction of lust, hatred, and ignorance—Nirvana, not the annihilation of personality, but complete attainment of perfect love and righteousness—The law of Karma is binding even after the attainment of Nirvana, ideals of Arhat and Jivanmukta compared—Peace, consolation, and hope attained in Buddhism—The true nature of Dharmakaya—Its universality—The origin of sorrow, anxiety and despair—The path of liberation—Freedom from suffering through the light of Dharmakaya—The all-embracing life of one who has attained Nirvana—The beatitude of Nirvana 199

THE ESSENCE OF BUDDHISM.

THE HISTORIC BUDDHA.

BUDDHISM, or, as it is known among its followers, the Dharma, is the religion preached by the Buddhas. A Buddha is one who has attained *bodhi*. By bodhi is meant an ideal state of intellectual and ethical perfection, which can be attained by man by purely human means. Of the many that have attained bodhi the one best known to history is Gautama Sākyamuni.

Gautama Sākyamuni is generally spoken of as the founder of the Dharma. But Sākyamuni himself refers in his discourses to Buddhas who had preached the same doctrine before him. Nor can we speak of the Buddha as the founder of Buddhism in the same sense as we speak of the founder of Christianity or Mahomedanism The founder of the former religion is essentially a supernatural being ; he is the incarnation of the son of God, who is no other than God himself. No one can call himself a true Christian, who does not accept the divinity of Jesus, and who does not believe that Christ rose from the dead after dying on the cross to take upon himself the sins of all those who believe in him. Mahomed, the founder of the latter religion, though not an incarnation of God or any of his relations or servants, is yet a privileged human being, who was chosen as the special vehicle for the communication of a supernatural revelation to mankind, and no man can call himself a Mahomedan, who does not believe that Mahomed is the prophet of God. But the Buddha nowhere claims to be anything more than a human being. No doubt we find him a full and perfect man. All the same he is a man among men. He does not profess to bring a revelation from a supernatural source. He does not proclaim himself a saviour who will take upon himself the sins of those that follow him. He distinctly tells us that every one must bear the burden of his own sins, that not even a God can do for man what self-help in the form of self-conquest and self-emancipation can accomplish. We read in the *Dhammapāda*, a collection of verses attributed to the Blessed Sākyamuni :

" All that we are is the result of what we have thought : it is founded on our thoughts, it is made up of our thoughts "

" By oneself evil is done ; by oneself one suffers ; by oneself evil is left undone ; by oneself one is purified. Purity and impurity belong to oneself ; no one can purify another."

" You yourself must make an effort ; the Buddhas are only preachers The thoughtful who enter the way are freed from the bondage of sin."

" He who does not rouse himself when it is time to rise, who, though young and strong, is full of sloth, whose will and thoughts are weak, that lazy and idle man will never find the way to enlightenment."

" Strenuousness is the path of immortality, sloth the path of death. Those who are strenuous do not die ; those who are slothful are as if dead already."

Again in the *Mahāparinibbāṇa Sutta* the Buddha gives the following admonition to Ānanda, one of his beloved disciples :

" O Ānanda, be ye lamps unto yourselves. Be ye refuges to yourselves. Hold fast to the Dharma as a lamp. Hold fast to the Dharma as a refuge. Look not for refuge to any one beside yourselves."

" And whosoever, Ānanda, either now or after I am dead, shall be a lamp unto themselves and a refuge unto themselves......it is they, Ānanda, among the seekers after Bodhi who shall reach the very topmost height."

Not only did the Buddha offer no support to favourable interference from supernatural agencies on behalf of man, not only did he offer no promise of exemption from suffering and sorrow as a reward of simple belief in him, but he went further in admonishing his disciples not to attach importance to his individual personality but to remember always the ideal. It is said in the *Vajracchēdika* : " He who looks for me, *i.e.*, the true Tathāgata, through any material form, or seeks me through any audible sound, that man has entered on an erroneous course, and shall never behold

Tathāgata." Similarly in another place we read: "Who say you see me and yet have transgressed the Dharma, are not seen by me, but as though you were distant by ten thousand miles, whereas the man who keeps the Dharma dwells ever in my sight." The same truth is much more impressively brought out in a conversation between the Blessed One and the Brahman Droṇa. Once upon a time the latter seeing the Blessed One sitting at the foot of a tree, asked him: "Are you a *deva*?" And the Exalted One answered: "I am not." "Are you a *gandharva*?"—"I am not"—"Are you a *yaksha*?"—"I am not." "Are you a man?"—"I am not a man." On the Brahman asking what he might be, the Blessed One replied: "Those evil influences, those lusts, whose non-destruction would have individualised me as a deva, a gandharva, a yaksha, or a man I have completely annihilated. Know, therefore, O Brahman, that I am a Buddha." Now the practical lesson of this anecdote is obvious. According to Hindu ideas a deva, a gandharva, a yaksha could assume a human form. It was therefore natural for the Brahman to ask if the being in human form before him was a deva, a gandharva, or a yaksha. But what perplexed the Brahman was that he received a negative answer to each one of his questions, and this led him to his general question. Buddha's answer to it was unequivocal. What was of importance in his eyes was not his form (*rupa*) but his character (*nāma*), the embodiment in practical life of the ideas of compassion and wisdom summed up in the word *bodhi*. He was not only Sākyamuni, but he was also Tathāgata. The eternal truths he taught were nothing but what he himself was in the quintessence of his personality. No wonder therefore that the personality that dominates Buddhism is not Sākyamuni but the Buddha.

Though what is of primary importance is the life in accordance with the Dharma, yet the personality of the Great Teacher is not without value. In so far as that personality is the practical embodiment of his teachings, it serves as a model for the disciple to imitate and follow. As the *Amitāyur-dhyāna Sutra* says: "Since they have meditated on Buddha's body, they will also see Buddha's mind. The

Buddha's mind is his absolutely great compassion for all beings." But it must at the same time be remembered that the teaching of the Blessed One does not rest for its validity on any miracle or any special event in his life as is the case in many another religion. Should the events in the life of Gautama Sākyamuni turn out to be unhistorical, that would not in the least detract from the merit of his teachings. As the Blessed One himself has said, the teaching carries with it its own demonstration.

Stripped of mythical embellishments, the principal events in the life of Gautama Buddha are easily told. He was born about the middle of the sixth century before the Christian era in Lumbinī Park in the neighbourhood of Kapilavastu, now known as Padeira, in the north of the district of Gorakpur. To mark this spot as the birth of the greatest teacher of mankind and as a token of his reverence for him, Empeior Asoka erected in 329 B.C. a pillar bearing the inscription: " Here was the Enlightened One born."*

At Kapilavastu resided the chiefs of the Sākya clan, of whom little would have been remembered, had not Siddārtha been born among them. Gautama's father, Suddhodana, and his mother, Māya, the daughter of Suprabuddha, belonged to this clan. The mother of Siddārtha died seven days after his birth. Under the kind care of his maternal aunt, Prajāpati Gautāmi, Siddārtha spent his early years in ease, luxury and culture. No pains were spared to make the course of his life smooth. At the age of sixteen he was married to his cousin, Yasodhara, the daughter of the chief of Koli, and they had a son named Rāhula. For twenty-five years Siddārtha saw only the beautiful and pleasant. About this time the sorrows and sufferings of mankind affected him deeply, and made him reflect on the problem of life. Impelled by a strong desire to find the origin of suffering and sorrow and the means of extirpating them, he renounced at the age of twenty-nine all family ties and retired to the forest, as was the wont in his day.

After this great renunciation (*abhinishkramaṇa*) the Bodhisattva, the seeker after bodhi, placed himself under the

* Hida bhagavam jāteti.

spiritual guidance of two renowned Brahman teachers, Ārāda Kālāma and Udraka Rāmaputra. The former lived at Vaisālī and was the head of a large number of followers. He was evidently a follower of Kapila, the reputed founder of the Sāṅkhya system of philosophy, and laid great stress on the belief in an *ātman*. He regarded the disbelief in the existence of a soul as not tending towards religion. Without the belief in an eternal immaterial soul he could not see any way of salvation. Like the munja grass when freed from its horny case, or like the wild bird when liberated from its trap, the soul, when freed from its material limitations (*upādhi*), would attain perfect release. When the ego discerned its immaterial nature, it would attain true deliverance. This teaching did not satisfy the Bodhisattva, and he quitted Ārāda Kālāma, and placed himself under the tuition of Udraka Rāmaputra. The latter also expatiated on the question of "I," but laid greater stress on the effects of Karma and the transmigration of souls. The Bodhisattva saw the truth in the doctrine of Karma, but he could not bring himself to believe in the existence of a soul or its transmigration. He therefore quitted Udraka also, and went to the priests officiating in temples to see if he could learn from them the way of escape from suffering and sorrow. But to the gentle nature of Gautama the unnecessarily cruel sacrifices performed on the altars of the gods were revolting, and he preached to the priests on the futility of atoning for evil deeds by the destruction of life and the impossibility of practising religion by the neglect of the moral life.

Wandering from Vaisālī in search of a better system he came to a settlement of five pupils of Udraka, headed by Kaundinya, in the jungle of Uruvilva near Gayā in Magadha. There he saw these five keeping their senses in check, subduing their passions and practising austere penance. He admired their zeal and earnestness, and to give a trial to the means employed by them he applied himself to mortification. For six years he practised the most severe ascetic penances, till his body became shrunken like a withered branch. One day after bathing in the river Nairañjanā (modern Phālgu) he strove to leave the water, but could not rise on account of his weakness. However with the aid of the stooping branch of a tree he raised himself and left the river. But while returning to his abode he again staggered and fell to the ground, and might perhaps have died, had not Sujātā, the eldest daughter of a herdsman living near the jungle, who accidentally passed by the spot where the Bodhisattva had swooned, given him some rice-milk. Having thus refreshed himself he perceived that asceticism, instead of leading him to the goal he sought, brought about only an enfeeblement of both body and mind. Accordingly he gave up all ascetic practices, and paying due attention to the needs of the body he entered upon a course of reflection and self-examination, trusting to his own reason, the light which each one of us carries within himself to attain the truth. One night, while sitting in deep meditation under a fig tree (ficus religiosa), the consciousness of true insight possessed him. He saw the mistaken ways of the faiths that then obtained, he discerned the sources whence earthly suffering flowed, and the way that led to their annihilation. He saw that the cause of suffering lay in a selfish cleaving to life, and that the way of escape from suffering lay in the attainment of the ten perfections (*daśa pāramitās*). With the discernment of these grand truths and their realization in life the Bodhisattva became enlightened; he thus attained *Sambodhi* and became a Buddha. Rightly has *Sambodhi* been called *Svabodhanam* to emphasise the fact that it can be accomplished only by self help without the extraneous aid of a teacher or an *Īsvara*. As the poet says,

> "Save his own soul's light overhead,
> None leads man, none ever led."

Now arrived the most critical moment in the life of the Blessed One. After many struggles he had found the most profound truths, truths teeming with meaning but comprehensible only by the wise, truths fraught with blessings but difficult to discern by ordinary minds (*prathakjana*). Mankind were worldly and hankering for pleasure. Though they possessed the capacity for knowledge and virtue and could perceive the true nature of things, they remained in ignorance, entangled by deceptive thoughts. Could they comprehend the law of Karma, the law of concatenation of cause and effect in the moral world? Could they rid themselves of the animistic idea of a soul and grasp the true nature of man? Could they overcome the propensity to seek salvation through a mediatorial caste of priests? Could they understand the final state of peace, that quenching of all worldly cravings which leads to the blissful haven of *Nirvāṇa?* Would it be advisable for him in these circumstances to preach to all mankind the truths he had discovered? Might not failure result in anguish and pain? Such were the doubts and questions which arose in his mind, but only to be smothered and quenched by thoughts of universal compassion. He who had abandoned all selfishness could not but live for others. What could be a better way of living for others than to show them the path of attaining perfect bliss? What could be greater service to mankind than to rescue the struggling creatures engulfed in the mournful sea of *samsāra?* Is not the gift of Dharma the greatest of all gifts? When the Perfect One considered how sorrow and suffering oppressed all beings, he became very compassionate, and made up his mind to preach to all mankind the eternal truths he had discovered.

With this firm resolve he started for Benares which has been famous for centuries as the centre of religious life and thought. On his way the Blessed One met one of his former acquaintances, Upaka, a naked Jain monk, who, struck by his majestic and joyful appearance, asked: "Who is the teacher under whose guidance you have renounced the world?" The Enlightened One replied: "I have no master. To me there is no equal. I am the perfect One, the Buddha. I have attained peace. I have obtained Nirvāṇa. To found the kingdom of righteousness I am going to Benares. There I shall light the lamp of life for the benefit of those who are enshrouded in the darkness of sin and death." Upaka then asked: "Do you profess to be the Jina, the conqueror of the world?" The Buddha replied: "Jinas are those who have conquered self and the passions of self, those alone are victors who control their passions and abstain from sin. I have conquered self and overcome all sin. Therefore I am the Jina."

At Benares he saw Kaundinya and his four companions in the Deer Park, Isipaṭaṇa. When these five (the *Pañcha-*

vaggiya) saw the Tathāgata coming towards them, they agreed among themselves not to rise in salutation, nor greet him, nor offer him the customary refreshments, when he came, for he had broken his first vow by giving up ascetic practices. However when the Tathāgata approached them, they involuntarily rose from their seats, and in spite of their resolution greeted him and offered to wash his feet and do all that he might require. But they addressed him as Gautama after his family. Then the Lord said to them: "Call me not after my private name, for it is a rude and careless way of addressing one who has become an *arhat.* My mind is undisturbed, whether people treat me with respect or disrespect. But it is not courteous for others to call one who looks equally with a kind heart upon all living beings by his familiar name. Buddhas bring salvation to the world, and therefore they ought to be treated with respect as children treat their fathers." Then he preached to them his first great sermon, the *Dharmachakrapravartana Sutra*, in which he explained the Four Great Truths and the Noble Eightfold Path, and made converts of them. They received the ordination and formed the first nucleus of the holy brotherhood of disciples known as the *Saṅgha.* Soon after, one night the Blessed One met Yaças, the youthful son of a nobleman of Benares, who was wandering like a madman much distressed by the sorrows of this world. The Tathāgata consoled him by pointing out the way to the blessedness of Nirvāṇa, and made him his disciple. Seeing that Yaças had become a bhikshu, his former fifty-four jovial companions also joined the Saṅgha. The Blessed One sent out these sixty as missionaries in different directions to preach his universal religion. Shortly afterwards the Buddha had an accession of a thousand new disciples by the conversion of three leading fire-worshipping ascetics, Uruvilva Kāsyapa, Nadī Kāsyapa and Gayā Kāsyapa, all brothers, with all their followers. To these he preached on a hill near Gayā a sermon on the fire sacrifice. In this discourse he explained how ignorance produced the three fires of lust, hatred and delusion, which burnt all living beings, and how these three fires might be quenched by the giving up of sin and the pursuit of right conduct.

From Gayā followed by his numerous disciples the Blessed One proceeded to Rājagriha, the capital of Magadha. After his great renunciation Siddārtha passed through Rājagriha, and Bimbisāra, the king of Magadha, failing to dissuade him from his resolve to attain bodhi, requested the Bodhisattva to come back to Rājagriha after the accomplishment of his purpose and receive him as his disciple. In compliance with this request the Blessed One now visited Rājagriha. King Bimbisāra, hearing of the arrival of the World-Honoured, went with his counsellors and generals to the place where the Blessed One was, and after hearing a discourse on the nature of the self, became a lay disciple. The purport of this discourse was that the self, the so-called lord of knowledge, was born of sensation and recollection, and its constancy was a mere delusion. After taking refuge in the Buddha the king invited the Blessed One to the royal palace, entertained him and his bhikshus and presented to the Saṅgha his pleasure garden, the bamboo grove *Vēṇuvana*, as a dwelling-place for the homeless disciples of the Great Teacher.

A much more important event connected with the Blessed One's stay at Rājagriha was the conversion of Sāriputra and Maudgalyāyana, both pupils of the wandering monk Sañjaya. One day as Asvajit, one of the first five that were ordained by the Buddha, was going on his alms-seeking round, Sāriputra saw the noble and dignified mien of Asvajit, and asked him who his teacher was and what doctrine he professed. Asvajit replied that his teacher was the Blessed One and that following the Tathāgatha's teaching he had renounced the world. On hearing this Sāriputra went to Maudgalyāyana and told him what he had heard. Then both of them went with all their followers to the Tathāgata and took their refuge in the Buddha, the Dharma and the Saṅgha. The Buddha held both of them in high estimation for their intelligence and learning. Some of the books of the Abhidharma, the philosophical part of the Tripitaka, are ascribed to these two learned bhikshus. Another worthy acquisition to the faith during the Master's stay in the Bamboo Grove was the Brahman sage, Mahā Kāsyapa, who had renounced his virtuous wife, his immense wealth and all his possessions to find out the way of salvation. It was he, who, after the *parinirvāṇa* of the Lord, held a council at Rājagriha under the patronage of King Ajātasatru, and collected the Tripitaka, the Buddhist canon, with the help of a large number of bhikshus. He was in fact the first patriarch of the Buddhist Church.

During his active life as a teacher, the Blessed One made many converts. High and low, rich and poor, educated and illiterate, Brahmans and Chandālas, Jains and Ājīvakas, house-holders and ascetics, robbers and cannibals, nobles and peasants, men and women--all classes and conditions of men furnished him with many disciples, both ordained and lay. Among his converts were King Prasenajit of Kosala, Panchasikha the follower of Kapila, Mahā-Kātyāyana of Benares, King Udayana of Kausāmbi, Kuṭadanta the head of the Brahman community of the village of Danamati, Krishi Bhāradvāja of the Brahman village of Ekanāla, Aṅgulimāla the bandit and assassin who was the terror of the kingdom of Kosala, Āḷavaka the the cannibal of Āḷavi, Ugrasena the acrobat, Upāli the barber who had the honour of reciting the *Vinaya* collection of the Tripitaka in Kāsyapa's Council, and Sunita the scavenger who was despised of men. Some of the members of the Sākya clan who were the close kith and kin of Siddārtha also became the followers of Sākyamuni. Suddhodana, the father of Siddārtha, became a lay disciple, and Rāhula, his son, joined the Saṅgha. Yasodhara, the wife of Siddārtha, and Prajāpathi Gautāmi, his aunt, both joined the order of bhikshunis, which was established with some reluctance by the Master owing to the importunities of Prajāpati Gautāmi and the intercession of Ānanda. Ānanda, who was the Buddha's constant companion and personal attendant, was one of his cousins.

Another of his cousins was Devadatta who became notorious in later days by attempting to found a new sect of his own with severer and stricter rules than those prescribed by the Buddha. When he did not succeed in getting many followers, even though he had a special Vihāra built for him by King Ajātasatru, the son of King Bimbisāra, he plotted many schemes to take the life of Sākyamuni. Murderers were set up to kill the Lord, but they were converted as soon as they saw him and listened to his preaching. The rock hurled down from the Gridhrakuta hill to hit the Master split in twain, and haply both pieces passed by without doing him much harm. The drunken elephant that was let loose on the royal highway just at the time when the Blessed One was coming along that path became docile in his presence. After these failures Ajātasatru, suffering greatly from the pangs of conscience, sought peace in his distress by going to the Blessed One and learning the way of salvation.

Twelve of Buddha's disciples became famous as preachers. These were Ajnāta Kaundinya, Asvajit, Sāriputra, Maudgalyāyana, Mahā Kāsyapa, Mahā Katyāyana, Anuruddha, Upāli, Pindola Bharadvāja, Kausthila, Rāhula, and Purna Maitrāyaniputra. In the conversation with Subhadra just before his death, the Blessed One said: "Save in my religion the twelve great disciples, who, being good themselves rouse up the world and deliver it from indifference, are not to be found."

Among the many patrons and benefactors of the Buddha no names are more famous than those of Anāthapindika, the supporter of the orphans, Jīvaka the physician, Visākha, the mother of Migāra, and Ambapāli, the courtezan of Vāisalī. Sudatta, called Anāthapindika on account of his charities to the orphans and the poor, was a merchant of Srāvashti of immense wealth. He bought at an enormous price a magnificent park at Srāvashti, from Prince Jeta, and built the splendid Jetavana Vihāra for the Buddha and his ordained disciples. Jīvaka was the renowned physician-in-ordinary to Bimbisāra, and was appointed by the king to undertake medical attendance on Buddha and his followers. It was at his instance that the bhikshus, who were previously wearing only cast-off rags, were permitted to accept robes from the laity. Visākha was the daughter-in-law of Migāra, a rich Jain merchant of Srāvashti, but she was generally known as the mother of Migāra, as she was the cause of Migāra's conversion to the Buddhist faith. She was the first to become a matron of the lay sisters, and obtained permission from the Lord to provide the chief necessaries of life on a large scale to the bhikshus and bhikshunis. Another service of hers was the erection of the Vihāra of Pūrvārāma near Srāvashti, which in splendour was inferior only to the Vihāra built by Anāthapindika. Ambapāli, who combined in her not only great beauty but also rare musical talent, presented to the Master her stately mansion and mango grove and became a bhikshuni.

In the time of Sākyamuni India was in a state of great intellectual ferment. There were many other religious teachers less known to fame than Gautama Buddha. The Buddhist books make special mention of at least six heretical teachers. One of them, Sanjaya Belatthiputta, repudiated all knowledge of the self, and propounded a kind of pyrrhonism. Ajita Kesakambala rejected all claims to knowledge by higher insight, and admitting no other life, resolved man into the four elements—earth, water, air, fire—which dispersed at death. Pūraṇa Kāsyapa was an indifferentist, who acknowledged no moral distinctions, and consequently no merit or demerit. Makkhali Gōsala, probably the founder of the sect of Ājīvakas, was a fatalist who admitted no voluntary action and karma. According to him everything was impelled by *niyati* or fate to work out the law of its nature. Man had no power to shape his own life. Everything went through a fixed series of rebirths, and at the end of these the fool as well as the wise put a stop to pain. The Blessed One condemned Makkhali's teaching as the worst of all errors. Nighanta Nātaputta, better known as Mahāvīra among the Jains, was one of the renovators of the Jain faith. He taught the reality of individual souls and the continuance of personal identity after death. He not only believed in transmigration, but also carried down the course of metempsychosis below the level of animal existence to plants and inanimate things. His way of salvation was based on asceticism and inaction. He commended suicide as "good, wholesome, proper, beautifying, meritorious." The Jains claim that Mahāvīra had in his days nearly two hundred thousand followers, including monks, nuns, and laymen.

The great popularity of the Master and the gifts which the pious laics bestowed on his followers created a jealousy in the hearts of the leaders of heretical sects. These conspired to sully the reputation of Sākyamuni and ruin him in the eyes of the people. They induced a heretical nun, Chiñchā, to accuse the Master of adultery before the assemblage. Her calumny was exposed and she was made to suffer terribly for her misdeed. Not baffled by this failure the heresiarchs made a second attempt to slander the Master. This time they induced one Sundarī, a member of one of the heretical sects, to spread a rumour that she passed one night in the bed-chamber of the Teacher. After this slander had been made sufficiently public, the heretics bribed a gang of drunkards to assassinate Sundarī. These scoundrels killed her, and threw her corpse in the bushes close to the Jetavana Vihāra. The heresiarchs then loudly clamoured for the institution of legal proceedings against the Lord. Luckily their plan failed owing to the imprudence of the assassins, who, reuniting after the murder in a tavern and excited by strong drink, quarrelled among themselves and reproached one another of having committed the crime. They were immediately arrested by the police and brought before the royal tribunal. When they were questioned as to the murder of Sundarī, the scoundrels openly confessed their guilt, and declared also the names of those who had employed them to commit the crime. The king ordered the assassins as well as the instigators of the crime to be put to death. On another occasion the heretics instigated Srīgupta to take the life of the Master by poisoning his food and misleading him into a pit of fire, but by pity and calm forgiveness the Holy One

> "Saved Srīgupta from spite and crime
> And showed how mercy conquers e'en a foe,
> And thus he taught Forgiveness' rule sublime,
> To free his followers from the world and woe."

The manner in which the Enlightened One ordinarily spent each day was very simple. He used to rise up early, wash and dress himself without assistance. He would then meditate in solitude till it was time to go on his round for a meal. When the time arrived, he would, dressing himself suitably, with his bowl in hand, alone or attended by some disciples, visit the neighbouring town or village. After finishing his meal in some house, he would discourse on the

Dharma to the host and his family with due regard to their capacity for spiritual enlightenment, return to his lodgings and wait in the open verandah till all his followers had finished their meal. He would then retire to his private apartment and, after suggesting subjects for thought to some of his disciples, take a short rest during the heat of the day. In the afternoon he would meet the folk from the neighbouring villages or town assembled in the lecture hall, and discourse to them on the Dharma in a manner appropriate to the occasion and suited to their capacities. Then, at the close of the day, after refreshing himself with a bath when necessary, he would explain difficulties or expound the doctrine to some of his disciples thus spending the first watch of the night. Part of the remainder he spent in meditation walking up and down outside his chamber, and the other part sleeping in his bed-chamber. During the nine months of fair weather, the Lord was wont to go from place to place walking from fifteen to twenty miles a day. During the rainy season he generally stayed in the Jetavana Vihāra or in the Purvārāma.

The Blessed One's method of exposition was generally adapted to the capacities of his hearers. His discussions with the learned were more or less formal and often coldly logical. But in his conversation with ordinary men the Master generally resorted to similes and parables, fables and folklore, historical anecdotes and episodes, proverbs and popular sayings. The parable of the mustard seed, described in the next chapter, illustrates how the Holy One brought home plain truths to the minds of simple folk. In the conversion of the wealthy Brahman, Krishi Bhāradvāja, the Buddha worked out the process of agriculture into an elaborate allegory. One day while staying in the southern district of Magadha (*Dakshinagiri*) the Buddha visited the Brahman village of Ekanāla. Bhāradvāja was then superintending the labourers in his field. With alms-bowl in hand the Blessed One approached the Brahman. Some went up and paid reverence to the Lord, but the Brahman reproached the Master saying: "O, Sramaṇa, I plough and sow, and having ploughed and sown, I eat; it would be better if you were in like manner to plough and sow, and then you would also have food to eat." "O Brahman," replied the Buddha, "I too plough and sow, and having ploughed and sown, I eat." "But," said the Brahman, "if you are a husbandman, where are the signs of it? Where are your bullocks, the seed, and the plough." Then the Teacher answered: "Faith is the seed I sow; devotion is the rain that fertilizes it; modesty is the plough-shaft; the mind is the tie of the yoke; mindfulness is my ploughshare and goad. Truthfulness is the means to bind; tenderness, to untie. Energy is my team and bullock. Thus this ploughing is effected, destroying the weeds of delusion. The harvest that it yields is the ambrosia fruit of Nirvāṇa, and by this ploughing all sorrow is brought to an end." Then the Brahman poured milk-rice into a golden bowl and handed it to the Lord saying: "Eat, O Gautama, the milk-rice. Indeed, thou art a husbandman; for thou, Gautama, accomplishest a ploughing, which yields the fruit of immortality." When the Holy One desired to point a moral or convey a reproof, he related an anecdote or a fable treating its characters as representing the previous existences of himself and the other persons concerned. Such anecdotes are known as *Jātakas* or birth stories. More potent than his word and his method was his wonderful personality. When he talked with men, his lovely voice struck them with rapture and amazement. Could mere words have converted the robber Aṅgulimāla or the cannibal of Āḷavi? To have once come under his spell is to be his for ever. To meet him is to be penetrated by his love (*maitri*), and to know him is to love him for ever

In his last preaching tour the Master came to the town of Pāvā, and there in the house of Chunda, a worker in metals, he had his last repast. After this he became ill, and moved to Kusinagara in the eastern part of the Nepalese Terai, where he died at the ripe age of eighty about 477 B. C.*

* The actual cause of the death of the Buddha was, coupled with extreme old age, an attack of dysentery induced by a meal of *sukara-maddava*. Some think that the dish consisted of the succulent parts of a young wild boar, while others suggest that sukara-maddava was an edible fungus or mushroom. One suggestion is that the dish consisted not of boar's flesh, but of *sukara kanda*, the root of a bulbous plant which is an article of vegetarian diet.

Even in his last moments he received a monk Subhadra, explained to him the Noble Eightfold Path, and converted him to the true faith. His last words to his disciples were: "Decay is inherent in all compound things. Dharmakāya alone is eternal. Seek wisdom and work out your salvation with diligence."

The remains of the Blessed One were burnt by the Mallas of Kusinagara with all the honours and pomp worthy of a king of kings. After cremation the relics were carried to the town-hall, and guarded there for a week covered by a cupola of lances in an enclosure of bows and honoured with garlands, prefumes, music and dances. When Ajātasatru, the king of Magada, heard of the death of the Lord at Kusinagara, he sent an ambassadaor to the Mallas of that place to demand of them a portion of the relics, as he desired to erect a tumulus (stupa) in honor of these relics. The same demand was also made by the Licchavis of Vaisāli, the Sākyas of Kapilavastu, the Bulis of Alahappa, the Koḷiyas of Rāmagrāma and the Mallas of Pāvā. A Brahman of Vethadvipa also demanded a share on the plea of his being a Brahman. At first the Mallas of Kusinagara were not willing to satisfy these demands, as the Lord attained *parinirvāṇa* in their territory. But on the advice of the Brahman Ḍroṇa, who pointed out to the Mallas the indecency of quarrelling over the relics of one who had preached universal brotherhood, the Mallas of Kusinagara changed their mind. Drona was then entrusted with the distribution, and he took for himself the urn, over which he desired to erect a stupa. After the division the Mauryas of Pippalavana sent an envoy for demanding some relics, but they had to content themselves with the charcoal from the funeral pyre. Those that received a share of the relics (*dhātu*) preserved them in dāgobas (*dhāthugarbhas*) erected in their respective countries. It is said that Emperor Asoka opened these ancient dāgobas and distributed the relics contained in them all over his wide empire, and built more than eighty thousand stupas and dāgobas for their preservation.

Such is, freed from the fanciful additions of a pious posterity, the life of the historic Buddha. How much of it is real history, is rather difficult to say. But as to the historicity of Gautama Sākyamuni himself there can be no doubt. As Minayeff remarks in his *Recherches sur le Buddhisme*, it is beyond doubt that grand historical personalities always appear specially at the commencement of great historic movements, and certainly it has been the case in the history of Buddhism, and we cannot doubt that its development also began with the work of a historical personality. There are, however, some orientalists like M. Emil Senart, who, while not altogether denying the existence of the historic Buddha, try to make out that the few historic elements are so much encrusted with mythical outgrowths that it is almost impossible to determine the former with certainty. "It is necessary," says M. E. Senart in his *Essai sur la Legende du Buddha*, "to recognise that, on the whole, excepting a few authentic souvenirs which easily slip through our fingers, the legend of Buddha represents not a real life, nor even a life coloured with fanciful inventions, but it is essentially the poetical glorification of a mythological and divine type that popular veneration has fixed as an aureole on the head of a perfectly human real founder of a sect."

Examining this view of M. Senart in his monograph on *Māra und Buddha*, Dr. Ernst Windisch writes: "When we consider how long he (Gautama Sākyamuni) lived, how far he travelled, how well-known he must have been to his contemporaries; when we further consider how old certain texts, at least parts of the *Vinayapitaka*, are, it is certainly not uncritical to regard as historical what seems to be a historical reality. This is more in accordance with the historic method than to regard the simple narrative of the life and events of the time as the transfiguration of a myth into ordinary life. Besides, this process must have been effected in a tolerably short time. For, against M. Senart's assertion that the mythical tendency can be traced back to the earliest days of Buddhism, I venture to point out that in the oldest Buddhist literature we meet with only such tendencies as are generally characteristic of ordinary life, persons and events in which no impartial observer can find any trace of a myth. To the historical events which, according to M. Senart, can have only a mythical meaning, belongs above all the tradition that the Buddha attained the highest wisdom under a *nyāgrodha* tree." The same scholar notices in passing the view put forward by Dr. H. Kern that the legend may be taken as perfectly true if we regard it as a mythical transformation of astronomical phenomena, and disposes of it with the remark that Dr. Kern's remarkable knowledge of astronomy enables him to see stars twinkling in regions where there is not the smallest ground for any such assumption.

Whatever may be the verdict of historic criticism on the details of the life of Gautama Sākyamuni, there can be no doubt that among the founders of religions he occupies a marked place. His dignified bearing, his high intellectual endowments, his penetrating glance, his oratorical power, the firmness of his convictions, his gentleness, kindness, and liberality, and the attractiveness of his character—all testify to his greatness. "Among heathen precursors of the truth," writes Bishop Milman, "I feel more and more that Sākyamuni is the nearest in character and effect to Him who is the Way, the Truth, and the Life." Similarly, says even Barthelemy Saint-Hilaire, who has no end of charges against Buddhism: "Than Buddha there is with the sole exception of the Christ no purer, no more touching figure among the founders of religions. His life is without blemish; he is the finished model of heroism, the self-renunciation, the love, the sweetness he commands." But the impartial philosophic critic finds that Gautama Sākyamuni towers above the founders of all other religions by his life, by his personal character, by the methods of propagandism he employed, and by his final success. Gautama Buddha, though born of an aristocratic and ruling class, lived the life of an ordinary man, discarding the narrow distinctions of caste, rank and wealth. He knew the world. He was son, husband, father, and devoted friend. He was not only a man, but never professed to be anything more than a man. He gave a trial to the creeds of his ancestors, but ultimately made for himself a nobler faith. His teaching was perfect, but never pretended to be a supernatural revelation. He did not doubt the capacity of man to understand the truth. He based all his reasoning on the fact of man's existence, and developed his practical philosophy by the observation and minute study of human nature. In an age innocent of science he found for the problems of the Whence, the Whither and the Why solutions worthy of a scientific age. His aim was to rescue mankind from the fetters of passion and avarice and to convince them of an ideal higher than mere worldly good. He preached the gospel of renunciation attainable by meditation, a renunciation which did not lead one to the dreamy quietism of pantheistic or nihilistic philosophy but to the purification of one's activity by intellectual and ethical enlightenment so as to bring one to the love of all beings by faith in an eternal Dharmakāya.

Among the world's religious teachers Gautama Sākyamuni alone has the glory of having rightly judged the intrinsic greatness of man's capacity to work out his salvation without extraneous aid. If "the worth of a truly great man consists in his raising the worth of all mankind," who is better entitled to be called truly great than the Blessed One, who, instead of degrading man by placing another being over him, has exalted him to the highest pinnacle of wisdom and love? "It was the genius unequalled among the sons of men that inspired the Buddha's teaching. It was genius commanding in its dictatorial strength that held together his order. It was genius, the first and last that India saw, that in its lofty aims and universality, foreshadowed the possibility of uniting the people into one great nationality, if such had ever been possible." Indeed the Tathāgata is the Light of the World. No wonder that even those who first rejected his teaching had at last to include him in their pantheon by making him an avatār of one of the very gods whom he had himself discarded!

To the unbiassed thinker even the legends which enshroud the life of Sākyasimha are not without significance. They set before him a truly admirable figure: a man of quiet majesty, of wisdom and pleasant humour, consistent in thought, word and deed, of perfect equanimity and moral fervour, exempt from every prejudice, overcoming evil with good, and full of tenderness for all beings. When surrounded by all his retinue of followers, and glorified by the whole world, he never once thought that these privileges were his; but went on doing good, just as the shower brings gladness, yet reflects not on its work. The Burmese relate that, hearing all people singing his praises, the Blessed One called Ānanda and said : "All this is unworthy of me. No such vain homage can accomplish the words of the Dharma. They who do righteously pay me most honour, and please me most." In some of the legends, the so-called birth-stories, the Buddha is represented as having voluntarily endured infinite trials through numberless ages and births, that he might deliver mankind, foregoing the right to enter Nirvāṇa and casting himself again and again into the stream of human life and destiny for the sole purpose of teaching the way of liberation from sorrow and suffering. The ideal of persistent energy thus held up before the disciple is intensely human. And even if the virtues of the Tathāgata are infinitely superior to those of ordinary men, still the ideal can serve as a pattern and guide. The disciple can always take the Buddha as his model so that the recollection of his heroic and saintly life may assist him to be a hero and a saint as well. In his unbounded love for all beings Sākyamuni stands unparalleled. And it is not a poetic fancy but a profound philosophic truth that makes him the best

"who loveth best
All things both great and small."

THE RATIONALITY OF BUDDHISM.

BUDDHISM is more a system of philosophy and practical ethics than a religion. If by religion we mean something which inspires enthusiasm and fervour, Buddhism is certainly a religion, as it has given spiritual enthusiasm and joy to nearly five hundred millions of the world's population, and has served to carry men through material pains and evils and to make them their conquerors. But if we take as the beginning of religion the fear of God, or the dread of the unknown, or the hankering for the unseen and the unintelligible, or the feeling for the infinite, Buddhism is certainly not a religion. The most striking feature of Buddhism is that it eschews all hypotheses regarding the unknown, and concerns itself wholly with the facts of life in the present work-a-day world. The Blessed One once told a Brāhman: "There are, O Brāhman, many Sramaṇas and Brāhmaṇas that maintain that night is day, and day is night. But I, Brāhman, maintain that night is night and day is day." To another Brāhman he flatly said: "The Tathāgata is free from all theories." The starting point for Buddhism is not dogma or belief in the supernatural, but the fact of the existence of sorrow and suffering, not merely the sorrow and suffering of the poor and the wretched, but also of those that live in the lap of luxury. Its goal is not heaven or a union with God or Brahman, but to find a refuge for man from the miseries of the world in the safe haven of an intellectual and ethical life through self-conquest and self-culture.

Standing on the firm rock of facts, Buddhism, unlike the so-called revealed religions, has never contested the prerogative of reason to be the ultimate criterion of truth. The Blessed One exhorted his disciples thus: "Do not believe in traditions merely because they have been handed down for many generations and in many places; do not believe in anything because it is rumoured and spoken of by many; do not believe because the written statement of some old sage is produced; do not believe in what you have fancied, thinking that because it is extraordinary, it must have been implanted by a deva or a wonderful being. After observation and analysis, when it agrees with reason and is conducive to the good and benefit of one and all, then accept it and live up to it."* Accordingly Buddhism requires nothing to be accepted on trust without inquiry. It does not want one to believe in order to understand. To no question does it answer : "It is believable, because it is so absurd; it is true, because it is so impossible." It has been sometimes said that the "will to believe" plays a more important part in life than reason. If we once grant the will to believe, we must equally grant the will to disbelieve. Further, what is the will to believe, but the will to hold something certain which one feels to be uncertain, the determination to beguile and hypnotise oneself in such a way as to accept as true what is clearly perceived to be error? The will to believe is nothing else than the will to deceive, first oneself and then, naturally, others. It is only a euphonious name for hypocrisy, which may be good for a church or a Jesuit, but not for religion or the seeker after truth.

The Blessed One rejects as worthless all recourse to authority and revelation for deciding between truth and error. The Buddha regards the frequent citation of the "holy" words of the Vedas by the Brāhmans as the vain repetition of the words of others and not as indicative of faith. "It is as if a number of blind men were leading one another; the first one does not see; neither does the middle one see; nor does the last see." The Enlightened One draws a clear distinction between "the mere reception of the truth" and "the knowledge of the truth." Just as a spoon holding honey knows not the flavour of what it holds, so does a man who has simply received the truth with a believing heart. Just as a slave mounting up to the place from which a king has addressed his retinue and repeating the same words cannot become a king, just as the mere writing on the sand of the words "come hither" cannot make the bank of a river move from one side to the other, similarly the mere acceptance of doctrine or dogma on the authority of others can never

* *Kālāma Sutta, Anguttara Nikāya.*

lead to enlightenment, to that spiritual comprehension which alone can bring about freedom from sorrow. On the other hand the knowledge of the truth involves both a subjective and an objective element, and therefore possesses two criteria. Firstly the perception of truth is possible only for a mind free from prejudice and passion. Secondly, as truth never lies on the surface, it needs pains to dive deep and grasp it. Higher than the knowledge of the truth is its internal appropriation, the practical realization of the truth through suitable training and development of one's intellectual and moral powers, the acquisition of enlightenment by investigation and contemplation coupled simultaneously with moral rectitude and love for all beings.

In Buddhism there are no beliefs which are not the outcome of knowledge. It does not constrain the rational human mind to dwell upon insoluble problems. Is the world eternal, or is it not eternal? Is the world finite, or is it not finite? Such questions have no value for Buddhism. "These inquiries," says the Blessed One in *Poṭṭhapāda Sutta*, "have nothing to do with things as they are, with the realities we know; they are not concerned with the law of life; they do not make for right conduct; they do not conduce to the absence of lust, to freedom from passion, to right effort, to higher insight, to inward peace." Nor does Buddhism contain anything esoteric or mystic. In his last moments the Lord said to Ānanda: "I have preached the truth without making any distinction between exoteric and esoteric doctrine; for in respect of the Dharma, Ānanda, the Tathāgata has no such thing as the closed fist of a Teacher who holds something back." On another occasion the Buddha said: "Secrecy is characteristic of three things: women who are in love seek secrecy and shun publicity; so also do priests who claim to be in possession of special revelations, and all those who stray from the path of truth. Three things shine before the world and cannot be hidden. They are the moon, the sun, and the truth proclaimed by the Tathāgata. There is no secrecy about them." Such dicta flatly contradict the oft-repeated assertion that the Buddha taught during his lifetime secrets to his favourite disciples, or left a so-called "esoteric doctrine" to be treasured and handed down among a select few, but held back from the common herd. Nor is there the smallest justification for classing Buddhism with the various oriental mystifications. On the other hand it is found to be the very negation of all mysticism in both religion and philosophy. It is the only religion which does not lean for its support on the glamour of the unintelligible. It is the only religion which is *a priori* not in contradiction with the discoveries of science. No divorce between science and religion will ever be possible in Buddhism as in other religions. Though the Buddha had not the same detail of scientific information at his disposal as we possess to-day, he was still familiar with the essential problems of psychology, philosophy and religion. He saw in broad outline the correct solution of the problem of religion. He taught a religion based upon facts to replace a religion based upon the assumptions of dogmatic belief.

Though the Dharma does not ask you to believe blindly, still it lays great stress upon the cultivation of faith (*sraddha*). By faith of course is not meant the belief in something which is irrational and absurd, or the belief in creeds or dogmas, or the determination to be satisfied with unproved and unwarranted statements, but the conviction that truth can be found. While reason enables man to arrange and systematise knowledge so as to construct truth, faith gives him determination to be true to his convictions and ideals. Faith becomes superstition when it parts company with reason, and worse still when it fronts it in flat contradiction, but reason without faith would turn a man into a machine without enthusiasm for his ideals Reason seeks disinterestedly to realise right order where it is not, but faith gives character and strength of will to break through the five hindrances of mental sloth, lust, malice, spiritual pride and pyrrhonism. While reason rejoices in the truths it has already found, faith helps it onward to further conquests, to aspire after the attainment of what has not yet been attained, to work strenuously for the realisation of what has not yet been realised. It is faith alone that can transform cold abstract rationalism into a religion of fervent hope and love. The Blessed One said:

"By faith one crosses over the stream,
By strenuousness the sea of life;
By steadfastness all grief he stills,
By wisdom is he purified."

People fancy that they can look for Buddhism in books and scriptures. It is no doubt true that the Buddhists all over the world possess books, called the *Tripitaka*, which are divided into *Sutra*, *Vinaya*, and *Abhidharma*; the first containing the conversations of the Buddha with some one of his audience, the second the discipline established by him for his ordained disciples, and the last the discussions by known authors on philosophical subjects. But ever since the earliest times the Buddhist brotherhood has been divided into many schools and sects. There have been four *nikāyas* and eighteen sects. The members of one and the same *nikāya* have never been in perfect agreement among themselves, not to speak of their disagreement with the other groups. Traditions have been opposed to traditions. In each sect again there have been Sautrāntikas, Vaināyikas, and Ābhidharmikas. The Sautrāntikas and the Ābhidharmikas of one and the same sect have never agreed with each other, and the Sautrāntikas of one sect have been opposed by those of a rival sect. Even at the present day the Buddhists may be classified into three groups: the Southern, who abide in Ceylon, Burma, Siam and Anam; the Northern who live in Tibet, China, Manchuria, Mongolia, and Siberia; and the Eastern who are found in Japan and Formosa The southern Buddhists follow the Hīnayāna or the Lesser Vehicle; the northerns are Lamaistic and highly ritualistic; and the easterns are followers of the Mahāyāna or the Greater Vehicle. Now the Tripiṭaka of the Hinayānikas is not the same as that of the Mahāyānikas Which of these schools then has really preserved the words of the Teacher? There is only one way out of the difficulty, and that is the one pointed out by the author of *Çikshāsamucchaya*: "*Yadkinchid subhāshitam tad sarvam buddhabhāshitam.* Whatsoever is rightly spoken and free from error, that is the teaching of the Buddha." Nothing can be the teaching of the Lord which does not conform to reason and experience. Such was also the dictum laid down by the Council of Vaisālī which met a hundred years after the death of the Master to settle the disputes between the rival sects into which the Buddhist community had become split up.*

Truly speaking there is only one way (*ekayāna*) shown by the Lord to the *summum bonum*, and that is the way of reason (*tatvayāna*), but from a practical point of view one may distinguish three means. These means are, in plain language, piety, philosophy, and striving for the welfare of one's fellow beings. These are respectively designated by the terms *Srāvakayāna*, *Pratyekabuddhayāna*, and *Bodhisatvayāna.* Higher than the simple piety of the *srāvaka* or *upāsaka*, is the self-acquired enlightenment of the *pratyekabuddha* or *arhat;* higher than this enlightenment for one's own salvation is the unselfish devotion of the *bodhisattva* to the spiritual elevation of others. The highest unity which embraces all these three is that of the *samyak sambuddha*, who, like Gautama Sākyamuni, becomes the universal teacher of the world. That such is the manner in which the so-called vehicles are to be understood is shown by the parable in the *Satdharmapundarīkam* of a man who, seeing his house on fire and his children playing unconcernedly within it, induces them to come out by the promise of toys. Here the Tathāgata is the father who sees his children playing in the consuming fire of worldliness and employs different expedients to bring them out of this burning house and lead them to the safe asylum of Nirvaṇa. These different *yānas* prove the universality of Buddhism, making it suitable for the highest as well as the lowest order of intelligence; the former being supplied with the religion of the intellect and the latter with the religion of the emotions.

Some of the popular phases of Buddhism, such as reverence paid to the Master's relics and images and the frequent invocation of the name of Amita, seem to conflict with its highly rationalistic character. But it must

* "In their philosophical expositions," says Wassiljew in his *Buddhismus* (p. 288), "the Buddhists set aside the Sutras, which serve as the basis of their religion. They have regard only for the general validity of ideas and for logical and psychological laws and only with the help of these they give a conspectus of their views and interpret them."

not be forgotten that the religion of the common people is never a true picture of the religion they profess. In every form of Buddhism the road to the attainment of the *summum bonum* lies always through the contemplation of the Four Great Truths and the pursuit of the Noble Eightfold Path. But, as Itsing, the Chinese pilgrim, remarks, "the meaning of the truths is so profound that it is a matter beyond the comprehension of vulgar minds, while the ablution of the holy image is practicable to all. Though the Great Teacher has entered Nirvaṇa, yet his image exists, and we should revere it with zeal as though in his very presence. Those who constantly offer incense and flowers to it are enabled to purify their thoughts, and those who frequently bathe this image are enabled to overcome their sins that involve them in darkness." In the same strain said the Regent of Tibet to Col. Younghusband: "When Buddhists look upon an image of the Buddha, they put aside thoughts of strife, and think only of peace." In the reverence paid to the images or the relics of the Blessed One there is no implication of grace, of providence, of recompense effected by a God, or of succour furnished by a saviour. On the other hand such a notion is categorically discarded by the Buddhists. As the commentator on the *Bodhicharyāvatāra* says: "*Sukhasya dhukkasya no kopi dāta, parodadātīti kubuddhirēsha.* It is a foolish idea to supose that another can cause us happiness or misery." The result of devotion is independent of the object worshipped and is entirely subjective. Says Nāgasena in *Milindapanha:* "Men by offering reverence to the relics of the jewel treasure of the wisdom of the Tathāgata, though he has died away and accept it not, cause goodness to arise within them, and by that assuage and allay the torment of the threefold fire." Devotion is beneficial and salutary, because it favours humility and destroys the thought of self.

Just as the Buddha resorted to tales and parables as a means of moral and spiritual instruction, so also the Buddhist philosophers employed the imagination as an instrument for the spiritual elevation of ordinary mankind. But it is evident from their philosophical works that they did not themselves believe in the reality of their fanciful creations. Among such creations are to be included the various *Dhyāni-bodhisattvas* and *Dhyāni-buddhas.* The former enabled Buddhism to coalesce readily with the pre-existing religions of the various peoples to whom it passed, though such coalition not infrequently proved disastrous to the Dharma itself by making it lose its specific features. By the application of one of their fundamental doctrines, namely, the Jātaka theory, the Buddhists transformed the gods of the peoples they came in contact with into Bodhisattvas or Avatāras of the primordial Buddha. The Dhyāni-buddhas are supposed to represent the ideal counterparts of the actual Buddhas. Amitābha, the ideal counterpart of the historic Gautama Buddha, is regarded as dwelling in Sukhāvati, the land of bliss, but represents nothing more than the infinite light dwelling in the hearts of men, which, if followed, will lead to the blissful port of Nirvāṇa. It is the name of this Dhyāni-buddha that is often invoked by the Japanese Buddhists.

In what spirit the Japanese Buddhist invokes the name of Amita is revealed by the following quotation from a leaflet published by the Buddhist Propagation Society of Japan. "Rejecting all religious austerities and other action, giving up all idea of self-power, we rely upon Amita Buddha with the whole heart for our salvation in the future life, which is the most important thing: believing that at the moment of putting our faith in Amita Buddha our salvation is settled. From that moment the invocation of his name is observed to express gratitude and thankfulness for Buddha's mercy; moreover, being thankful for the reception of this doctrine from the founder and succeeding chief priests whose teachings were so benevolent and as welcome as light in a dark night, we must ever keep the laws which are fixed for our duty during our whole life." Nevertheless all cult of adoration is foreign, not to say antagonistic, to the most elementary principles of Buddhism. As the author of the *Bodhicharyāvatāra* says: "*Hitāsamsana mātrena buddhapuja visishyate.* It is by the practice of good deeds we render to Buddha the most perfect adoration." In another verse the same author interprets the worship of the

Tathāgata as the getting rid of the sorrows of the world and giving happiness to all beings.

Not infrequently people confound the Buddhist *triçaraṇas*, or the vows of taking refuge in the Buddha, the Dharma and the Saṅgha, with what is ordinarily called prayer. In Buddhism there is no such thing as prayer. The Blessed One rejects all prayer for an object, which, as George Meredith says, is "the cajolery of an idol, the resource of superstition." In the place of prayer we have what is called *pranidhāna*. But this is no begging. It is only a self-discipline which is capable of producing nothing more than subjective results. No more is expected from it than what Kant speaks of as the natural effects of prayer, namely, that the dark and confused ideas present in the mind are either clarified, or that they receive a higher degree of intensity, or that the motives of a virtue receive greater efficacy.

Rationality and sanity are in evidence in all points of Buddhism. The Buddha does not claim superiority by virtue of any transcendental peculiarity of his nature, surpassing everything terrestrial. It may be true that one of the eighteen sects, the *Lokottaravādina*, contend that the Tathāgata is not subject to worldly laws. But this is a small minority. And the Buddha himself has clearly told us how he became a Buddha by a course of moral preparation and by the acquirement of the necessary knowledge, which it is in the power of every mortal to attain by a severe struggle. The Buddha did not say: "You must not trust to yourself. You must depend wholly on me. You cannot be righteous except through a power implanted in you from above"; but he has repeated times without number: "You must trust to yourselves. You can take nothing from me. You must be righteous through your own efforts. You have to depend on yourselves for the final getting rid of all selfishness and hence all suffering." In his last moments he spoke to Ānanda as follows: "Surely, Ānanda, should there be any one who harbours the thought, 'It is I who will lead the brotherhood,' or 'the Order is dependent on me,' it is he who should lay down instructions in any matter concerning the Order. The Tathāgata thinks not, Ānanda, that he should lead the Brotherhood or the Brotherhood is dependent on him. Why, then, should he leave instruction in any matter concerning the Order? Therefore, O Ānanda, be ye lamps unto yourselves. Be ye refuges to yourselves. Hold fast to the truth as a lamp. Hold fast as a refuge to the truth. Look not for refuge to any one beside yourselves."

Another testimony of the rationality of Buddhism is its attitude towards miracles and wonders. That in a religion which recognises no supernatural or extramundane god there can be no miraculous interference from outside nature needs so special proof. Nevertheless the possibility of acquiring wonderful powers by wholly natural means is not denied. The Buddha is described in the legend as acquiring the six *abhijnās* with the attainment of perfect enlightenment. Further the legend speaks of the concurrence of wonderful natural phenomena, such as earthquakes and thunderstorms, with events of extraordinary ethical significance. Still the disciples of the Buddha are not permitted under any circumstances to work wonders or boast of supernatural powers to raise themselves in the esteem of others. The legend says that Piṇḍola, being challenged by heretics to work a miracle, flew up into the air, and brought down an alms-bowl which had been fixed on a pole. The Buddha reprôved him for this, and forbade his disciples to work miracles for display. On one occasion some of his adherents entreated the Buddha to permit his missionaries to work wonders, as that would elevate them in the eyes of others. The Buddha replied as follows:* "There are three kinds of miracles. The first is the miracle of power, in which extraordinary power is manifested, as in walking on water, exorcising devils, raising the dead and so forth. When the believer sees such things his faith may become deepened, but it would not convince the unbeliever, who might think that these things are done by the aid of magic. I therefore see danger in such miracles, and I regard them as shameful and repulsive. The second is the miracle of prophecy, such as thought-reading, soothsaying, fortune-telling, etc. Here also there would be disappointment, for these too in the eyes of the unbeliever would be no better than extraordinary magic. The last is the miracle of instruction. When any of my disciples brings round a

* Kevaddha Sutta.

man by instruction to employ rightly his intellectual and ethical powers, that is the true miracle." Thus did the Blessed One without denying the possibility of all miracles forbid the making of converts by all other means than argument and instruction.

What methods the Blessed One employed when he was expected to work a miracle is clearly shown by the interesting legend of Kisāgotamī. Kisāgotamī, a young woman, had an only son, and he died. In her grief she carried the corpse from house to house, asking for medicine. The people reproved her saying: "You have lost your senses you are asking medicine for your dead boy." At last one man advised her to go to Sākyamuni, the Buddha, who was the Great Physician that could give aid to all. So Kisāgotamī repaired to the Blessed One and implored him to give the medicine that would cure her boy. The Buddha answered: "I shall cure your boy, if you bring a handful of mustard seed from a house where no one has lost a child, husband, parent or friend." So she wandered from door to door, and the people, through pity, readily offered her mustard seed. But when she questioned if a son or daughter, a father or mother had died in the family, the answer she received everywhere was: "Alas! the living are only few, but the dead are many." All day long she wandered through the city, and at last when night set in she began to think: "Ah, it is a difficult task. I thought that my son alone died, but in this city the dead are more numerous than the living.

"This is the law not only for villages or towns,
Not for one family is this the law;
For all the wide worlds, both of men and gods,
This is the law—that all must pass away."

When she thought so, her selfish affection for her child disappeared. She went to the forest, buried the child, and returned to the Blessed One. The Holy One comforted her by preaching to her the Dharma, which serves as a soothing balm to all troubled hearts.

Of Buddhism alone can it be affirmed that it is free from all fanaticism. Its aim being to produce in every man a thorough internal transformation by self-culture and self-conquest, how can it have recourse to might or money or even persuasion for effecting conversion? The Tathāgata has only shown the way to salvation, and it is left to each individual to decide for himself if he would follow it. Every religion ministers to certain needs and inclinations, and, however superstitious it may appear at first sight, contains some germs of truth. Buddhism endeavours to point out those germs of truth and nourish them by giving a new and better interpretation. The Master has said:

> "Revere your own, revile no brother's faith.
> The light you see is from Nirvāṇa's sun,
> Whose rising splendours promise perfect day.
> The feeble rays that light your brother's path
> Are from the self-same sun, by falsehoods hid,
> The lingering shadows of the passing night."

Accordingly the Buddhist kings of the world have been the most tolerant and benign. Emperor Asoka, though an ardent Buddhist himself, showered his gifts on the Brāhmans, the Jains, the Ājīvakas as well as the Buddhists. In his twelfth rock-edict Asoka says: "Whosoever raises his own sect to the skies, and disparages all other sects from special attachment to his own with a view to encourage it, does thereby much harm to his own sect." The Buddhist kings of Ceylon in the Middle Ages were kind and considerate to the followers of the other faiths that then prevailed in their country. The Pāla kings of Bengal, who were zealous Buddhists, bestowed gifts also upon the Brāhmans. But Pushyamitra, who adored and sacrificed to the Devas, destroyed many Sanghārāmas and killed the bhikshus who dwelt there. Sulapāṇi, the great founder of the Bengal school of law, made the very sight of a Buddhist atonable only by the most severe penances. The Brāhmans make a boast of their persecution of the Buddhists and the Jains. In China the Buddhists were thrice persecuted very severely by the Confuçianists. Nor did Buddhism escape persecution at the hands of the Japanese Shintoists. Islam was perpetuated by persecution and bloodshed. Christianity has cost two thousand years of war, persecution, millions of money and thousands of human lives. But Buddhism, even where it was persecuted has never persecuted in return. Nowhere in the Buddhist books do we find such sentiments as are breathed by the following: "But these mine enemies which would not that I should reign over them, bring hither and slay before me." "And whosoever shall not receive you, nor hear your words......it shall be more tolerable for the land of Sodom and Gomorrah in the day of judgment than for them." Compare with these words the following admonition of the Blessed One in the *Saddharmapundarīkam*: "The strength of charity is my abode; the apparel of forbearance is my robe; and voidness (self-lessness) is my seat; let (the preacher) take his stand on this and preach. When clods, sticks, pikes, or abusive words, or threats fall to the lot of the preacher, let him be patient thinking of me." The model placed before the Buddhist preacher is Purṇa, an emancipated slave, who, after becoming a rich merchant, renounced everything and became a bhikshu. When he was informed of the perils of his enterprise to preach the Dharma to a wild tribe, he replied: "When I am reproached, I shall think within myself that these are certainly good people, since they do not beat me. If they begin to beat me with fists, I shall think they are mild and good, because they do not beat me with clubs. If they proceed to this, I shall think that they are excellent, for they do not strike me dead. If they kill me, I shall die saying: 'How good they are in freeing me from this miserable body.'"

The missionary impulse of Buddhism is a product *sui generis*. It is wholly foreign to Brahmanism; the Brahman loves and lives a lonely supercilious life. On the other hand the Buddhist can not do without propagating his faith. The psychology of Buddhism leads to those universal relations between man and man which are summed up in the idea of brotherhood. And it is this universal idea which produces the universal feeling termed the missionary motive. Of all gifts the gift of the Dharma is the greatest. "Go ye, O bhikshus, for the benefit of the many, for the welfare of mankind, out of compassion for the world. Preach the doctrine which is glorious in the beginning, glorious in the middle, and glorious in the end, in the spirit as well as in the letter. There are beings whose eyes are scarcely covered with dust, but if the doctrine is not preached to them they can not attain salvation. Proclaim to them a life of holiness. They will understand the doctrine and accept it." Such were the loving words addressed by the Exalted One to his disciples. In strict accordance with this mandate, the disciples of the Great Teacher have always considered others first and themselves afterwards. Forgetful of home and life, indifferent to renown and failure, they have laboured to open the eyes of the crowds deceived by false teaching. To spread the holy doctrine they travelled over lands and seas, crossed through snowy mountains and sandy deserts, braved all toils and dangers. The names of Kumārajīva, Fā Hian, Huen Thsang, Hui Shen, Dipānkara Srignāna are sufficient evidence of the strength and enthusiasm which the Dharma can inspire into the minds of its adherents.

Without the aid of the sword, or Maxim guns, or howitzers, Buddhism carried its message of peace and good-will to the barbarous hordes of the most populous parts of Asia and civilized them. "How a religion which taught," says Max Muller, "the annihilation of all existence, of all individuality and personality as the highest object of all endeavours, could have laid hold of the minds of millions of human beings, and how, at the same time, by enforcing the duties of morality, justice, kindness, and self-sacrifice, it could have exercised a decidedly beneficial influence not only on the natives of India, but on the lowest barbarians of Central Asia, is a riddle which no one has been able to solve." But the riddle is by no means insolvable, if due regard is paid to the spirit of tolerance that characterizes the religion of the Blessed Teacher. It was its benign tolerance that enabled Buddhism to accommodate itself to the minds and ways of animistic and ancestor-worshipping races and vastly elevate them in the scale of civilization. Without its character of universality the Dharma would never have been capable of developing those marvellous faculties of assimilation which we observe in its attitude to the Bon in Tibet, the Tao in China, the Shinto in Japan, the Nāt in Burma, and the Prēta in Ceylon. It is its character of being an *āgama*, a preparation for the attainment of truth, and not a dogmatic religion like Christianity or Islam, that gives Buddhism sufficient breadth and suppleness to comprehend theism as well as atheism, monism as well as dualism, polytheism and pantheism, fetichism and animism, idolatry and iconomachy, contemplative quietists and boisterous jumpers, gods and demons, saints and heroes, higher beings and lower beings, worlds above and worlds below, heavens and hells; and yet makes it the one religion which imposes no dogma or article of faith on any of its followers. If on the whole the underlying spirit leads to a beautiful and noble life, and manifests itself in kindness, charity and tolerance, in forbearance and forgiveness, in fortitude and cheerfulness, in a sense of the largeness and mystery of things, why should not a little superstition be permitted?

Among religions, Buddhism is the only one that breathes a spirit of unbounded generosity and compassion for all beings. Nowhere in the life of the Buddha do we come across the drowning of pigs by handing them over to devils, or the cursing of fig trees for not bearing fruit out of season. Buddhism has always shrunk from inflicting pain even in self-defence. Not only did it teach that knowledge (*pragnā*) without benevolence (*maitri*) is barren, but it carried out this teaching so consistently in practice as even to endanger its own existence. It has always deprecated war between nation and nation. It has constantly discouraged capital punishment. It sought everywhere to abolish bloody sacrifices. As the *Mahāvastu* says, it is the advent of the Buddha that put an end to *asvamēdham*, *purushamēdham*, *pundarīkam* and other kinds of abominations in India.

A tangible way in which a religion manifests its actual influence upon civilization is art. The great glory of Buddhism is that it has always ministered to the satisfaction of aesthetic aspirations. Wherever Buddhism has prevailed, artistic pagodas, vast vihāras, beautiful stupas have come into existence. The finest buildings in Japan are the Buddhist temples. The beauty and charm of the frescoes of Ajanṭa caves serve as monumental proofs of the wonderful inspiration which the religion of the Tathāgata imparted to art. Brahmanism had no art of its own in India, and the plastic arts of later Vaishnavism and Saivaism are the bastard children of the sculpture of the bhikshus. As Dr. Grünwedel[1] says, "the figurative part of Brahman art, so far as we are now acquainted with it, is based essentially upon Buddhist elements—so much so indeed that the Saiva figures which originated at the same time as the Northern Buddhist,appear to have fixed types, whilst the iconography of the Vishnu cult embraces chiefly Buddhist elements to which different interpretation has been given. But still more dependent on Buddhism are the representations of Jaina arts." In satisfying the æsthetic aspirations of its adherents Buddhism has in no way deviated from its fundamental principles. For the Buddhist all enjoyment is negative, and only by the perpetuation of this negation can selfishness be destroyed. In the appreciation of the artistic and the beautiful one loses one's self. Hence a fostering of the love of the beautiful can not but minister to individual salvation, and the promotion of art necessarily serves as a means of universal salvation.

Not only for the arts, such as architecture and sculpture, painting and engraving, is India indebted to Buddhism, but also for science and culture in general. The best era of Indian medicine was contemporary with the ascendancy of Buddhism. The ancient Brahmans might have derived the rudiments of anatomy from the dissection of animals in sacrifices. But the true schools of Indian medicine rose in the public hospitals established by Asoka and other Buddhist kings in every city.[2] Charaka, the author of the well-known *Charakasanhita*, was the court physician of the Bhuddhist king Kanishka. Nāgārjuna[3] infused new life into the science of Āyur Veda. To his lofty intellect and extensive scholarship India owes the revised edition of *Suçruta* now in use. The latter part of Suçruta's treatise, which bears the name of *Uttaratantra*, is entirely the work of Nāgārjuna's independent research and thought. In the spirit of a true Buddhist Nāgārjuna popularised the science of Āyur Veda by teaching it without reserve to all classes without distinction of caste. All sciences and arts were studied

[1] Buddhistische Kunst in Indian.

[2] The Buddha taught: "Whosoever would wait on me, let him wait on the sick"—Mahāvagga.

[3] He was the fourteenth patriarch.

in the chief centres of Buddhist civilization, such as the great Buddhist university of Nālandā. According to the great orientalist Theodore Benfey the very bloom of the intellectual life of India, whether it found expression in Buddhist or Brahminical works, proceeded substantially from the Dharma, and was contemporaneous with the period in which Buddhism flourished. "The noblest survivals of Buddhism in India," says Sir W. W. Hunter, "are to be found, however, not among any peculiar body, but in the religion of the people; in that principle of the brotherhood of man, with the reassertion of which each new revival of Hinduism starts; in the asylum which the great Vaishnava sect affords to women, who have fallen victims to caste rules, to the widow and the outcaste; in that gentleness and charity to all men, which take the place of a poor law in India, and give a high significance to the half satirical epithet of the 'mild' Hindu." When Buddhism took root in China, it started a new development and gave such a great impetus to Confucianism as to produce in it some deep thinkers like Luh Siang San, Chu Tze and Wan Yang Ming. Wherever Buddhism entered into the life of a people, it always gave them refinement and embellishment. In his *Things Japanese* Prof. Basil Hall Chamberlain says: "All education was for centuries in Buddhist hands, as was the care of the poor and sick. Buddhism introduced art, introduced medicine, moulded the folklore of the country, created the dramatic poetry, deeply influenced politics and every sphere of social and intellectual activity. In a word Buddhism was the teacher under whose instruction the Japanese nation grew up."

The tree is known by its fruits. Buddhism put reason in the place of authority; it discarded metaphysical speculation to make room for the practical realities of life; it raised the self-perfected sage to the position of the gods of theology; it set up a spiritual brotherhood in place of hereditary priesthood; it replaced scholasticism by a popular doctrine of righteousness; it introduced a communal life in the place of isolated anchoret life; it infused a cosmopolitan spirit against national exclusiveness. Dogma and miracle are wisdom to the Christian; kismet and fanaticism are wisdom to the Moslem ; caste and ceremonialism are wisdom to the Brahman ; asceticism and nakedness are wisdom to the Jain ; mysticism and magic are wisdom to the Taoist ; formalism and outward piety are wisdom to the Confucian ; ancestor-worship and loyalty to the Mikādo are wisdom to the Shintoist ; but love and purity are the first wisdom to the Buddhist. To work out his salvation the Buddhist must renounce all selfish desires, and live to build up a character of which the outward signs are purity of heart, compassion for all, courage and wisdom born of calm insight into truth, and that tolerance and freedom of thought which does not hinder one's house-mates in possessing their beliefs in peace. Of Buddhism alone can it be said that it has discarded all animism, all dogmatism, all sensuality, all asceticism, all ceremonialism, that it consists in charity and benevolence, self-denial and self-consecration. It alone teaches that there is hope for man only in man, and that

> "that love is false
> Which clings to love for selfish sweets of love."

THE MORALITY OF BUDDHISM.

THE goal of Buddhism is the freedom from sorrow and suffering. This cannot be attained except by the destruction of all selfish cravings. The self as such manifests its activity in *trishṇā* or grasping desire. If the self is to be annihilated, *trishṇā* must be suppressed. For the annhilalation of an organ really consists in reducing the interval of time between two inhibitory states of that organ. Accordingly, if the self, considered as the organ producing sorrow and misery, is to be annihilated, it can be effected only by the infinite prolongation of the state in which all *trishṇā* or *upādāna* is absent, that is to say, only by the continual avoidance of all evil and the doing of good.

"If the Noble Path be followed,
Rest and freedom will be man's;
If selfishness be his guide,
Sin and trouble will drag him along."

All acts of human beings become evil by ten transgressions, and by the avoidance of these their conduct becomes good. These ten transgressions are the three sins of the body, the four sins of speech, and the three sins of the mind. The three sins of the body are murder, theft and adultery. The four sins of speech are lying, slander, abuse and idle talk. The three sins of the mind are covetousness, hatred and error. "If a man having such faults," says the Blessed One, "does not repent, but allows his heart to remain at rest, sins will rush upon him like water to the sea. When vice has thus become more powerful, it is still harder than before to abandon it. If a bad man, becoming sensible of his faults, abandons them and acts virtuously, his sins will day by day diminish and be destroyed, till he obtains full enlightenment." Accordingly the Enlightened One taught the following ten precepts* for the guidance and salvation of his followers.

* These ten precepts (*daçakuçalāni*) should not be confounded with the ten precepts (*daçaçikshapada*) specially intended for the Sramaneras. The ten virtues here enumerated are to be practised by all Buddhists.

I. From the meanest worm up to man you shall kill no animal whatsoever, but shall have regard for all life.

" Let him not destory, or cause to be destroyed, any life at all, or sanction the acts of those who do so. Let him refrain even from hurting any creature, both those that are strong, and those that tremble in the world."—*Dhammika Sutta.*"

" Suffuse the world with friendlines; let all creatures, both strong and weak, see nothing that will bode them harm and they will learn the ways of peace."—*Chulla Vagga.*

In accordance with the spirit of this precept Buddhists all over the world have abstained from killing animals either for pastime or for sacrifice. In Ancient India before the birth of Buddhism the slaughtering of animals for sacrifice was exceedingly common. In the *Satapatha Brāhmaṇa*, it is stated that men, horses, bulls, rams and she-goats were used for sacrifice. In the *Asvalāyana Sutra* mention is made of several sacrifices in which the slaughter of cattle formed a part. One of them is called *Sulagāva* or " spitted calf,' and from the directions given for eating the remains of the offering it is evident that the animal slaughtered was intended for food. Manu (v. 35) declares that the man who, having in due form performed a (*mathuparka* or other) ceremony, fails to eat flesh meat will be doomed to be born an animal for twenty generations. A guest was called *goghna*, cow-killer, because a cow used to be killed on the arrival of a distinguished guest. The *Mahābhārata* bears testimony to the high value of flesh as an article of diet. Bloody offerings are still common in many of the temples of Northern India. Nevertheless we find in the mouth of every Hindu the well-known saying *Ahimsā paramo dharma.* How has this change been brought about? We cannot say that it is wholly due to a natural disposition to benevolence. For we find a learned and thoughtful Hindu like Saṅkara defending the *Jyotishṭoma* sacrifice as a holy act, though it involves the shedding of blood, on the ground that that sacrifice is enjoined by the Vedas as a duty. The true reason of the change of feeling towards bloody sacrifices, is given by the author of the *Nirṇaya Sindhu.* This writer says: " The slaughter of large bulls and large sheep for Brahmans versed in the Vedas, though duly ordained, should not be effected being detested by the public. Further the rule, let a cow fit for offering to Mitra and Varuṇa, or a barren cow, or one that has ceased to bear after first calving be sacrificed, is duly ordained, but such sacrifice, being opposed to public feeling, should not be performed." What could have been instrumental in producing this revulsion of public feeling against the ordinances of the Vedas, were it not the Buddhist denunciation of all bloody sacrifices? "Here (*i.e.*, in my kingdom) no animal," promulgated Emperor Asoka, "shall be slaughtered for sacrifice, nor may holiday-feasts be held, for His Majesty King Priyadarsin sees manifold evil in holiday-feasts." The Buddhist appeal to humanity was so strong that it created a horror against the vain sacrifice of animal life, which even a devout belief in the authority of the Vedas and the Smrithis could not overcome.

Not only does the Buddhist abhor the vain destruction of animal life, but he also regards it as his duty to care for the well-being of all animals. The second edict of Asoka says: "Everywhere in the dominions of His Majesty King Priyadarsin, and likewise in the neighbouring realms...everywhere, on behalf of His Majesty King Priyadarsin, have two kinds of hospitals been established, hospitals for men, and hospitals for beasts. Healing herbs, medicinal for man and medicinal for beast, wherever they were lacking, have everywhere been imported and planted. In like manner, roots and fruits, wherever they were lacking, have been imported and planted. On the roads, trees have been planted, and wells have been dug for the use of men and beast." Everywhere in Buddhist countries is the love for animals widely spread.

Another result of the observance of the precept against the destruction of life is the strong partiality for a vegetarian diet noticed in all Buddhist lands. In the first edict of Emperor Asoka, we read: "Formerly, in the kitchen of His Majesty King Priyadarsin, each day many thousands of living creatures were slain to make curries. At the present moment, when this pious edict is being written, only these three living creatures, namely two peacocks and one deer, are killed daily, and the deer not invariably. Even these three creatures shall not be slaughtered in future." Such

Buddhists as eat meat will not themselves slaughter the animals whose flesh they eat. But there seems to be no reason to suppose that the Buddha strictly prohibited the use of meat. In the *Amagandha Sutta* a Brāhman, abstaining from meat on the ground of its defiling him, is told that what defiles a man is not the eating of flesh, but a bad mind and wicked deeds. When the schismatical Devadatta requested the Blessed One to prohibit his bhikshus from using salt, milk, curds and meat, he refused to impose such stringent rules, as they would lead more to asceticism than to the Middle Path which he taught. Once the naked Nirgranthas, learning that the Buddha was given food with meat in it at an entertainment given to him by a layman, went about sneering the Master for eating meat specially prepared for him. The Master hearing of this said: "My disciples have permission to eat whatever food it is customary to eat in any place or country, provided that it is done without indulgence of the appetite, or evil desire." The last repast which the Master partook in the house of Chunda, the metal worker, is said to have contained dried boar's flesh, but it has also been pointed out that the Pali word generally interpreted as boar's flesh might also mean boar's wort which is a kind of edible mushroom.

The question of food cannot be solved by psychological or ethical principles, but only in accordance with physiology and hygienic experience. The best food for man seems to be a mixed diet, as his teeth and his digestive apparatus are composite. He possesses certain carnivorous teeth, and certain glands which hardly exert their function except under the stimulus of meat. His digestive apparatus produces some ferments which can do nothing else than digest starch. It may be possible for man to subsist on a purely vegetable diet. Abstention from all animal food may have beneficial results under certain conditions. But all people, ancient and modern, have used a mixed diet. People that profess to abstain from meat, use milk, curds, butter, cheese, eggs. It cannot be denied that flesh speedily increases strength and ordains great development and that there is no food superior to flesh. All that hygiene has to teach us in this respect is that the simpler food of the less civilized peoples is preferable to the refined dishes of the civilized nations.

Devout Buddhists have sometimes pushed to extremes their observance of this precept. They have observed it more in the letter than in the spirit. In the seventh century an imperial decree was issued in Japan forbidding the people to eat the flesh of cattle, horses, dogs, monkeys, or fowls. The Chinese Buddhists are reported to have once prevailed upon a pious emperor to prohibit the manufacture of silk, because the worms in the cocoons had to be killed before their threads could be utilized. But this exaggeration has not the approval of the Blessed One. The life of animals is indeed sacred, but it cannot be as sacred as human life. Animals are tended and cared for, because they in some way subserve general happiness. The exaggerated regard for animal life shown by the pious Buddhists would prove disastrous to the very animals on whose behalf the appeal is made. Our only obligation to animals is to give them a happy life and a painless death. Even the practice of vivisection, if guarded from all abuse, is justifiable in so far as it subserves general happiness.

Though the Buddha has not told us precisely his views as to war, yet there are many passages in the *Sutras* from which we may surmise his attitude. He has deprecated all killing, whether it be for pastime, or for sacrifice, or in warfare. But he has also taught that he who wages war in a righteous cause after having exhausted all means of preserving peace is not blameworthy. In the description of his fight with Māra, the personification of evil, the Tathāgata compares himself to a king who rules his kingdom with righteousness, but being attacked by envious enemies goes out to wage war against them. He who goads others to wage war in a righteous cause suffers the consequences of his own evil doing. Devout Buddhist kings did not shrink, when necessary, from waging war in a righteous cause, though they lamented the vain shedding of blood. When there is just cause for war, war must be waged openly and resolutely but without cherishing feelings of hatred and revenge. Nowhere does the Buddha approve of that ovine indolence which would not resist evil even by right methods. When Prince Abhaya was stirred up by Nātaputra to tax the Blessed One with having used unkind language to the schismatic Devadatta, the Blessed One explained that a word which is true and is intended to do good, though it give pain, is right. So also war in a righteous cause, which is intended to teach a lesson to the evil doer, is right, though it may involve the shedding of blood. But Buddhism is wholly opposed to that militarism which represses all sympathetic feelings, developes the cruel side of human nature, and commends hatred of enemies and revengefulness as the highest virtues. On the other hand, it inculcates long suffering, forgiveness and loving kindness which show not only goodness of heart but also deep wisdom.

The most noteworthy result of the strict observance of this precept is the spirit of tolerance so characteristic of Buddhism. It is the only religion which has never sought to extend itself by the sword or by might. Indeed the Buddhist holds his religion to be the truth, but he lets others hold their beliefs in peace. The twelfth edict of Asoka reveals to us the true motive of this toleration. "His Majesty King Priyadarsin does reverence to men of all sects, whether ascetics or householders, by donations and various modes of reverence. But His Majesty cares not so much for gifts or external reverence as that there should be a growth of the essence of the matter in all sects. The growth of the essence of the matter assumes various forms, but the root of it is restraint of speech, to wit, a man must not do reverence to his own sect by disparaging that of another man for trivial reasons. Depreciation should be for adequate reasons only, because the sects of other people deserve reverence for one reason or another. By thus acting a man exalts his own sect, and at the same time does service to the sects of other people. By acting contrariwise a man hurts his own sect, and does disservice to the sects of other people. For he who does reverence to his own sect, while disparaging all other sects from a feeling of attachment to his own on the supposition that he thus glorifies his own sect, in reality by such conduct inflicts severe injury on his own sect. Concord is, therefore, meritorious, in that one hearkens to the teachings of others and hearkens willingly." This spirit of tolerance proved disastrous to Buddhism, especially where it came in contact with Islam.

II. You shall neither rob nor steal, but help every one to be the master of the fruits of his labour.

"A disciple knowing the Dharma should refrain from stealing anything at any place, should not cause another to steal anything, should not consent to the acts of those who steal anything, should avoid every kind of theft."—*Dhammika Sutta.*

"He is the greatest gainer who gives to others, and he loses most who receives from others without giving a compensation."—*Dhammapāda.*

In abstaining from theft the chief motives ought to be contempt for wealth and the conviction that the mere accumulation of property is a hindrance to the higher life. The Buddhist has certainly to acquire wealth, but not accumulate property for himself. Said the Blessed One to Anāthapindika: "It is not life and wealth and power that enslave men, but the cleaving to them. He who possesses wealth and uses it rightly, will be a blessing unto his fellow beings." Whatever the Buddhist acquires is for the benefit of all mankind. This is one of the several reasons for the Buddhist bhikshu's vow of poverty. The individual bhikshu is poor, but the *Saṅgha*, the community of aspirants for bodhi all over the world, may be rich. He whose thought and labour are expended altogether upon his family is only one step above the man who labours and plans solely for himself. Such a man, though often an angel to his family, may prove a demon to all the rest of the world. Do not diamonds for the wife often cost the bread of the poor?

The spirit of Buddhism is essentially socialistic, that is to say, it teaches concerted action (*samānārthā*) for social ends. It is therefore totally opposed to that industrialism which with its unremitting, sordid, unscrupulous and merciless struggle for wealth as the one supreme object of human effort is eating the very vitals of the so-called advanced nations of the world. This fascination for the pursuit of wealth has produced within trade circles perfect callousness to the feeling of human brotherhood. "If success attends upon a man in his commercial warfare, if his intrigues are only wide enough to give him plunder on a vast scale, he passes for a merchant-prince, the rightfulness of whose transactions is little questioned, and men poorer but of noble sentiment, extend to him the hand of fellowship and call him a gentleman." The accumulation of capital in the hands of a few can have no ethical justification. Capital is not, as some economists contend, the result of individual saving, but is the surplus seized from producers, many of whom are reduced to a condition of slavery for the comfort and the enjoyment of a few. How does this differ from theft? There are still other kinds of theft. "It can never be pretended that the existing titles to such property (landed property) are legitimate......Violence, fraud, the prerogative of force, the claims of superior cunning—these are the sources to which these titles may be traced." So said Herbert Spencer in the first edition of his *Social Statics.* Matters have not changed much since then, and his remark is as true now as then. Even the so-called imperialism of modern times is but a manifestation of a robbing propensity, for it means nothing else than the lust of conquest and the greed of commercial gain. Buddhism prohibits theft of every form, whatever may be the euphemistic name by which it may be known. Even in extreme need, when no other means of relief may be available, there can be no justification for seizing others' goods.

III. You shall not violate the wife of another nor even his concubine, but lead a life of chastity.

"A wise man should avoid unchastity as if it were a burning pit of live coals. One who is not able to live in a state of celibacy should not commit adultery."—*Dhammika Sutta.*

"Guard against looking on a woman. If you see a woman, let it be as though you see her not. If you must speak with her, let it be with a pure heart. If the woman be old, regard her as your mother; if young, as your sister; if very young, as your child."

"Guard yourself against a worldly woman who is anxious to exhibit her form and shape, whether walking, standing, sitting, or sleeping, and is desirous of captivating with the charms of her beauty. Restrain the heart and give it no unbridled license. Lust beclouds a man's heart when it is confused with woman's beauty and the mind is dazed."

Religions have generally denounced the sexual impulse and even recommended its absolute repression. This attitude may be irrational but not unjustifiable. There may be nothing undignified or immoral in the proper exercise of the sexual function. It may be even true that all such noble traits as sympathy, fidelity, affection, self-sacrifice, which are included under the term altruism spring from the reproductive instinct. But the excesses connected with the satisfaction of the sexual appetite have been so frightful as to justify the feeling of sinfulness attached to it. The overmastering power of the reproductive instinct has often proved too great even for religion in some forms not to succumb to it. A great number of religious rites and usages are nothing else than symbolic representations of sexual practices. The sexual orgies of the religious festivals of past times and many extravagant religious rites of more recent times owe their origin to the overpowering character of the reproductive impulse. It is, therefore, only natural that special injunctions should be laid down against the improper exercise of the sexual function.

Though the Dharma prohibits all illegitimate sexual relations, it does not follow that sexual intercourse is completely interdicted to those who aspire for the higher life. Were all sexual intercourse in its very nature an obstacle to the higher life, it ought not to have been possible for Siddārtha to attain bodhi. Siddārtha was not only married, but lived in luxury. Why the Dharma condemns sexual indulgence is that it creates a craving for enjoyment, and is the chief cause of various nervous disorders. Though the ostensible object of marriage is the preservation of the species, in reality marriages are contracted not in the interests of the future generation, but solely with regard to the personal interests and enjoyments of the contracting parties. The choice of a wife or of a husband is determined so much by wordly conventions and material interests that neither health nor beauty nor intellect nor heart is considered to be of any value. The Dharma can have no objection to marriages with the high motive of propagating the species. Some

Buddhist schools have maintained that it is possible for a laic to become not only an *anāgāmin*, but also an *arhat.* Some Buddhist books, like the *Manichuda Avadāna*, even make marriage compulsory for the *bodhisattva*, the aspirant for *bodhi*, an idea which may have given birth to the married clergy of Japan. Many married men and women are spoken of in the Buddhist books as having entered the paths.

If the Blessed One left his wife and children and went into homelessness, it was because error prevailed and the world was plunged in darkness. Having reached the deathless Nirvāna he was bent wholly on the one aim of pointing out the path to others, and those of his followers, who like him have left the world, live a life of poverty and celibacy, not for their own sake, for they have given up all attachment to self, but for the sake of the salvation of the world. *Bhikshuta* consists not in wearing the yellow robe but in *bhinna kleçata*, the freedom from sorrow; it is not the mere observance of rules that makes the *arhat*, but the deliverance, the purification of thought and life.

IV. You shall speak no word that is false, but shall speak the truth with discretion, not so as to harm, but with a loving heart and wisely.

"When one comes to an assembly or gathering he should not tell lies to any one, or cause any to tell lies, or consent to the acts of those who tell lies; he should avoid every kind of untruth."—*Dammika Sutta.*

"Speak the truth; do not yield to anger; give if you are asked: by these three steps you will become divine."—*Dhammapāda.*

The Dharma regards lying as one of the gravest of offences that man may commit. There is scarcely a crime or vice into which lying does not enter as an important element. Not only does lying involve an abuse of confidence, but in its essence it is cowardice, "the desire to gain an advantage or inflict an injury which we dare not effect by open means, or to escape a punishment or avoid a loss which we have not the courage to face squarely or submit to." Calumny, flattery, perjury are different forms or grades of lying.

Hypocrisy, which is want of consistency in thought, speech and action, is a form of lying which is fostered largely by churches. Writing on the ethics of conformity, a well-known writer on ethical subjects says: "The student of history sees that hypocrisy and insincere conformity have always been the besetting vice of the religious, and a grave drawback to their moralising influence. Just as lying is the recognised vice of diplomats, chicanery of lawyers, and solemn quackery of physicians."

"Tell a lie and shame the devil" is a proverb that originated from a church whose early representatives, according to Lecky, "laid down a distinct proposition that pious frauds were justifiable and even laudable."

A question of some importance in relation to lying is the lie of necessity. Is lying under all circumstances wrong, or are there conditions under which it is permissible or necessary? "In the case of sexual gratification, of marriage, of food eaten by cows, of fuel for a sacrifice, of benefit or protection accruing to a Brāhman, there is no sin in an oath": says the Code of Manu. But in the matter of lying Buddhism is uncompromising, although it attaches great importance to the motive* that determines an action. Its only behest is: Speak the truth with discretion, but always be truthful; never alter or disguise the truth whatever may be the case; love the truth even to martyrdom.

V. †You shall not eat or drink anything that may intoxicate.

"The house-holder who delights in the Dharma should

* In the sixth lecture of Sutrakritānga the Buddhists are severely ridiculed by the Jains for maintaining that it depends upon the intention of a man whether a deed of his be a sin or not.

† The ten sins which should not be committed are generally enumerated as follows: (1) Killing a living being (praṇātipāda); (2) Stealing (adattadāna); (3) Committing adultery (kāmamithyāchāra); (4) Lying (mṛshāvāda); (5) Slander (paiçunya); (6) Abusive language (pārushya); (7) Frivolous talk (sambhinnapralāpa); (8) Avarice (abhidhya); (9) Evil intent (vyāpāda); (10) False view (mithyādṛshti). But in the treatment adopted in this book drunkenness (surāpāna) has been made the fifth evil, as its avoidance finds a place in the *pancha çīla*, which are obligatory on all Buddhists. The evils represented by (6) and (7) in the above list have been incorporated and dealt with together.

not indulge in intoxicating drinks, should not sanction the actions of those who drink, knowing that it results in insanity.

"The ignorant commit sins in consequence of drunkenness, and also make others drink. You should avoid it as it is the cause of demerit, insanity and ignorance—though it be pleasing to the ignorant."—*Dhammika Sutta.*

"Drunkenness is the cause of the loss of goods and reputation, of quarrels, diseases, immodesty of dress, disregard of honour and incapacity of learning."—*Sigālovāda Sutta.*

The use of intoxicating drinks was exceedingly common in Ancient India. The Vedic Brāhmans indulged largely both in *soma* beer and strong spirits. The most acceptable and grateful offering to their gods was *soma* beer. In the *Rig Veda* we read: "The sacred prayer, desiring your presence, offers to you both, Indra and Agni, for your exhilaration, the *soma* libation. Beholders of all things, seated at this sacrifice upon the sacred grass, be exhilarated by drinking of the effused libation." The object of drinking *soma* is expressly stated to be intoxication. *Sura*, a distilled liquor, was likewise offered to the gods. In the *Sautrāmani* and *Vajapeya* rites libations of strong arrack formed a prominent feature.

At no time in their history have the Hindus as a people abstained altogether from the use of intoxicating liquors as a means of gratification. In the Dharma Sutras beside the *soma* and the *sura* of the *Saṇhitas* we find mention of *madvika* or mowa, *tāla* or toddy spirit, and other liquors. In the Rāmāyaṇa Visvāmitra is said to have been entertained by Vasishta with *maireya* (rum) and *sura.* Sita, when crossing the Ganges on her way to the wilderness, promises to worship the river goddess with a thousand jars of arrack on her return home. Similarly on crossing the Yamuna Sita promises to worship the river with a hundred jars of arrack after the accomplishment of her husband's vow. In the last book of the Rāmāyana, Rāma makes Sita drink pure *maireya*, and both are entertained by hosts of apsaras, who have been exhilarated with wine. In the Mahābhārata, Krishna and Arjuna are described as having their eyes reddened by drinking *madhvi* and *āsava.* Manu says that "there is no turpitude in drinking," though "a virtuous abstinence from it produces a signal compensation." According to the *Mītākshara* the Brāhmans alone have to abstain from all kinds of spirituous liquors, the Kshatriya and Vaishya from arrack or *paishti*, and Sudras may indulge in whatever they liked. In one of the tāntric books Siva addresses his consort thus: "O sweet speaking goddess, the salvation of Brāhmans depends on drinking liquor. I impart to you a truth, a great truth, O mountain-born, that the Brāhman who attends to drinking and its accompaniments forthwith becomes a Siva."[1]

The Buddhists were the first to enjoin total abstinence from strong drinks in India. The reason why the Dharma prohibits strong drink is that intoxication incapacitates a man for rational deliberation without hindering him from acting irrationally. Drunkenness leads the drunkard to treat others irrationally and possibly to abuse them. That drunkenness is the cause of many crimes is a wellknown fact. Hence to put oneself in such a condition is a source of insecurity to others.

Alcohol is more a heat-producer than a tissue-former. It is certain that a portion of the alcohol absorbed undergoes combustion; but a great part of it is disengaged in the form of vapour, as is proved by the breath of drunkards, and the combustion takes place without any special benefit for the regeneration of the tissues. Even the experiments of Dr. Atwater have not proved alcohol to be a veritable food, that is to say, something which is capable of being incorporated into the organism. Alcohol employed in small doses acts as a stimulant to the nervous system; in very feeble doses and in certain cases it may be useful as a medicine. But its abuse is more productive of mischief than good.

According to Buddhism the love of intoxicating liquors is one of the six ruinous things. The other five are wandering about the streets at unreasonable hours; too great a passion for dancing, games and spectacles; gambling[2]; frequenting

[1] See Rajendralal Mitra's Essays on Indo-Aryans, Vol. II.

[2] No vice was so universal as deceit and gambling. Perjury also was not uncommon, and there was no lack of robbers and thieves.—*Zimmer's Altindish Leben.*

vicious company; slothfulness and negligence in the performance of one's duty. "Unseasonable wanderings expose a man to great dangers, and by keeping him from his family oblige him to leave the chastity of his wife and daughters unprotected; and moreover, his possessions are thus liable to depredations. He may likewise be taken in the company of thieves and punished with them. A passion for shows draws a man from his occupations, and hinders him from gaining his livelihood. In gambling success is followed by intrigues and quarrels; loss by bitterness and sorrow of heart as well as dilapidation of fortune. The gambler's word has no weight in a court of law, he is despised by his friends and his kinsmen, and he is looked upon as ineligible for marriage. Frequenting the company of the vicious will lead a man into the houses of women of ill-fame, into drunkenness and gluttony, into deceit and robbery, and all kinds of disorders. Finally the sluggard who neglects his duties fails to acquire new property and that which he possesses dwindles away."

VI. You shall not swear nor indulge in idle and vain talk, but speak decently and with dignity to the purpose, or keep silence.

"The man seeking the higher life must renounce wordly ambition and all luxurious tastes, and unprofitale amusements; he must refrain from idle as well as mischievous words; he must not gossip about great people; he must not speak at all about meats, drinks, clothes, perfumes, couches, equipages, women, warriors, demigods, fortune-telling, hidden treasures, short stories, nor about empty tales concerning things that are and things that are not."

VII. You shall not invent evil reports, nor repeat them. You shall not carp, but look for the good sides of your fellow-beings, so that you may with sincerity defend them against their enemies.

The invention of evil reports and repeating them are only different forms of lying. "One must regard oneself as wicked and others as good; one must therefore give up the evil in him and try to copy the good in others." So says the *Bodhicharyāvatāra*.

VIII. You shall not covet your neighbour's goods, but rejoice at the fortunes of other people.

"Liberality, courtesy, benevolence, kindness—these are to the world what the linchpin is to the rolling chariot."—*Sigālovāda sutta.*

"The wise man who lives a virtuous life, who is gentle and prudent, who is lowly and teachable, shall be exalted. If he be resolute and diligent, unshaken in misfortune, persevering and wise, he shall be exalted. Benevolent, friendly, grateful, liberal, a guide, instructor and trainer of men, he shall attain honour."—*Dhammapāda.*

It is selfish to seek one's own advantage, regardless of others, or at the expense of others. Jealousy is an intense form of selfishness which takes pleasure in the distress and sufferings of others without advantage to self. Ceaseless competition has bred a propensity, in proportion as one covets success, to hate those who succeed better and to rejoice in their calamity, if eventually they fall. The poet has rightly described jealousy as "the fire of endless night, the fire that burns and gives no light."

IX. You shall cast out all malice, anger, spite and ill-will, and shall not cherish hatred even against those who do you harm, but embrace all living beings with loving kindness and benevolence.

"Let a man overcome anger by love; let him overcome evil by good; let him overcome the greedy by liberality, and the liar by truth. For hatred does not cease by hatred at any time; hatred ceases by love, this is its true nature."—*Dhammapāda.*

"To the man who foolishly does me wrong I shall return the protection of my ungrudging love; the more the evil that comes from him, the more the good that shall go from me."—*Sutra of forty-two sections.*

"Returning good for good is very noble, but returning good for evil is nobler still"—*Bodhicharyāvatāra.*

Justice, concerned with man as he is at present, demands that we should respect and protect the rights of others as well as our own by lawful means. So it says: Do unto others what you wish they should do unto you, that is to say, render to each one that which is his due. But morality with its eye directed to the future man tells us that the duty of justice should be supplemented by equity and magnanimity. Equity demands that we should resign claims and acts to which we have an unquestionable theoretical right, so that the advancement of our interests may not cause relatively greater damage to those of others. Magnanimity requires us to overlook personal injuries and not to embrace the opportunity of revenge, though it present itself.

The teaching "love thy neighbour as thyself" is not only vague, but may also lead to mischievous consequences. If a man love himself meanly, childishly, timidly, even so shall he love his neighbour. If a man hate himself, it must follow that he must hate others too. The teaching of Buddhism is definite, and requires us to love ourselves with a love that is healthy and wise, that is large and complete. To be effectually generous one must have a confident, tranquil and clear comprehension of all that one owes to one'sself. If you are asked to love your enemy and return good for evil, it is because, as the *Bodhicharyāvatāra* says, "an enemy is one who is capable of helping you to acquire bodhi, if you can only love him." One should hate hatred and not the person who hates him. This does not mean that one should show the left cheek, when smitten on the right, but it means that we must fight evil with good. Passive non-resistance of evil is no morality at all. The meekness of the lamb is praiseworthy, but if it could lead only to becoming a prey to the rapacity of the tiger, it is not worth possessing.

The Blessed One again and again impressed upon his followers the duty of practising *maitri* or universal love. *Maitri* must not be confounded with *kāma* and *prēma* (*priya*, *prīti*). The former stands for sexual love, which is regarded as a hindrance (*saṁyojana*) to spiritual progress. The latter represents the natural affection and friendliness, such as exists between parents and children, or brothers and sisters. But, as this is not completely free from the taint of selfishness, it is not considered the highest ideal. *Maitri* represents the perfection of loving kindness, as it "does not cling to love for selfish sweets of love." In the *Metta Sutta* of *Sutta Nipāta* it is said: "As a mother, even at the risk of her own life, protects her son, her only son so let every man cultivate *maitri* without measure among all beings. Let him cultivate *maitri* without measure toward the whole world, above, below, around, unstinted and unmixed with any feeling of difference or opposition. Let a man remain steadfastly in this state of mind all the while he is awake, whether he be standing, walking, sitting, or lying down. This state of heart (*chetovimukti*) is the best in the world."

> " Do not deceive, do not despise
> Each other, anywhere;
> Do not be angry, nor should ye
> Secret resentment bear.
> For as a mother risks her life
> And watches o'er her child,
> So boundless be your love to all
> So tender, kind and mild.
>
> " Yea, cherish goodwill right and left
> All round, early and late,
> And without hindrance, without stint,
> From envy free and hate,
> While standing, walking, sitting down,
> Whate'er you have in mind,
> The rule of life that's always best
> Is to be loving kind." *

From *maitri* originate *karuṇa* (compassion) and *mudita* (goodwill), and therefore it is higher than both of these. All pious deeds, all gifts, are nothing compared to a loving heart. In another place the Holy One says: "Who, O bhikshus, in the morning, midday and evening, cherish love in their hearts only for one moment acquire thereby greater merit than those who, morning, midday and evening, make presents of hundreds of bowls of food." With a few exceptions the disciples of the Buddha have always followed his exhortation to practise love.

How the bhikshus practised love towards one another is illustrated by the following anecdote. "Once the Blessed One happened to visit the *Prăchīnavamsadāva*, the eastern bamboo forest. Then there lived the venerable Anuruddha, the venerable Nandika and the venerable Kimbila. The keeper of the forest, seeing the Buddha coming towards him, cried out: "O bhikshu, do not enter this forest. Here live three great men free from

* Dr. Paul Carus: Gems of Buddhist poetry.

all troubles and sorrows, do not disturb them!" The venerable Anuruddha, hearing how the forester addressed the Blessed One, said: "Brother forester, do not obstruct the Blessed One. Our Blessed Master is there." And the venerable Anuruddha went to the venerable Nandika and the venerable Kimbila, and said to them: "Come, Venerable One, come, Venerable One, our Blessed Teacher is there." And the venerable Anuruddha, the venerable Nandika, and the venerable Kimbila, went to the Blessed One. One removed his robe and alms-bowl, one arranged for him a suitable seat, the other brought him a foot-stool, a basin and water to wash his feet. The Blessed One seated himself on the seat prepared for him and washed his feet. And after the venerable disciples had finished their greeting ministrations, they sat by his side. And the Blessed One spoke to the venerable Anuruddha as follows: "How do you do, O Anuruddha? Have you enough to live on? Have you no need of alms?" "We are doing well, O Blessed One. We have enough to live on, O Blessed One, and we have, O Lord, no need for alms." "Do you live together, O Anuruddha, in concord, without strife, peaceably looking at each other with friendly eyes." "We live together, O Lord, in concord, without strife, peacefully viewing each other with loving eyes. "And how do you do this, O Anuruddha?" "I think, O Lord, that it is for me a gain and a blessing that I live together with such fellow bhikshus. In me has grown, O Lord, towards these Venerable Ones a love which actuates openly and in secret all my deeds, words and thoughts. I always attempt, O Lord, to suppress my own will and act according to the wills of these venerable men. And I have, O Lord, suppressed my will and acted according to the wills of these Venerable Ones. Though our bodies, O Lord, are different, our heart, I believe, is one and the same." On questioning Nandika and Kimbila the Blessed One obtained the same answer.

Attempts have sometimes been made to belittle the importance of love in Buddhism. In certain Jātakas, such as the Visvāntara Jātaka, the bodhisattva is represented as giving away his wife and children in the practice of *dāna pāramitā*. From this it is argued that heartless inhumanity passes in the eye of the Buddhist for beneficence and charity. Such a misconception apparently owes its origin to a misunderstanding of the purpose and meaning of the Jātakas. As already stated, a Jātaka is a historiette, an anecdote, or a fable employed as an illustration either to convey a reproof, or point a moral, or bring out in relief some essential of Buddhahood. Most of the Jātakas are devoted to the last purpose, and in these not infrequently emphasis is placed on some one essential of bodhi without due regard being paid to the others. Thus in the Hare Jātaka stress is laid on charity (*dāna*); in the Saṁkhapāla Jātaka on morality (*çīla*); in the Lesser Sutasoma Jātaka on renunciation (*nishkāmya*); in the Sattubhatta Jātaka on wisdom (*pragnā*); in the Greater Janaka Jātaka on courage and fortitude (*vīrya*); in the Khantivāda Jātaka on patience and forbearance; (*kshānti*) in the Greater Sutasōma Jātaka on steadfastness (*adhisṭhāna*); in the Ekarāja Jātaka on benevolence (*maitri*); in the Lomahaṁsa Jātaka on equanimity (*upeksha*); and so forth. But it does not follow that one can attain bodhi without practising all the essential virtues. Consequently, in comprehending the full import of the Jātakas we must take them in their ensemble. It would be as absurd to condemn Buddhism on the ground of what we find in a few Jātakas as to condemn Jesus either by his cursing of the fig-tree, or by his drowning of the Gadarene pigs.

It is often said that Christianity is the only religion of love. But a close investigation of the nature of love shows that the claim of Christianity to this title, even in its early stage, is not borne out by facts. In his *Der Buddhismus als Religion der Zukunft** Th. Schultze has made a searching examination of this question, which he concludes thus: "If we examine those passages of the New Testament which deal with love, we find none among them in which at least an attempt is made to set forth minutely the nature of love as an internal (subjective) mental condition. They either speak approvingly of love; or give the motive which actuates or should actuate love (such as that God has or-

* Zweite Auflage, pp. 62-68.

dained it, or that God himself is love); or deal with the outward expression of love, its beneficial effects, and the practical relations which are, or should be, determined by it; or simply make mention of the reward of love. What strikes us in all this is that we are involved in a circle, for, on the one hand, love is said to spring from obedience to God's commandments, and, on the other hand, love itself is said to lead to the obeying of God's laws." While in Christianity love is exacted by means of external authority, loving kindness (*maitri*) is a logical consequence of the Buddhist doctrine of *nairātmya*. If the New Testament contains a song in praise of *agapy*, the *Itivuttaka* contains an equally charming praise of *maitri*. Further, the Buddhists all over the world have strictly adhered to the ideal of their Master in extending loving kindness to all living beings, while the life of Christendom is a standing testimonial of its divergence from the ideal of the New Testament.

X. You shall free your mind of ignorance and be anxious to learn the truth, lest you fall a prey to doubt which will make you indifferent, or to errors which will lead you astray from the noble path that leads to blessedness and peace.

The attitude of Buddhism towards doubt is unique among religions. The Buddha nowhere asks us to give our unqualified assent to propositions the truth of which is not clear and distinct. He does not say: "Thou shouldst never wrangle about Dharma and then seek to have those doubts solved into which thou mayest arrive. Let no doubts like these ever take possession of thy mind. Do thou obey what I say without scruple of any kind. Follow me like a blind man or like one who, without being possessed of sense himself, has to depend upon that of another."* On the other hand the Blessed One has repeatedly asked his disciples not to accept anything merely on the authority of others. He has distinctly laid down that the investigation of the Dharma is one of the essentials of *bodhi*. Accordingly Buddhism does not underestimate the value of doubt during the period of investiga-

* This is the advice of Bhishma to Yudhisthira. See *Anuçāsana Parva*, Mahābhārata.

tion. But the doubt it sets store by is of that sort whose whole aim is to conquer itself by high aspiration, renewed effort, and incessant toil, and not of that other sort which, born of flippancy and ignorance, tries to perpetuate itself as an excuse for idleness and indifference. Herein lies an essential difference between Buddhism and vulgar scepticism. The sceptic regards hopeless suspense as an end in itself, but the Buddhist, ever full of hope and aspiration, treats it as a mere stepping stone to his final goal, the attainment of truth.

The somewhat detailed consideration given above to the special precepts naturally leads to the discussion of certain general questions which concern them all in common. Buddhism is a nomistic religion, that is, a religion on which the great personality of an individual founder has left an indelible impression, and as such it belongs to an advanced stage of thought. No religion or ethical system is fabricated out of the brain of one individual. The founder of a religion may modify, criticise, and even negate the beliefs and practices of his time, but he cannot ignore them. A religion without an organic historical nexus with the past will find no soil in which it can take root and receive nourishment. We may, therefore, safely admit that Buddhism has its roots deep down in the great past of India, and that the Dharma represents the noblest product of the Indian mind. But there can be difference of opinion as to the Buddhists having borrowed their teachings from the Brāhmans. Whether the codes of sacred laws ascribed to Apastambha, Baudhāyana and Gautama and the so-called earlier Upanishads are really anterior to the time of Sākyamuni we have no means of deciding. Nor have we any evidence to show that the Buddha was acquainted with them, even if they were composed before him. Says Dr. G. Thibaut: "There is, so far as I know, no evidence of Buddha himself having been acquainted with philosophical views of the type of those which find their expression in the Chāndogya or Brihadāraṇyaka, and generally, I fail to see why a doctrine essentially and fundamentally non-brāhminical must be held to depend on brāhminical works in any way, even if only in the way of contrast or reaction. There may have been in

Ancient India more centres of independent religious and speculative thought than is generally assumed, and the popular theory of a direct filiation of the great systems may be a fiction."*

Between the ethical teachings of Buddhism and the moral codes of the Brāhmans there is a remarkable difference. No doubt the earlier and later Dharma Sāstras of the Brāhmans inculcate bravery, loyalty, hospitality, and prohibit stealing, lying and illegal injury to others, and in a few cases also enjoin self-restraint. "But if these laws," as Prof. E. W. Hopkins points out, "be compared with those of savage races, it will be found that most of them are also factors of primitive ethics. Therefore we say that the Hindu Code as a whole is antique and savage, and that, excluding religious excess and debauchery, it is on a par with the modern ethical code only nominally. In reality, however, this savage and ancient code is not on a level with that of to-day. And the reason is that the ideal of each is different. In the savage and old world conception of morality, it is the ideal virtue that is represented by the code. It was distinct laudation to say of a man that he did not lie, or steal, and that he was hospitable. But to-day, while these factors remain to formulate the code, they no longer represent the ideal virtue. Nay rather, they are but the assumed base of virtue, and so thoroughly is this assumed that to say of a gentleman that he does not lie or steal is not praise, but rather an insult, since the imputation to him of what is but the virtue of children, is no longer an encomium when applied to the adult who is supposed to have passed the point where theft and lying are moral temptations, and to have reached a point where, on the basis of these savage, antique, now childish virtues, he strives for a higher moral ideal. And this ideal of to-day, which makes fairmindedness, liberality of thought, altruism the respective representatives of the savage virtues of manual honesty, truth-speaking and hospitality, is just what is lacking in the more primitive ideal formulated in the code of savages and of the Brāhman alike. It is not found at all among savages, and

* Address to the graduates of the University of Allahabad.

they may be left on one side. In India all the factors of the modern code are entirely lacking at the time when the old code was first completely formulated. Liberality of thought comes in with the era of the Upanishads, but it is restricted freedom. Altruism is unknown to pure Brāhminism. But it obtains amongst Buddhists who also have liberality of thought and fairmindedness. Hence from the point of view of higher morality, one must confess that Buddhism offers the best parallel to that of to-day. On the other hand Buddhistic altruism exceeds all others."* Nay more; the fundamental idea of Buddhism is *maitri*, universal love.

Nevertheless some critics would make out that the ethics of Buddhism is egoistic, because its final aim is individual perfection. But a slight reflection will show the absurdity of this charge. What differentiates man from other animals is his possession of certain intellectual and ethical powers. Only by the harmonious and perfect development of these powers can each one of us truly realise his humanity and make himself serviceable to his fellows. Hence following the dictates of reason the true end of man can be nothing else than the perfection of his powers. If the striving after this perfection be selfish, it is such selfishness as cannot be dispensed with. A sound, good, fruitful self-love is the necessary basis for every virtue, and therefore also for a true, sound, good and fruitful love to others. As Maeterlinck says, "there is more active charity in the egoism of a clear-sighted and strenuous man than in all the devotion of the man that is blind and helpless, and before one exists for others, it behoves him to exist for himself."† In endeavouring to attain the perfection of bodhi, one perfects himself in order that he might work for the good of others. "*Bodhichittam samutpādya sarva satva sukhecchaya.* It is with the desire to make all beings happy that one desires to attain bodhi." So says the *Bodhicharyāvatāra.* In Buddhism there can be no real morality without knowledge, no real knowledge without morality, and both are

* E. W. Hopkins: Religions of India, pp. 535, 536.

† La sagesse et la destinee.

bound up together like heat and light in a flame.* What constitutes *bodhi* is not mere intellectual enlightenment, but intellectual enlightenment combined with compassion for all humanity. The consciousness of moral excellence is of the very essence of *bodhi*. "Love thy neighbour as thyself" and "love thine enemy" are indeed noble precepts, but so long as one does not understand the reason why he should love his neighbour and even his enemy, these precepts must necessarily remain a dead letter. If it is selfish to love an enemy because such love will lead one to bodhi, it is worse still to do good to others for the sake of rewards in heaven or for fear of punishment in hell.

Buddhism does not teach that man is by nature evil. "*Atha doshāyam āgantukuh*," says the *Bodhicharyāvatāra*, "*satva prakriti pesalah*. The evil in men is not inborn; naturally they are good." Hence for its moral precepts the Dharma seeks no external source of authority. No Buddhist regards the various moral precepts as commandments by the Buddha. Coming as they do from him whom every Buddhist takes as his model of perfection, these precepts have indeed a higher value than any commandments. But still in no sense are they commandments, for no man has any right to command his brother-men. They are but the ways pointed out by the Blessed One for avoiding the evils of life, and he who does not tread on the path shown will have to bear the consequences. Though there are neither rewards nor punishments in a future world, yet there is the law of cause and effect, whose sway in the domain of ethics is as powerful as in the domain of physics. The Buddhist ethical system is emphatically "a study of consequences—of *karma* and *vipāka*, of seeing in every phenomenon a reaping of some previous sowing." The tiger will necessarily be hunted down, and the criminal will necessarily be punished. Whosoever is punished for his

* "In Buddha's thought there is no incompatibility between the ethical ideal and that devotion to mental training which is prominent in early Buddhism, but is not regarded as a requisite in Christianity. Christianity seldom emphasises, even when it permits, the utmost intellectual freedom, while Buddhism establishes the faith intellectually from the beginning."—*E. W. Hopkins.*

misdeeds suffers his injury, not through the ill-will of others, but through his own evil doing. Even the undetected criminal does not escape the effect of his deeds. If he is not one of those pitiable pathological cases, if his longings, impulses, and ideals are those which inspire the average man, he cannot escape the misery flowing from his misdeeds. Jean val Jean may become Father Madelaine, but he cannot escape the pangs of memory. Nor can it be doubted that the criminal, though he may get on well for some time, will in the long run be eliminated from off the face of the earth as surely as the tiger is being eliminated now. Such elimination is but a part of the eternal inevitable sequence that leads man in the end to wisdom and peace.

The Buddhistic ethics is purely autonomous, and not heteronomous like the Jewish-Christian or the Hindu. In the Jewish-Christian system the moral character of a man's actions is made dependent upon his obedience or disobedience to the commands of a supernatural being, who is supposed to have revealed himself to man at some particular time in some particular way. In Hinduism the Eternal Self is made the basis of morality, but as the existence of the Eternal Self, as Saṅkara says, cannot be proved by any amount of inferential reasoning and has to be accepted solely on the authority of the Vedas, the knowledge of one action being right and another wrong rests ultimately on the authority of scripture only.

That moral ideas have nothing to do with the belief in supernatural beings does not need much reasoning to prove. Supernatural beings are but creations of human fancy, and can be endued only with such qualities as man already possesses. How can a man love and reverence what he has not seen, unless he has already learnt to love and reverence what he has seen? Nor is man ethical for fear of an invisible police. Does a man love his parents, wife or children because otherwise he would be punished for it? The belief in future rewards and punishments in an invisible world may influence men's conduct, but it cannot be a moral force. "Could he be really honest, could he be called really virtuous," says Immanuel Kant, "who will gladly give himself up to his favourite vices if he feared no future punishment, and must not one rather say that he indeed shuns the practice of evil, but nourishes in his soul a vicious disposition ; that he loves the advantage of conduct seemingly virtuous, while he hates virtue itself ? "

As regards the Eternal Self, even if it existed, it can have no value in ethical considerations. Being an eternal spiritual principle, the Eternal Self transcends all time. But all ethical questions deal with empirical wants and aspirations which are time processes. How can the self-same Eternal Self be enriched by acts of virtue or impoverished by vice ? Can it be affected by all the vicissitudes of life and still retain its timeless self-sameness ? What part can such a "self" play in ethical life ? Perhaps it may be said that morality consists in the realization of the Eternal Self. But if one's Eternal Self is real already, what has one to realize ? He might, for aught we know, be realising his Eternal Self as much in a vicious life as in virtuous deeds, in indolence as much as in strenuousness. *Be yourself !* may be a valuable moral precept to such as have already framed for themselves a worthy idea of manhood, but for others it can convey no meaning.

Buddhism rejects both of these flimsy supports for the moral life. It makes the basis of morality purely subjective. It appeals to the natural needs of man. Man desires to get rid of the sorrows and sufferings of this life ; he desires to enjoy endless bliss. How can he attain this ? First of all, as the *Bodhicharyāvatāra* argues, *puṇyam* makes the body happy. If a man is compassionate and serviceable to others, they will not prove a source of trouble to him. No man can realise all his desires without the help of others. Hence if he desires the help of others, he must have sympathy and compassion for them. As they also desire happiness, he must endeavour to get rid of their sufferings and sorrows. How can the suffering of one affect another ? In the same way as the suffering of one's foot affects his hand. Though the body consists of different parts, we treat it as one and protect it. Similarly there may be different beings in this world, still they should all be treated as one, for all are endeavouring to avoid suffering and attain happiness. One's body is the product of the combination of the sperm and germ of others, but by custom one speaks of one's body as one's own. If what is the product of others can be regarded as one's self, where is the difficulty of regarding the bodies of others as one's own? That one is always the same person is not true; yet one imagines himself to be the same person. Is it more difficult to imagine one's oneness with others? If there is no *ātman*, all beings are equally void. Is not then the fundamental oneness of all beings obvious? Such is the manner in which the Buddhist argues. For the ordinary Buddhist the doctrine of Karma may serve as the all-important motive force for the moral life. But for the wise man the main—stay of morality is the internal perception of *nairātmya*, the realization of the selflessness (*çunyata*) of all beings and the consequent fundamental equality of all beings with one another. It is this realization which forms the well-spring of cheerfulness (*mudita*), compassion (*karuṇa*), and benevolence (*maitri*), which are the bases for all good deeds.

With deep insight did the Blessed One percieve two thousand years ago truths which modern science declares to us at the present day. "Man," teaches Science, "is but a single cell in the organism of humanity. His worth as an individual is nothing apart from the rest of the organism. Apart from other human beings the individual cannot be so much as begotten and born. All his latent powers he owes to the ancestral lives that are seeing within his eyes and listening within his ears. Even his natural endowments and capabilities can find no suitable employment and proper development apart from the society of other human beings. Only in and with the grand life of mankind as a whole can the individual live as a human being. Not only has he been produced by the vital energies of mankind, but they also maintain him till death. With the elevation of humanity the individual rises in the scale of being, and with its downfall he degenerates. Being but an insignificant episode in the life of mankind, he can lay no claim to everlasting life. But as the generations before him have contributed to his being, so can he also contribute to the well-being of future generations. If the individual desires perpetual life, he can secure it only by living in the whole and for the whole.

Hence what is good for all mankind, what creates better conditions for its existence and its perfectation, is also good for the individual. What jeopardises the life of humanity or degrades it is also bad for him. A perfected humanity is his heaven, a decaying humanity is his hell. To preserve and enhance the worth of human life is virtue; to degrade humanity and lead it to perdition is vice."

If a man desires to hasten his deliverance from sorrow and suffering, he must necessarily follow the laws of the good. This motive is indeed egoistic, but it alone can work with dynamic precision. A man will necessarily desist from injuring others, if he sees clearly that his interests are bound up with theirs. He will even forego some of his own goods for the sake of others, if he is sure that his sacrifice will redound to his own advantage. A man will not hate his enemy, if he knows that the love of his enemy will carry him forward to *bodhi*. No man loves others merely from his love for them. On the other hand he loves others because for some reason they please him. In the *Brihadāraṇyaka Upanishad* Yāgnavalkya says rightly to his wife Maitreyi: "Not out of love for the husband is a husband loved, but the husband is loved for love of self. A wife is loved, not out of love for the wife, but for love of self. Children are loved, not out of love for children, but for love of self. Wealth is loved, not out of love for wealth, but for love of self. The priestly order is loved, not out of love for that order, but for love of self. The order of the warrior is loved, not out of love for that order, but for love of self. The states are loved, not out of love for the states, but for love of self. The gods are loved, not out of love for the gods, but for love of self. Existence is loved, not out of love for existence, but for love of self. Not out of love is any loved, but for love of self are all loved." King Prasenajit once asked his wife Mallika: "Have you ever loved any better than yourself?" With surprising naïveté she answered: "Truly, great king, I have not loved any one better than myself". Undaunted the king said the same thing of himself, and they both communicated their conversation to the Blessed One, who good humouredly replied as follows:

"I have through all regions wandered;
Still have I none ever found
Who loved another more than himself.
So is one's own self dearer than another,
Therefore out of love to one's own self
Doth no one injure another."

In Buddhism morality rightly rests on egoism, and altruism becomes applied egoism. No more solid basis can be found in this world for the love of one's neighbour than the love of one's self. As Hume says, "whatever contradiction may vulgarly be supposed between the selfish and social sentiments or dispositions, they are really no more opposite than selfish and ambitious, selfish and revengeful, selfish and vain. It is requisite that there be an original propensity of some kind, in order to be a basis for self-love, by giving a relish to the objects of its pursuit; and none more fit for this purpose than benevolence or humanity. The goods of fortune are spent in one gratification or another. The miser who accumulates his annual income, and lends it out at interest, has really spent it in the gratification of his avarice. And it would be difficult to show why a man is more a loser by a generous action, than by any other method of expense; since *the utmost which one can attain by the most elaborate selfishness, is the indulgence of some affection.*" So far from saying that men have naturally no affection for anything beyond themselves, we ought to say that though it may be difficult to find one who loves any single person better than himself, still it is as difficult to find one in whom the sympathetic affections taken together do not overbalance the selfish.

In the Vedānta also morality is made to rest on egoism. The wise man perceives the *ātman*, the self, to be identical with *Brahmaṁ*, the universal self. Hence the I is all, and all is I. So my neighbour is identical with myself. I must love my neighbour not like myself, but as my own self. When I see another suffer or enjoy, it is myself that suffers or enjoys. The apparent duality between myself and others is only an illusion (*Māya*). To the enlightened man all differences vanish, and everything is self. *Tat tvam asi.* That thou art. I love everything because everything is myself. Thus by broadening the idea of self the egoism of the

Vedānta becomes transformed into an altruism. However, between the egoism of the Vedānta and that of Buddhism there is an essential difference. Buddhism denies the existence of an *ātman*, and its self is consequently illusory. As there is no real self, all possibility of a real egoism disappears. With the Vedānta, on the other hand, the egoism is real, and its morality consists in the knowledge that all is I. But in Buddhism the knowledge of *anātmata* only leads the way to the moral life. Just as sunlight cannot be perceived and utilized except by reflection, so the internal perception of *nairātmya* cannot be attained except by right relationship to your fellows in thought, word and deed. Only when this internal perception has found its fullest expression in love (*maitri*), compassion (*karuṇa*), cheerfulness (*mudita*), and equanimity (*upeksha*) will perfect bliss be attained.

In another respect also the Vedānta differs from Buddhism. In the Vedānta only the three higher castes, the "twiceborn", are spiritually qualified for salvation. On the contrary, Buddhism throws its doors open to all men without any distinction. Further, the Vedānta lays great stress on the efficacy of rites and purificatory ceremonies, whereas Buddhism regards these as an obstacle to the attainment of salvation. In this respect the Sāṁkhya resembles Buddhism, but it lays no weight on morality. Besides, the Sāmkhya and its later development, the Yoga, sharply differ from Buddhism in enforcing asceticism. The Buddha found out the inefficacy of asceticism as a means to salvation while dwelling in the forest of Uruvela, and entirely discarded it.

The end and aim of man cannot be the acquisition of wealth or the satisfaction of natural inclinations. But, as the Dharma teaches, it is the attainment of that perfection which consists in perfect wisdom, perfect charity and perfect freedom. Can this faith in the future perfection of mankind inspire man with enthusiasm? Yes; it has acted in the past as an impelling force leading mankind upward. And there is apparently no reason why it should not be equally serviceable now or in the future. Humanity, as we see it now, consisting of poor pitiful beings, "with their wild hopes and vain attempts to realise them, with their struggles and failures and successes more bitter than failures, or, worst of all, with the resignation of an irremediable despair: all alike, young and old, rich and poor, good and bad, drifting down the long thoroughfare of life, with no end before them but the grave," may excite more pity than enthusiasm. But an ideal humanity, like the Buddhas ever abiding in the *Dharmakāya*, would necessarily arouse in man an enthusiasm driving to action. "The mind by an original instinct tends," says Hume, "to unite itself with the good, and to avoid the evil, though they be conceived merely in idea, and be considered to exist in a future period of time." And history shows how strongly man has been moved by the contemplation of ideal objects, whose existence he may not assert. Nay more; history proves how men have sacrificed their possessions, their blood, and their everything for ideal aims. Even in religious belief the most effective part has been similar to that which we have in the objects of imagination. Nor is an ideal at any time absolutely non-existent. It is always partially realized, even though the extent of such realization may be infinitesimally small. In man are always present the traces of what he may become, the germs of enlightenment that even in savage bosoms stir up

> "longings, yearnings, strivings
> For the good they comprehend not."

BUDDHISM AND CASTE.

"THE Tathāgata recreates the whole world like a cloud shedding its waters without distinction. He has the same sentiments for the high as for the low, for the wise as for the ignorant, for the nobleminded as for the immoral. His teaching is pure, and makes no discrimination between noble and ignoble, between rich and poor. It is like unto water which cleanses all without distinction. It is like unto fire which consumes all things that exist between heaven and earth, great and small. It is like unto the heavens, for there is room in it, ample room for the reception of all, for men and women, boys and girls, the powerful and the lowly." Such were the words in which Gautama Sākyamuni impressed on his disciples the universality of the salvation he brought into the world. How this spirit of universality has been carried out in practice is well shown by the attitude of Buddhism towards the baneful Hindu institution of caste.

On one occasion Ānanda, one of the oldest disciples of the Buddha, passing by a well, where a girl of the Mātanga caste was drawing water, asked her for some water to drink. She answered: "How dost thou ask water of me, an outcast who may not touch thee without contamination?" Ānanda replied: "My sister, I ask not of thy caste, I ask thee water to drink." The Chandāla girl was overjoyed and gave Ānanda water to drink. Ānanda thanked her and went his way, but the girl, learning that he was a disciple of the Blessed One, repaired to the place where the Buddha was. The Blessed One, understanding her sentiments towards Ānanda, made use of them to open her eyes to the truth, and took her among his disciples.

On the admission of this Chandāla woman into the order of bhikshunis, King Prasenajit and the Brāhmans and the Kshatriyas of Srāvashti, feeling greatly scandalised, came to remonstrate with the Lord on his conduct. The Blessed One demonstrated to them the futility of caste distinctions by the following simple reasoning.

Between ashes and gold there is a marked difference, but between a Brāhman and a Chandāla there is nothing of the kind. A Brāhman is not produced like fire by the friction of dry wood; he does not descend from the sky nor from the wind, nor does he arise piercing the earth. The Brāhman is brought forth from the womb of a woman in exactly the same way as a Chandāla. All human beings have organs exactly alike; there is not the slightest difference in any respect. How can they be regarded as belonging to different species? Nature contradicts the assumption of any specific inequality among mankind.

The Brāhman is a specifically Indian phenomenon. In the neighbouring countries no Brāhman exists. In those countries there are only masters and slaves. Those who are rich are masters, and those that are poor are slaves. The rich may become poor, and the poor rich. Even in India when a Kshatriya, a Vaisya, or a Sudra abounds in wealth, the members of the Brāhman caste serve him; they wait for his commands and use soft words to gratify him. To minister to his wants they rise before him in the morning and go not to sleep until he has retired to rest. Where then is the difference between the four castes? The declaration of the Brāhmans that they alone are the high caste, and others are of low caste is an empty sound.

If a Brāhman commits sin, he suffers for it like every other man. Like every other man the Brāhman also has to abstain from sin, if he desires salvation. Does not the ethical world order also give the lie to the theory of specific inequalities among mankind? Are not also the native capacities and talents the same everywhere? Is not the Sudra who is despised for his caste capable like the Brāhman of good thoughts and noble deeds? If a bath can purify a Brāhman from dust and dirt, can it not equally purify every other man? If water shows no special preference for the Brāhman, does fire show any special regard to differences of caste? Does not the fire obtained by the members of the so-called highest caste by rubbing costly fragrant sticks arise just in the same way as when the members of the so-called lowest caste rub pieces of wood from a dirty foulsmelling dog-trough or swine-trough? Further, when crossing takes place between the members of different castes, do not the children in all cases take after the mother as well as the father, and are we not able to assign them to their proper parents? Is it not otherwise with brutes among which the crossing of a mare with an ass produces a mule? What support then is there for supposing the existence of different species among mankind? On the contrary the good sense of the Brāhmans themselves proves that it is the ethical worth of an individual that confers superiority. For in distributing alms they prefer an ethically good-natured man, even when he may exhibit no distinguishing marks, nay even when he may not have gone through the initiatory ceremony known as "second-birth." Accordingly it follows that, while it is possible to obtain exact information concerning the purity or impurity of an individual's conduct, no exact information can be obtained as regards birth and descent.

In plants, insects, quadrupeds, snakes, fishes, and birds the marks that constitute the species are abundant, whereas amongst men this is not the case. Neither the hair, nor the formation of the skull, nor the colour of the skin, nor the vocal organ, nor any other part of the body exhibits any specific differences. By birth and descent all men are alike. They become different only through differences in occupation, and they are designated accordingly. Some are called husbandmen, some artisans, some merchants, some kings, some robbers, some priests, and so on. In one and the same caste different members follow different professions. Have we not among the Brāhmans physicians; necromancers; musicians; merchants; agriculturists owning cattle, poultry and slaves; wealthy landholders who give much wealth as the portion of their daughters, and receive much when their sons are married; butchers who kill animals and sell their flesh; those that provide gratification for the lust of others; those who tell lucky hours; those who sit *dhāraṇa*; those who live like savages in the wilderness; those who get their livelihood after the manner of those who break into houses to steal; beggars with long hair, dirty teeth, immense nails, filthy bodies, and heads covered with dust and lice; and those who profess to be released from all desires and to be ready to release others also?

If we look closely, we see no difference between the body of a prince and the body of a slave. What is essential is that which may dwell in the most miserable frame, and which the wisest have saluted and honoured. The talk of 'high and low castes,' of 'the pure Brāhmans, the only sons of Brahma,' is nothing but empty sound. The four castes are equal. He is a Chandāla who cherishes hatred; who torments and kills living beings; who steals, or commits adultery; who does not pay his debts; who maltreats aged parents, or fails to support them; who gives evil counsel and hides the truth; who does not return hospitality nor render it; who exalts himself and debases others; who ignores the virtues of others and is jealous of their success. Not by birth, but by conduct, is one a Chandāla. He is a Brāhman* who is free from sin. He is an outcast who is angry and cherishes hatred; who is wicked and hypocritical; who embraces error and is full of deceit. Whosoever is a provoker and avaricious, has sinful desires, is not afraid and ashamed to commit sins, he is an outcast. Not by birth does one become an outcast, not by birth does one become a Brāhman; by deeds one becomes an outcast, by deeds one becomes a Brāhman.*

> "'T is he is a Brāhman indeed
> Who knows the births that he has lived before;
> And sees (with heavenly eye) the states of bliss,
> And states of woe, that other men pass through;
> Has reached the end of all rebirths, become
> A sage, perfect in insight, *Arahat*
> In these three modes of knowledge, three fold wise
> Him do I call a Brāhmaṇa, three fold wise,
> And not the man who mutters o'er again
> The mystic verse so often uttered through before."*

* "A Brāhman, O king, means one who has escaped from every sort and class of becoming, who is entirely free from evil and from stain, who is dependent on himself"—Milindapanha.

* Assalāyana Sutta, Mathura Sutta, Ambaṭṭa Sutta, Vaseṭṭa Sutta, and Dasa Brāhma Jātaka.

* *Aggañña Sutta, Dīgha Nikāya.*

From the point of view of religion the Dharma makes no difference between one caste and another. All are admitted without distinction and difficulty into the Saṅgha. Only minors, soldiers, slaves, invalids and cripples are not permitted to join the order. These are inevitable exceptions. For the defence of even the best governed country soldiers are necessary, and they cannot be allowed to give up their work without sufficient reason. But with the permission of the government they may join the order. Like minors slaves are not free, and their admission into the Saṅgha before emancipation may prove harmful to their masters. But it is not to be supposed that the Dharma encourages slavery. On the contrary it teaches one to attain the highest freedom. Still slavery was an existing institution which the Buddha had to reckon with. To take off the sting from slavery the Blessed One specially taught that masters should provide for the welfare of their slaves by apportioning work to them according to their strength, supplying suitable food and wages, tending them in sickness, sharing with them unusual delicacies and occasionally granting them holidays. In one of his rock edicts Asoka emphasises the fact that the Dharma consists in kind treatment of slaves and servants, obedience to father and mother, charity, and respect for the sanctity of life. It is opposed to the spirit of Buddhism to regard one class of men as having been created for the purpose of serving another class. It is possible for every one to attain that self-culture and self-control which is designated by the word Nirvāṇa, whether he be a Brāhman or a Chandāla, a white man or a black man.

Invalids and cripples are disallowed because they are incapable of the effort needed to attain *bodhi*. For *bhikshuta* does not consist in leading an indolent and idle life, but in a strenuous active life for the good of others. "O bhikshus," says the Blessed One, "be not afraid of good works: such is the name for happiness, for what is wished, desired, dear, and delightful,—namely good works."

For those that join the Saṅgha there is no caste. As the great streams, however many they may be, the Ganga, the Yamuna, the Achiravatī, the Sarayu, the Mahānadi, when they reach the great ocean, lose their old name and their old descent, and bear only one name, "the great ocean," so also the disciples of the Buddha, to whatever caste they may belong, when they join the order, lose their old name and old paternity and bear only the one designation of Sâkya-bhikshus.

Among the elders mentioned in the *Theragâtha* we find Angulimâla, the dreaded robber; Sunita, the scavenger; Svapâka, the dogeater; Svâti, the fisherman; Nanda, the cowherd; and Upâli, the barber. Among the bhikshunis were Ambapâli, the courtezan; Vimalâ, the daughter of a prostitute; Pūrṇâ, the daughter of a slave woman; and Châpâ, the daughter of a hunter. The story of the conversion of Sunita, as given by himself, shows how easy it was for the members of the so-called lower classes to join the Saṁgha. Says Sunita: "I came of a humble family. I was poor and needy. The work which I performed was lowly,—sweeping the withered flowers. I was despised of men, looked down upon, and held in low esteem; with submissive mien, I showed respect to many. Then I beheld the Buddha and his band of bhikshus, as he passed to Magadha. I cast away my burden and ran to bow myself in reverence before him From pity for me he halted, he the highest among men! I bowed myself at the Master's feet and begged of him, the highest of all beings, to accept me as a bhikshu. Then said unto me the gracious Master,—'Come, O bhikshu'—that was all the initiation I received. 'O bhikshu,' said the Master, 'let your light so shine before the world, that you, having embraced the religious life according to so well-taught a doctrine and discipline, are seen to be mild and forbearing."

While those that joined the order had to give up caste, the Buddha does not seem to have insisted on his lay followers doing likewise. The social conditions prevalent during the time of Gautama Sâkyamuni did not probably necessitate the preaching of a general crusade against caste. Caste, like every other social institution, is a product of natural growth. In the Rig Veda there is, with the single exception of *Purushasuktam*, no clear indication of the existence of caste in the Brâhmanical sense of the word. In the Vedic hymns two classes of society, the royal and the priestly classes, are recognised as above the *vis*, or bulk of the community. But the Brāhmans had not yet established their claims to the highest rank in the body politic. In the Buddha's time the Brāhmans were perhaps endeavouring to assert their superiority over the Kshatriyas. In the *Ambatta Sutta* the Blessed One claims superiority for the Kshatriya. "So it is clear, whether you regard it from the male or from the female side, that it is the Kshatriyas who are the best people, and the Brāhmans their inferiors. Moreover it was the Brahma Sanam Kumāra who said—'The Kshatriya is best among folk who heed lineage. He who knows and acts aright is best among gods and men.' Now this stanza Ambaṭṭa was well-sung and not ill-sung by the Brahma Sanam Kumāra, well-said and not ill-said, sensible and not senseless. I too, Ambaṭṭa, join in saying that the Kshatriya is best among folk who heed lineage."* "There is no evidence," as Dr. Rhys Davids remarks, "to show that at the time of the rise of Buddhism there was any substantial difference in the valley of the Ganges and their contemporaries, the Greeks or Romans, dwelling on the shores of the Mediterranean Sea. The point of greatest weight in the establishment of the subsequent development, the supremacy in India of the priests, was still being hotly debated. All the new evidence tends to show that the struggle was being decided rather against than for the Brāhmans. What we find in the Buddha's time is caste in the making. The great mass of people were distinguished quite roughly into four classes, social strata, of which the boundary lines were vague and uncertain. At one end of the scale were certain outlying tribes and certain hereditary crafts of a dirty or despised kind. At the other end the nobles claimed the superiority. The Brāhmans by birth (not necessarily sacrificial priests, for they followed all sorts of occupations) were trying to oust the nobles from the highest grade. They only

* In the Mahābhārata (*Vanaparva*) Sanatkumāra says: "The Kshatriya is the best of those among this folk who put their trust in lineage. But he who is perfect in wisdom and righteousness is the best among gods and men."

succeeded long afterwards, when the power of Buddhism had declined."*

The caste distinctions which might have obtained among the Buddhist laity in India had no religious consecration. They had only a social significance. On the other hand, in Hinduism, that is to say, that religion which refers to Brāhmanic scriptures and tradition for its orthodoxy, which worships the Brāhmanic deities and their incarnations, which enjoins veneration for the cow and certain rules concerning intermarriage and interdining, and which enforces the presence of the Brāhman at all ceremonies, caste distinctions have not only a social but also a religious significance. One is a Brāhman, a Kshatriya, a Vaisya, or a Sudra solely by his birth. The status of a Brāhman, it is said, is incapable of acquisition by a person belonging to any of the three other orders. That status is the highest with respect to all creatures. We are told in the *Mahābhārata*: "From the order of brute life one attains to the status of humanity. If born as a human being, he is sure to take birth as a Pukkasa or a Chandāla. One having taken birth in that sinful order of existence, one has to wander in it for a very long time. Passing a period of one thousand years in that order, one attains next to the status of a Sudra. In the Sudra order one has to wander thirty thousand years before one acquires the status of a Vaisya. After wandering for a time, that is, sixty times longer than what has been stated as the period of the Sudra existence, one attains to the Kshatriya order. After wandering for a time that is measured by multiplying the period last named by two hundred one becomes born in the race of such a Brāhman as lives by the profession of arms. After a time measured by multiplying the period last named by three hundred, one takes birth in the race of a Brāhman that is given to the recitation of the *Gāyatri* and other *mantras*. After a time measured by multiplying the last named by four hundred, one takes birth in the race of such a Brāhman as is conversant with the Vedas and the scriptures." Only the Brāhman as such, by subjugating joy and grief,

*Supplement to the Encyclopædia Britannica, Vol. II, Art. Buddhism.

desire and aversion, vanity and evil speech, can attain salvation. Hence the Brāhman is something transcendently divine. "By his very origin the Brāhman is a god, even to the gods." "A Brāhman, whether he be learned or unlearned, is a great divinity." He shall not rise to receive a Kshatriya or Vaisya, though they may be learned. If a Brāhman serves a Sudra, he commits a sin which can be wiped off only by bathing for three years at every fourth meal time. A Brāhman may seize without hesitation, if he be distressed for a subsistence, the goods of a Sudra. If a Sudra comes as a guest to a Brāhman, he shall first be made to do some work and then be fed. Immoral Brāhmans shall be worshipped, but not Sudras even though they may have subdued their passions. Although Brāhmans may employ themselves in all sorts of mean occupation, they must invariably be honoured. The kingdom of that king, says Manu, who stupidly looks on while a Sudra decides causes, shall sink like a cow in deep mire. The duty of the Sudra cannot be any other than servitude, because such a man was created by the self-existent for the purpose of serving Brāhmans. A Sudra, though emancipated by his master, is not released from a state of servitude, for from a state natural to him by whom can he be divested. In the very nature of things the Sudra can have no claim to salvation, for by his birth he has no spiritual capability for it.

Whatever may be the origin of the system of caste, there can be no doubt that its development is largely due to the ambition and selfishness of those who profited by it.* The system of caste was indeed profitable to the Brāhmans, and naturally they fostered and turned it to their own advantage. Wherever they went, they sought to perpetuate their own social ascendancy by inculcating the doctrine of their own superiority as custodians of a divine revelation and as expounders of sacred laws. Wherever they spread over India, they defined the duties and privileges of the different classes, assigned to them definite places in the graduated scale of

* Among the ancient Romans the pontifices became mighty and influential owing to their knowledge of the all important details of sacrificial ceremonies. For a similar reason the Brāhmans became powerful in India.

the community, and secured for themselves the best places. The attitude of the later Buddhists towards the claims arrogated to themselves by the Brāhmans is best illustrated by the *Vajrasuchi*, a small tract ascribed to Asvagosha, the well-known author of the *Buddhacharitra*, who lived in the latter half of the first century before Christ. The argument of the *Vajrasuchi* may be thus summarised.

Granted that the Vedas, the Smritis and the Dharmasastras are true and valid, and that all the teachings at variance with them are invalid, still the assertion that the Brāhman is the highest of the four castes cannot be maintained.

What is Brāhmanhood? Is it the life principle *(jīva)*; or descent; or the body; or learning; or rites (*āchāra*); or acts *(karma)*; or knowledge of the Vedas?

If the life principle constituted Brāhmanhood, how could, as is stated in the Vedas, quadrupeds and other animals have become gods? According to the *Mahābhārata* seven hunters and ten deer of the hill Kalinjala, a goose of the lake Mānasasāra, a Chakravāka of Sharadvipa were born as Brāhmans in Kurukshetra, and became very learned in the Vedas. In his *Dharmasastra* Manu says: "Whatever Brāhman learned in the four Vedas with their *angas* and *upāngas* receives gifts or fees from a Sudra, shall for twelve births be an ass, for sixty births a hog, and seventy births a dog." Hence it is evident that it is not the life principle that constitutes Brāhmanhood.

If Brāhmanhood depended on descent or parentage, how could this be reconciled with the statement of the *Smriti* that many Munis had no Brāhman mothers? Achala Muni was born of an elephant; Keça Pingaḷa of an owl; Suka Muni of a parrot; Kapila of a monkey; Sringa Rishi of a deer; Vyāsa Muni from a fisherwoman; Kausika Muni from a female Sudra; Visvāmitra from a Chāndalini; and Vasishta Muni from a strumpet. If one born of a Brāhman father or mother is a Brāhman, then even the child of a slave (*dāsa*) or (*dāsi*) may become a Brāhman. If he alone is a Brāhman whose father and mother are both Brāhmans, then it must be established that the parents themselves are pure Brāhmans. But the mothers of the parent race of Brāhmans are not, any of them, free from the suspicion of having committed adultery with Sudras. "In human society," says Yudhsthira in the *Mahābhārata* (*Vanaparva*), "it is difficult to ascertain one's caste, because of promiscuous intercourse among the four orders. This is my opinion. Men belonging to all the orders begot (promiscuously) offspring upon women of all the orders. And of men, speech, sexual intercourse, birth and death are common. And to this the Rishis have borne testimony, by using at the beginning of a sacrifice, such expressions as—'of what caste soever we may be, we celebrate the sacrifice.'" Further according to the *Mānavadharmasāstra* the Brāhman who eats flesh loses instantly his rank; and also he who sells wax, or salt, or milk, becomes a Sudra in three days. If Brāhmanhood depended upon birth, how could it be lost by any acts however degrading? Can an eagle by alighting on the earth be turned into a crow?

Is the body then the Brāhman? Then fire will become the murderer of a Brāhman, when it consumes his corpse, and such also will be every one of the Brāhman's relatives who may consign his body to the flames. Again, every one born of a Brāhman, though his mother be a Sudra, will be a Brāhman, being bone of the bone and flesh of the flesh of his father. But according to the *Mahābhārata* the son that is begotten by a Brāhman upon a Sudra wife is called *Pārāsava*, implying one born of a corpse, for the Sudra woman's body is as inauspicious as a corpse. Again, the virtue of the holy acts sprung from the body of a Brāhman is not, according to the Brāhmanical theories, destroyed by the destruction of his body. Hence Brahmanhood cannot consist in the body.

Is it learning that constitutes Brāhmanhood? If that were the case, many Sudras must have become Brāhmans from the learning they possessed. Many Sudras, even *Mlechchas*, are masters of the four Vedas, of Vyākaraṇa and Jyotisha, of the Mimāmsa and the Vedānta, and of Sāṁkhya, Nyāya and Vaisheshika philosophies; yet not one of them is or ever was called a Brāhman. Nor can *āchāra* and *karma* be said to constitute Brāhmanhood. For many Sudras are everywhere following practices appropriate to

Brāhmans, and are performing the severest and most laborious acts of piety.

Why then should the higher life be prohibited to the Sudra? Why is it laid down that for the Sudra service and obedience paid to Brāhmans are enough? Is it because in speaking of the four castes the Sudra is mentioned last? How can the order in which certain beings are named or written affect their relative rank and dignity? Does the Sudra become the lowest and meanest of beings, because his name is mentioned after the dog in a certain sutra? Are the teeth superior in dignity to the lips, because we find the latter placed after the former for the sake of euphony in some grammatical rule? No; nor any more is it true that the Sudra is vile and the Brāhman high, because we are used to repeat the *chatur varṇa* in a particular order. And if this is untenable, the inference from it that the Sudra must be content to serve and obey the Brāhman falls likewise to the ground.

Again, if as the Brāhmans say all men proceed from one Brahma, how then can there be a fourfold insuperable diversity among them? If one has four sons by one wife, the four sons, having one father and mother, must all be essentially alike. Among quadrupeds, birds, trees, we see differences of conformation and organization whereby we can separate them into distinct species. But all men are formed alike without and within, except in such non-essential differences as are observed in the children of one and the same parents. It is therefore evident that all men belong to one species. Further in the jack-tree the fruit is produced from the stem, the joints and roots as well as the branches. Is one fruit therefore different from another so that we may call that produced from the roots the Sudra fruit? Surely not; nor can men be of four distinct species, because, as the Brāhmans assert, they sprang from four different parts of one body. Besides, a Brāhman's sense of pleasure and pain is not different from that of a Chandāla. Both are born in the same way, both sustain life in the same manner, and both suffer death from the same causes. They differ neither in intellectual faculties nor in their actions, nor in the aims they pursue, nor in their subjection to fear and hope. Accordingly the talk of four castes is fatuous. All men are of one caste.

When such onslaughts of the Buddhists began to tell on Hindusim, various attempts seem to have been made by the Brāhmans to bolster up their religion. The result of one such attempt is apparently the *Bhagavatgīta.* To a thoughtful reader of the *Gīta* its underlying motive is obvious. The Buddhists reject absolutely the authority of the Vedas and the system of castes. But it is impossible for the Brāhmans to let go the authority of the Vedas or to give up their hierarchical system. They could, however, combine their own doctrines with the prevailing popular beliefs and supply a new basis for their hierarchy. This is just what has been done in the *Gīta.* The *Gīta* does not reject the Vedas absolutely, but shelves them. "To an enlightened man," the *Gita* says, "there is as much use in all the Vedas as there is in a reservoir for one who is surrounded by water on all sides." Again instead of asserting that a Sudra must become a Brāhman by going through a number of births and then attain salvation, the *Gita* says that " man attains salvation, devoted each to his own duty." It tries to place caste on a more tenable basis by saying that the duties of Brāhmans, Kshatriyas, Vaisyas and Sudras are divided according to the qualities of their nature. " Better is one's own duty though destitute of merit than the duty of another well performed. He who does the duty ordained by his own nature suffers thereby no demerit. Nature-born duty, though faulty, one ought not to abandon, for undertaking to do another's duty is fraught with evil." The Buddhists regard a Buddha as a man born to save the human race from impending ruin, whenever sin and ignorance gain the upper hand in this world. Thus in the *Saddharmapundarīkam* the Buddha says: " I am the Tathāgata, the Lord, who has no superior, who appears in this world to save." Similarly says Krishna in the *Gīta*: " Whenever there is a decay of religion and there is a rise of irreligion, then I manifest myself. For the protection of the good and the destruction of the wicked, for the firm establishment of religion, I am born in every age." Religion here means, as pointed out by Saṅkara, only such religion as is indicated by castes and religious orders. The real import of these teachings is very clear. They contain an admonition to the Sudra not to give up caste following the precepts of Gautama Sākyamuni and his disciples. In the view of the Brāhmans the greatest sin of Sākyamuni is that he, being a Kshatriya, transgressed the duties of his own class by assuming the function of a teacher and the right to receive gifts, which the Brāhmans regard as their exclusive privileges; and, worse still he instructed the members of the fourth caste whom the Brāhmans place outside the pale of instruction. The main object of the *Gīta* is to support covertly the domination and prestige of the Brāhman class while appearing to provide for the wants which Buddhism satisfied. Whatsoever is noble and sublime in the *Gīta* is what Brāhmanism has freely borrowed from its rival and utilized for its own purposes, especially to prevent the Sudras from seceding from their old faith. The rest is a conglomerate of repetitions, contradictions, absurdities, the result of an unsuccessful attempt to reconcile all phases of orthodox opinion. No wonder that the *Gīta* has been described as "the wonderful song, which causes the hair to stand on end!"

Caste has always formed the mainstay of Hinduism. "It is by means of these caste distinctions," says the Brāhman author of the *Hindu Dharma Tatva*, "that in the Bharatakhanda the Hindu religion has been so well preserved...... These caste distinctions are the chief support of the Hindu religion; when they give way there can be no doubt that the Hindu religion will sink to destruction." It is by means of the system of castes that the Brāhmans have always carried on their proselytising operations. All outsiders, so long as they do not interfere with the existing castes, are allowed to become Hindus without giving up any of their old customs and superstitions, gods and goddesses, provided they are willing to form themselves into a new caste subject to the Brāhmans. It is in this way that the uncivilised aboriginal populations have been gradually brāhmanised. We have no longer only four castes, but more than a thousand. Among the Brāhmans alone there are more than a hundred subdivisions. Almost every trade or profession now forms a caste of its own, having no social intercourse with nor patriotic feelings for the other castes. And what has been the baneful result of this parcelling of the Indian population into innumerable divisions? The vast continent of India with its hundreds of millions of inhabitants has for centuries been the prey of predatory conquerors. Ever since Alexander the Great conquered and humiliated India, her sovereigns have always been foreigners. India has had the unique distinction of being in succession subject to the Scythians, the Arabs, the Afghans, the Mongols, the Portuguese, the Dutch, the French, and the British. A small body of foreigners suffices to keep in check a host a thousand times larger than itself. Not only have the Hindus lost all power of resisting foreign invasion, they have also sunk into a state of intellectual immobility. As Mr. Crozier has pointed out, "where caste is absolute, and the barriers that separate class from class are insurmountable, mere rank is everything, and practical intellect, initiative, originality, and enterprise being alike unavailing to help a man out of the sphere in which he was born are held in a minimum of regard. The consequence is that these nations have long sunk into a settled and abiding intellectual stagnation."

Not satisfied with the pernicious results already produced, the modern upholders of Hinduism attempt to buttress caste by scientific props. Caste, they contend, has an ethnological basis. The Sanskrit word for caste being *varṇa*, which literally means colour, it is urged that between the higher castes, the so-called Aryans, and the lower castes, there is a racial opposition more or less absolute arising from a difference in colour. Apparently these neo-advocates of Hinduism are not acquainted with the fact that difference in colour does not represent any essential difference in quality. The microscope reveals no difference between the blond and the black. The human skin, whether it be the skin of the darkest Negro or of the whitest European, always contains only dark pigment. The colour of the white European is not produced by milk or the ichor of the gods of antiquity. The pigment is everywhere the same, and it is always dark. It differs not in quality, but only in quantity. In some cases the quantity of pigment is so large that it makes its appearance on the surface, while in other cases it lies hidden in the deeper layers. But the pigment is never absent. The new-born children of all people are of the same colour and equally fair. The children of the same father and mother are not always of the same colour. The colour of the skin changes with the climate. A long stay in the tropics turns the skin of the European brown, while the skin of the Negro becomes perceptibly bleached by long residence in the temperate zone.

All attempts to classify mankind into races have proved a signal failure. At best the so-called races of mankind, spoken of by anthropologists and ethnologists, are only hypothetical classifications for convenient description serving just the same purpose as the theories of physical science. They are, to use an expression of Lamarck, mere products of art, the results of mental gymnastics, which have no real counterparts in nature. "Much of our modern race-theory," says Prof. Josiah Royce, "reminds me of the conversations in the 'Jungle-Book'—of the type of international courtesy expressed in the 'Truce of the Bear'—too much, I say, to seem like exact science." At the present day the unity of the origin of mankind is a fact universally accepted. No classes of men are incapable of fruitfully mixing with one another. No race of man now in existence can be said to represent a pure unvarying type. Much more than anatomical and physiological considerations, the general similarity of mental and moral endowments and the oneness of the historical development of man in all climes and countries teach us to regard all humanity as a vast brotherhood.

The purity of blood for which some men stickle is a pure myth. The *varṇasaṅkrama* which the orthodox Hindu of the present day fears was accomplished centuries ago. In the veins of the Brāhmans of the present day flows the blood of the Sudras* of antiquity, just as in the veins of the

* It is said in the *Santiparva* of the Mahābbārata that "the Sudras and Vaisyas acting most wilfully began to unite themselves with the wives of Brāhmans." Without the least compunction Manu speaks of Chandālas and other lower classes as the off-spring of adulterous Brāhman women. The bovine practice said by Strabo to be common in Ancient India is attested by the Mahābhārata.

white Europeans of to-day runs the blood of the Negroes who lived on the continent of Europe during the quaternary period. To this intermixture is not improbably due the beauty of their women and their vitality. Dr. Tylor says that he saw the most beautiful women in the world in Tristan da Cunha among the descendants of the whites and the blacks. In South India we find the most brilliant specimens of female beauty among the freedom-loving Nair and Theeya women of the West Coast. The most remarkable examples of longevity, says M. Finot in his *Philosophie de la Longevite*, are found among Mulattoes. The infusion of new blood into families and peoples has always been productive of very beneficial results. Wherever crossing has taken place in normal conditions, the types called inferior have improved without causing any degeneracy in the representatives of the types called superior. The pessimistic assertions of the detractors of crossing are refuted by the fact that peoples who have freely mixed with one another have continuously progressed. Those who are in the vanguard of civilization and progress are those whose blood is most rich in heterogeneous elements. Even when we consider the case of superior individuals in different countries, we are astonished to find that almost all of them are the result of intermarriages. Havelock Ellis affirms that the best American writers and thinkers are descended from mixed families. The best known among the American inventors, Mr. Edison, belongs to the same category. We might cite a host of other names if necessary. On the other hand all attempts to preserve the purity of blood have produced disastrous consequences. History demonstrates how those among the aristocracy of Europe who have kept aloof from the plebeian classes have either degenerated or died out.

It is not uncommon at the present day to find people laying much stress upon heredity. Some even hope to bring into existence a race of ethical men by artificial selection and breeding, and thus to facilitate and ensure the ethical advancement of nations and thereby of all mankind. Such views and hopes could originate only from a complete misapprehension of the nature of morality. The ethical character of an individual is something purely psychical. It is so much the result of voluntary adaptation and activity that no one can definitely assert of another, or even of himself, that he has always been ethical, that is, that he has always been guided by ethical motives. Moreover, even in the highly developed ethical man, the in-born traits of average general development are so mighty that morality, which is essentially the product of individual development, can rarely be expected as a natural factor to exhibit greater power than the other factors. Were man left solely to the control of heredity, he would exhibit much more the character of an animal than of an ethical being. In short the ethical character is as little inherited as talent. Further, inherited morality, which would be lacking all the essentials of morality, such as sense of duty, freedom of resolve, &c., would have no value. The artificially bred ethical man, even if such a creature were possible, cannot stand much higher than the animal whose actions are impelled by instinct. The intellectual and ethical culture of an individual depends on voluntary conscious effort towards an end in view, and has therefore to do more with education than heredity. *Janmanā jāyate sudra, karmaṇā jāyate dwijāh.* Every one born of woman is a Sudra, but conduct makes him a twice-born man.

Those in power not infrequently suppose that they are necessarily more capable of development than those whom they regard as their inferiors. Such a supposition is unwarranted by the teachings of science. One well-established fact of evolution is that in the "higher" form of a species there is a tendency to revert to the typical form, and that in the "lower" form the tendency is to rise to this typical form. Hence it would seem possible that the descendants of those who are now thought low and base might, if time and opportunity are given them, rise to the typical form of the species, and even go beyond it, while it is not impossible that the successors of those who are now regarded as representing a higher type might revert to the typical form of the species, and even degenerate to a lower condition. Of this history furnishes ample proof.

From whatever point of view we may look at the question of caste, it is something noxious. True to human nature the

Buddha broke down the barriers of caste and preached the equality of all mankind. He proclaimed: "My dharma is a dharma of mercy for all. Proclaim it freely to all men; it will cleanse the good and evil, the rich and poor alike; it is as vast as the spaces of heaven that exclude none. Whoever is compassionate will feel the longing to save not only himself but all others. He will say to himself: 'When others are following the Dharma, I shall rejoice at it, as if it were myself. When others are without it, I shall mourn the loss as my own. We shall do much, if we deliver many; but more if we cause them to deliver others, and so on without end.' So shall the healing word embrace the world, and all who are sunk in the ocean of misery be saved." Working in this spirit the Dharma became a religion for all, and has spread over vast tracts in Asia, India, Burma, Ceylon, Tibet, China, and Japan, and is slowly leavening the thought and life of Europe and America. May we not hope for the day when its humanising influence will be so far-reaching and deep that the prejudices of class and colour which still persist in various quarters will be forced into the limbo of forgotten things?

"Pity and need
Make all flesh kin, there is no caste in blood,
Which runneth of one hue, nor caste in tears
Which trickle salt with all; neither comes man
To birth with *tilak*-mark stamped on the brow,
Nor sacred thread on neck. Who doth right deed
Is twice-born, and who doth ill-deeds vile."

WOMAN IN BUDDHISM.

THE wives of many noblemen, who had left their homes and joined the Saṅgha, desired to follow the example of their husbands. With Prajāpati Gautamī, the maternal aunt and foster mother of Siddārtha, as their leader, they beseeched the Blessed One to grant permission to woman also to enter the order. In strict accordance with his principles the Buddha could not refuse them admission. But he feared that the admission of women into the Saṅgha might give occasion for the heretics to speak ill of his institutions. He therefore advised Gautamī and her companions to find their lasting reward and happiness by wearing the pure white robe of the lay woman and leading a pure, chaste and virtous life. But this advice did not satisfy Gautamī. She counselled her companions to ordain themselves, and then go to the Buddha. So they cut off their hair, put on the proper robe, and taking earthen bowls journeyed with painful feet to the Buddha. And Ānanda, the faithful attendant on the Buddha, moved by their earnestness and zeal, brought their petition once again to the Master. The Blessed One admitted them into the Saṅgha with the following reply: "Are the Buddhas born only for the benefit of men? Have not Visākha and many others entered the paths? The entrance is open to women as well as men." Thus did the Buddha give woman an independent status and place her on a footing of equality with man.

Though perfectly consistent with the principles of the Dharma, which sees no difference between man and man, except that which may exist by superiority of virtue, yet the step taken by the Buddha and his followers was indeed bold, considering the depraved moral condition of Ancient India and the consequent low estimation in which woman was then held. Ancient India was notorious for the looseness of its morality. Vedic worship was highly sensual. Indra, the principal Vedic deity, was not only an indulger in the intoxicating *soma*, but alsoan adulterer. *Paundarīkam* was a sacrifice in which the sexual act was worshipped, and which in later times developed into the worship of the phallus as Mahādeva. The priests, who spoke of themselves as the representatives of gods on earth, indulged largely in sexual debaucheries. The priest was enjoined by a special rule not to commit adultery with the wife of another during a particularly holy ceremony, but if he could not practise continence, he might expiate his sin by a milk offering to Varuṇa and Mitra. Naturally the sentiment towards woman was low. An ancient verse, cited in the *Anabhirati Jātaka*, compares womankind to highways, rivers, court-yards, hostelries and taverns which extend universal hospitality to all alike and ends by saying that wise men never stoop to wrath at frailty in a sex so frail? We are told in the *Adiparva* of the *Mahābhārata:* "Women were formerly not immured within houses and dependent upon husbands and other relatives. They used to go about freely, enjoying as they liked best. They did not then adhere to their husbands faithfully, and yet they were not regarded sinful, for that was the sanctioned usage of the times. That very usage is followed to this day by birds and beasts without any exhibition of jealousy. That practice, sanctioned by precedent, is applauded by great Rishis. The practice is yet regarded with respect among the Northern Kurus. Indeed that usage so lenient to woman hath the sanction of antiquity." Again in the *Udyogaparva* of the same book it is said: "The birth of a daughter in the families of those that are well behaved and high-born and endowed with fame and humility of character is always attended with evil results. Daughters when born in respectable families, always endanger the honor of their families, *viz*, their maternal and paternal families and the family into which they are adopted by marriage." Still worse is the description of woman given in the *Anuçasanaparva*. Sukrati, the grandson of Janaka, the ruler of the Videhas, has declared: "There is the well-known declaration of the scriptures that women are incompetent to enjoy freedom at any period of their life. Even if high-born and endued with beauty and possessed of protectors, women wish to transgress the restraints assigned to them. There is nothing else more sinful than women." "Women are fierce. They are endued with fierce prowess.

There are none whom they love or like so much as those that have sexual congress with them. Women are like those (*atharvan*) incantations that are destructive of life. Even after they have consented to live with one, they are prepared to abandon him for entering into engagements with others."

That the Buddhist revolt against this depraved social condition proved a success is shown to us by the picture we find of it in the commentary on the *Therigātha*, a work containing verses ascribed to bhikshunis. "A good many of these verses," says Dr. Rhys Davids, "are not only beautiful in form but also give evidence of a very high degree of that mental self-culture which played so great a part in the Buddhist ideal of the perfect life. Many of the women who joined the order became distinguished for high intellectual attainments as well as for moral earnestness. Some women of acknowledged culture are represented not only as being the teachers of men and as expounding the deeper and subtler points of the Dharma, but also as having attained the Great Peace which is the final result of intellectual illumination and moral earnestness."

The Buddhist reformation being a moral reaction against a corrupt state of society, it was very necessary that the relations between the sexes should be guarded with care. Strict rules were therefore laid down for the intercourse of bhikshus with women and of bhikshunis with men. But nowhere in any of the utterances of the Buddha do we find anything to show that he made any difference between man and woman. If he honoured Maudgalyāyana and Sāriputra, he also held in high esteem Khema, the wife of King Bimbisāra, and Dhammadinna, the chief among the bhikshunis that preached the Dharma. In no religion has a woman played such a prominent part as Visākha has done in Buddhism. In the *Saddharmapundarīkam* the Blessed One appears on his holy mountain surrounded by multitudes of disciples, and among them are six thousand female saints. That the Blessed One often warned men against the dangers that lurk in man's attraction for woman does not prove that the Buddha regarded woman as naturally wicked. If people are warned to avoid a precipice, does it follow that there is something intrinsically bad about a precipice? If some people cannot see a precipice without wishing to throw themselves down, it is not the precipice that is to blame, but their bad circulation, and it is wise that such people should avoid precipices. Similarly, if some men cannot see a woman without devilish thoughts in their minds, is woman to blame for it? Wickedness is a thing that pertains to the heart. If a man could only be sure that he has no *trishṇa* for that which is specific in woman's organisation, he might mix with her as freely as he might like, whether he be an upāsaka or a bhikshu. Did not the Blessed One, when after his Enlightenment he visited Suddhodhana's palace, repair to the apartments of Yasodhara, the mother of Rāhula, to greet her, when she refused to come out? On that occasion the Blessed One said to Sāriputra and Maudgalyāyana, who accompanied him to the princess's chamber: "I am free; the princess, however, is not as yet free. Not having seen me for a long time, she is exceedingly sorrowful. Unless her grief be allowed its course, her heart will cleave. Should she touch the Tathāgata, the Holy One, you must not prevent her." The Buddha has not damned woman, because she is often a temptation to man to do evil, but he has only warned weakminded men against the dangers of her unconscious influence.

Theoretically man and woman are placed by the Buddha on the same footing of equality. But in practice the latter stands much lower. Her peculiar organization places more hindrances in the way of her attaining the goal. Before one can attain the Great Peace one must have purified oneself from all lust of the flesh by a severe struggle. Only a few men enter on this struggle, but most men seem capable of entering on the path. But most women are found in experience to be too scant in wisdom, too deeply immersed in vanity, and too frail for that renunciation and mastery of the passions which are demanded of those who aspire to reach the supreme heights of Nirvaṇa. This is why the Buddhists often say that most women must be born as men, before they can enter on the Noble Path that leads to the Great Deliverance. But the Dharma itself holds both men and women as equally fitted for the task. If women can only see the light and follow the path, they will reach the goal as well as men.

Buddhism being a matter of self-control and self-culture, it regards every individual, whether man or woman, as a complete whole. Accordingly the Dharma does not concern itself with those relations between man and woman in which one sex is regarded as completing the other. But in all Buddhist countries the influence of Buddhism has been such that woman has always had fair play. She is given perfect freedom and is bound by no rigid ties. Speaking of the influence of Buddhism on the Burmese, Talboys Wheeler says: "Their wives and daughters are not shut up as prisoners in the inner apartments, but are free as air to take their pleasure on all occasions of merry-making and festivals; and often they assume an independent position in the family and household, and gain a livelihood for themselves or superintend the affairs of husbands or fathers. Their affections are not pent up in little hotbeds of despotism as in Hindu households, but are developed by social intercourse into free and healthy play. Courting time is an institution of the country. On any evening that a damsel is desirous of receiving company she places her lamp in her window, and puts fresh flowers in her hair, and takes her seat upon a mat. Meantime the young men of the village array themselves in their best, and pay a round of visits to the houses where they see that a lamp is burning. In this manner attachments are formed; and instead of arbitrary unions between boys and girls, there are marriages of affection between young women and young men, in which neither parents nor priests have voice or concern."

Most Burmese women, even in the villages, are able to read and write. No obstacle is placed in the way of female education. "At an early age," writes a Burmese lady, "the girls go to their school, and learn to read and write, the Buddhist scriptures in Burmese, and sometimes in mixed Burmese and Pāli, forming the ground-work of their studies. All that they learn, their ideals of right and wrong, of the nature of the body and the mind, of illness and hygiene, comes from the same source; as also do those higher teachings of faithfulness, generosity and kindliness, which are perhaps the most eminent traits in the character of the Burmese women. Many learn at school the five duties of a wife :—to order her household aright, to be a hospitable housewife, to be a chaste and faithful wife, a thrifty housekeeper, and a skilful and diligent woman ; and together with this instruction in ethics they receive a practical training in the ways of life at home." Females of the higher classes in Burma do not contemn industry nor affect the listlessness of Hindu women. A large proportion of the retail trade in Burma is in women's hands, and women even make long trading voyages on their own account. In Siam men of all ranks are greatly aided by their wives especially in public affairs, and in their movements are as free as men. Even in lamaistic Tibet women are granted complete independence both in business and personal conduct. The Russian explorer G. Ts. Tsybikoff writes: "Women enjoy perfect freedom and independence and take an active part in business affairs, often managing extensive enterprises unaided."

Among the Buddhists the ceremony of marriage is very simple. There are no complicated superstitious observances connected with it. In Ceylon, Tibet, Mongolia, Japan and in all other Buddhist countries marriage is properly a civil contract witnessed only by parents and guardians, relations and friends. Marriage in Burma is a compact on the part of husband and wife which is made before the elders of the village. When a Burmese woman marries, she does not change her name, nor does she wear any outward sign of marriage, such as a *tāli*, or a ring, or a covering for the head. No stranger can find out either from a woman's name or by seeing her whether she is married or not, or whose wife she is. A husband has no power over his wife's property. Whatever she may bring with her, or earn for herself, or inherit subsequently, is all her own. She is absolutely the mistress not only of her own property but also of her own self. Among the Hindus a woman is always dependent. When young she is dependent on her parents, when married on her husband, and when old on her children. Among Europeans, a woman loses her own name when she marries, and becomes known only as the mistress of her husband.

In Burma a woman, though married, always remains mistress of herself, a companion of her husband. No wonder that Sir T. G. Scott says that "the Burmese woman enjoys many rights which her European sister is even now clamouring for!"

The Buddhist religion is a religion of free individuals. It enforces no obedience to any authority other than the law of righteousness. Among the several vows that a bhikshu takes on joining the order, there is no vow of obedience to any superior. How can such a religion make an unbreakable bond of marriage, as other religions have done? Hence in all Buddhist countries the ideal of marriage is that it is a partnership of love and affection, which, when these no longer exist, should be dissolved. In Burma for proper cause shown the marriage compact can be terminated by either party. And the grounds which suffice for the dissolution of the marriage tie are much more numerous than, and different from, those which obtain in Western countries. Drunkenness, the opium habit, difference of temperament, a nagging tongue, spendthrift ways—all these form, if proved, sufficient grounds for the elders to grant a divorce. In spite of this freedom the proportion of divorced to married couples is very small in Burma. On the other hand the facility of divorce has made men and women very careful in their behaviour towards each other.

A charge usually brought against the Dharma is that its teachings are destructive of the family life, as those that accept its teachings in all their fulness do not marry, or if they are already married, betake themselves to a homeless life, leaving their parents, wives and children. This is no new accusation. The Buddhist books tell us that the people of Rājagriha reviled the bhikshus for inducing young nobles to leave their homes and thus causing the extinction of many families. When this reviling was reported to the Blessed One, he said: "If people revile you, O bhikshus, say that it is by preaching the truth that Tathāgatas lead men. Self-control, righteousness and a clean heart are the injunctions of our Master." Self-control, righteousness and a clean heart cannot be acquired except by the renunciation of all sensual pleasure and the practice of perfect chastity. If voluntary chastity brings about the destruction of the family life, the loss is none too great for the true holiness and perfection thereby achieved. Not only Buddhism but all other religions also have laid greater or less stress on celibacy. But it might be asked, what would become of the human race if all abstained from the nuptial bed, which is the only means of propagating the species? Would that they did so with a pure mind and a clean conscience, with zeal and unselfishness so that they could soon become citizens of the kingdom of righteousness and hasten the end of Māra's dominion! Would not such extinction of mankind be nobler than destruction by war and tyranny, poverty and famine, plague and pestilence, earthquake and tidal wave? As Schiller says,

> "Das Leben ist der Güter Höchstes nicht."
> (Mere living is not the highest good.)

THE FOUR GREAT TRUTHS.

The main teachings of the Dharma have been summarised by the Blessed One in four propositions, which are generally known as the Four Great Truths or affirmations* (*chatur āryasatyāni*). They contain in a nutshell the philosophy and the morality of Buddhism. They are as follow:

The first great truth is that misery, that is to say, pain and suffering *(dukkha)*, is associated with all stages and conditions of conscious life. Birth is suffering; age is suffering; illness is suffering; death is suffering. Painful it is not to obtain what we desire. Painful again it is to be joined with that which we do not like. More painful still is the separation from that which we love.

The second great truth is that the cause of misery (*samudaya*) is *trishṇa*, the grasping desire to live for selfish enjoyment. Sensations (*vedana*), begotten by the surrounding world, create the illusion of a separate self. This illusory self manifests its activity in a cleaving to things for selfish enjoyment which entangles man in pain and suffering. Pleasure is the deceitful siren which lures man to pain.

The third great truth is that emancipation from misery (*nirodha*) is possible by abandoning selfish cravings (*upādānas*). When all selfish cravings are destroyed, there is necessarily an end of suffering. All selfish craving arises from want, and so long as it is not satisfied, it leads to pain. Even when it is satisfied, this satisfaction is not lasting, for this very satisfaction gives rise to new needs and therefore to new sorrows. The entire essence of man seems to be an unquenchable thirst for a thousand wants. How else could he get rid of sorrow but by abandoning this thirst?

The fourth great truth is that the Noble Eightfold Path (*ārya ashtānga mārga*) is the means by which man can get rid of all selfish cravings and attain perfect freedom from

* In the statement of these Four Great Truths, the language of Indian medical science has been employed.

suffering. He who has fathomed the Dharma will necessarily walk in the right path, and to him salvation is assured.

These four great truths form what may be called the articles of the Buddhist creed. But they are not put forward as dogmas which have to be accepted without inquiry. Dogmatism which prohibits investigation would, instead of leading to the Buddhist *summum bonum*, dissuade the aspirant from his duty and therefore from the Noble Path. Nowhere has the Buddha said: "Avoid inquiry, for it will lead you where there is no light, no peace, no hope; it will lead you into the deep pit, where the sun and moon and stars and beauteous heavens are not, but chilliness and barrenness and perpetual desolation."* On the other hand, it is clearly laid down that nothing can be the teaching of the Buddha which is not consistent with reason, which cannot be subjected to the dry light of investigation. The idea of a religious authority is incompatible with the Dharma, for it teaches that every man is his own architect and his own saviour. It is a childish idea to suppose that an authority, external to man, can have a religious value. An authority can only exist for one only in proportion as one recognises it as such either unconsciously and without understanding the motives that prompt him, or by virtue of an act of conscious reasoning. After all it is the adhesion of one's mind and will that can give weight to any authority. A Buddhist bhikshu, unlike the Christian monk, lays no claim to any authority, nor does he avow obedience to any authority. The aim set by the Blessed One before the aspirant being enlightenment, the belief in authority and dogma will be of no avail. The creed of Buddhism is, therefore, like the creed of every genuine science, a register of results.

No one can question the fact that misery is associated with conscious life. We live in a world which is full of evil and misery. Were there no misery, there would be no need for the struggle for existence which is always and everywhere in evidence. Hunger and fear are the boon companions of the great majority of human beings, not to speak of the animals in the same condition. Individual experience and history

*Cardinal Newman.

prove that optimism is the silliest nonsense that has been invented to console mankind. Even the most hardened optimist, if he would but open his eyes well, would be horrified to see the immensity of misery and suffering which surrounds man. Let him walk through hospitals, lazarettos, surgical rooms, through penitentiaries, dungeons, and slave kennels, through places of torture and execution, through battlefields, and then let him ask himself if this is the best of all possible words. He will no longer find it easy to doubt that

> "life from birth to death
> Means—either looking back on harm escaped,
> Or looking forward to that harm's return
> With tenfold power of harming?"

Schopenhauer has vividly described the misery of life as follows:

"Having awakened to life from the night of unconsciousness the will finds itself as an individual in an infinite and endless world among innumerable individuals, all striving, suffering, erring; and as though passing through a frightful unpleasant dream, it hurries back to the old unconsciousness. Until then, however, its wishes are unlimited, its claims inexhaustible, and every satisfied desire begets a new one. No gratification possible in the world could allay its cravings, put a final end to its longings, and fill the bottomless abyss of its heart. Consider, too, what satisfactions of every kind man generally receives: they are usually nothing more than the meagre preservation of this existence itself, daily gained by ceaseless toil and incessant care, in struggle against want, with death for ever in the van. Everything in life indicates that earthly happiness is destined to be foiled or to be avowed as a delusion. The causes of this lie deep in the nature of things. Accordingly the life of most of us proves sad and short. The comparatively happy are usually only apparently so, or are, like longlived persons, rare exceptions—left as a decoy for the rest.

"Life proves a continual deception in great as well as small matters. If it makes a promise, it does not fulfil it, unless to show that the coveted object was little desirable.

Thus sometimes hope, sometimes the fulfilment of hope, deceives us. If it gives, it is but to take away. The fascination of distance presents a paradise, like an optical illusion when we have allowed ourselves to be allured thither. Happiness accordingly lies always in the future or in the past; and the present is to be compared to a small dark cloud which the wind drives over a sunny plain. Before it and behind it all is bright, it alone casts a shadow. The present therefore is never satisfactory; the future uncertain; the past irrecoverable. Life with its hourly, daily, weekly, and yearly small, great and greater misfortunes, with its frustrated hopes and mishaps baffling all calculation, bears so plainly the impress of something we should become disgusted with that it is difficult to understand how any one could have mistaken this and been convinced that life was to be thankfully enjoyed and man destined to be happy. On the other hand the eternal delusion and disappointment as well as the constitution of life throughout seem as though they were intended and adapted to arouse the conviction that nothing whatever is worthy of our striving, driving and wrestling,—that all goods are nought, the world bankrupt throughout, and life a business that does not meet expenses,—so that our will may turn away from it.

"The manner in which this vanity of all objects of the will reveals itself, is, in the first place, time. Time is the form by means of which the vanity of things appears as transitoriness, since through time all our enjoyments and pleasures come to nought; and we afterwards ask in amazement what has become of them? Accordingly our life is like a payment which we receive in copper pence, and which at last we must receipt. The pence are the days, death the receipt. For, at last, time proclaims the sentence of nature's judgment upon the worth of all beings by destroying them.

> And justly so; for all things from the void
> Called forth, deserve to be destroyed.
> T'were better, there were nought created.—*Goethe.*

"Age and death, to which every life necessarily hurries, are the sentence of condemnation upon the will to live, passed by nature herself, which declares that this will is a struggling, that must defeat itself. 'What thou hast willed', it says, 'ends thus; will something better'.

"The lessons which each one learns from his life consist, on the whole, in this, that the objects of his wishes constantly delude, shake and fall; consequently they bring more torment than pleasure, until at length even the whole ground upon which they all stand gives way, inasmuch as his life itself is annihilated. Thus he receives the last confirmation that all his striving and willing were a blunder and an error.

'Then old age and experience, hand in hand,
Lead him to death, and make him comprehend
After a search so painful and so long
That all his life he has been in the wrong.'

"Whatever may be said to the contrary, the happiest moment of the happiest mortal is still the moment he falls asleep, as the unhappiest moment of the unhappiest mortal the moment he awakens." *

Despite the gruesome misery of life man does not grow desperate. True to his nature as a living being he is continually striving after self-preservation. With all his labour in civilisation man strives for nothing else than his salvation, his deliverance from sorrow and suffering. What man speaks of as pleasure or happiness is nothing else than deliverance from pain. We know nothing positive about pleasure. Some desire or want is the condition that precedes every pleasure. With the satisfaction of the want, the wish and, therefore, the pleasure cease. All that is given to us directly is merely the want, *i.e.*, the pain. Even when all other wants have been satisfied, there is one desire which man cannot attain. Man's instinctive impulse towards self-preservation has created in him a desire for changeless and deathless life, a desire to be free from old age and death. How can this desire be attained? How can man obtain deliverance from the inevitable doom of death? How is it possible to maintain a continuity in spite of the perpetual change going on in the great struggle of existence? This is everywhere the problem of religion. Everywhere religion is the instinct of self-preservation manifesting itself in the form of hope and

* The world as Will and Idea, vol II, Chapter 46.

aspiration. Wherever man meets with circumstances which cannot be made serviceable to him, but to which on the contrary he is obliged to suit himself and his life-aims, there arises religion. Religion, in the true sense of the word, has nothing to do with the origin or purpose of the world. As Prof. Leuba says, "not god, but life, more life, a larger, more satisfying life is, in the last analysis, the end of religion." With true insight and wisdom has the Buddha declared: "Have I promised to reveal to you secrets and mysteries? I have, on the contrary, promised to make known to you suffering, the cause of suffering, and the way of escape from suffering. As the vast ocean is impregnated with one taste, the taste of salt, so also my disciples, this Dharma, this teaching, is impregnated with one taste, the taste of deliverance."

In his attempts to find a perfect life, a life free from misery and death, man has through ignorance fallen a victim to the creations of his own fancy. To satisfy his longing for a deathless life he invented immortal souls which could survive the death of the body. Judging the unknown, upon which he found himself hopelessly dependent for the realisation of his desires, in the light of what was best known to him, that is to say, of what he fancied about his own nature, he peopled the universe with gods, souls like himself but more mighty and capable of doing him good or harm. To win the favour of the gods or avert their wrath, man invented all kinds of prayers, charms, magical formulæ, and bloody sacrifices. Especially the last have played such a prominent part in religion that many writers on anthropology have mistaken it for 'the fundamental doctrine of religion'. Even the very gods have been supposed to become incarnate human beings and offer themselves in sacrifice for the salvation of mankind.* But all these are not essential to religion, and the Buddha saw that clearly. He put an end to all kinds of sacrifices, rejected the use of charms and magical

* "A curious relic of primitive superstition and cruelty remained firmly imbedded in Orphism—a doctrine irrational and unintelligible, and for that very reason wrapped in the deepest and most sacred mystery: a belief in the sacrifice of Dionysos himself, and the purification of man by his blood."

formulæ, and pointed out the ineptitude of gods to save mankind. He taught that misery and suffering were not the result of the wrath of gods, but that they were the consequences of man's ignorance of his own nature and his surroundings. Nor is death the result of sin. Life and death are inseparable. All life is change; and what is change but the death of the present? Man shudders at and fears death, and yet death and life are not different. Just as all energy tends towards dissipation, so does all life tend towards death. All life is progressive death. The great Chinese philosopher Licius, pointing to a heap of mouldering human bones, rightly remarked to his scholars: "These and I alone have the knowledge that we neither live nor are dead." Similarly just before his death the Buddha said: "Everything that lives, whatever it be, is subject to the law of destruction; the law of things 'combined' is to 'separate.'"

The world process did not come into existence all perfected. It started with blind potentialities, and when self-conscious man made his appearance on the scene there, was already an outcrop of inherited tendencies. That man originated from an animal is no longer doubted. All known facts demonstrate that man, looked at from a purely zoological standpoint, is nothing more than a simian 'monster', a sort of arrested development in an anthropomorphic ape of an anterior epoch. He is only a prodigy child of an anthropoid born with a brain and intelligence more developed than those of its parents.* As a result of this origin there have survived in man qualities fitted for a nonmoral life. But his development gave rise to the necessity of associating with his fellows into families, and this has led to the growth of social life, a life of morality. What is called the feeling of sinfulness is nothing else than the consciousness that the actions suited to an individual life are not suited to the requirements of a social or moral life, a consciousness which varies in proportion to the development of social claims and the moral sense.

Evolution takes place through all forms, from the mineral through plants and all kinds of animal forms, until perfec-

* Elie Metchnikoff: Etudes sur la nature humaine.

tion is reached in the Buddha. All beings are what they are by their previous and present *karma*. The germ of enlightenment (*nirvāṇadhātu*) first manifests itself as sentient reflex activity, but gradually develops through the path of conscious concurrence into self-conscious rational reaction. In the initial stage of sentient reflex activity the living being acts under the influence of some inherent impulse which enables it to accomplish some good in a mechanical way. This reflex activity excludes all freedom and evil propensities ; the living being is devoid of all notion of good or evil, and it lives, so to speak, in unconscious communion with the whole of nature. In the middle stage of conscious concurrence the living being begins a life of individuality, differentiating itself more and more as it progresses from other beings and disputing with them for as large a share as possible of enjoyment and satisfaction. Though it has lost the primitive simplicity which, in the initial stage, enabled it to do some good unconsciously, yet it has acquired freedom. It is now constantly bent on evil, but when it does evil it knows not that it does evil.

During the final stage of self-conscious rational reaction the living being enters on the struggle for life, engages in the strife for pleasure and comfort, and sacrifices as many beings as it can for the satisfaction of its own egoistic appetites, but when it does evil there arises within itself a feeling of remorse. Gradually the notion of duty takes root in the heart of man, and it becomes a check to the free play of his passions. As he makes constant efforts to arrest his passions, his moral sense, the keen perception for improvement, becomes more and more active. He finds it necessary to wipe off the effects of his bad tendencies, and he resolves to suppress them in future. He thus gets a glimpse of the Noble Path that leads to perfection. The more intense this self-conscious reaction in a man is, the more does he feel a necessity to return to a stage similar to that of reflex activity, though acting in the full consciousness of freedom. He can henceforth do nothing else than good, but, instead of doing it in an involuntary mechanical way like the beings of the initial stage, he does it voluntarily with a view to accumulate merit. He does good to others, not in order that they may do good to him, but because by doing so, he does good to himself. How can one be good to others, if he is not good to himself? The deliberate accomplishment of good, even at the sacrifice of the demands of reflex activity and primal instinct, opens out to him the Noble Path of enlightenment. He now perceives under what conditions it would be possible to traverse the path. By means of the efforts he makes to produce a moral transformation in himself, he sees with certainty what further steps have necessarily to be taken to reach the goal. His final emancipation, his salvation from misery and death, is now assured. It is merely a question of time, for he is in possession of the means of hastening his emancipation. He suppresses more and more his egoistic inclinations and works for the good of all beings. When he has trained himself to feel his oneness with all that lives, with the generations past and the generations to come, not only with his fellow-beings, but with the whole world, with every creature that walks the earth, his progress is completed, and he has reached the blissful haven where there is no more struggle, no more pain, but unutterable peace. By breaking the chains which bind him to the world of individuality and growing to be co-extensive with all life, he secures for himself a life ever-lasting, where there is no more the taste of death.

> " 'Tis self whereby we suffer. 'Tis greed
> To grasp, the hunger to assimilate
> All that earth holds of fair and delicate,
> The best to blend with beauteous lives, to feed
> And take our fill of loveliness, which breed
> This anguish of the soul intemperate.
> 'Tis self that turns to harm and poisonous hate
> The calm clear life of love that Arhats lead.
> Oh! that't were possible this self to burn
> In the pure flame of joy contemplative!
> Then might we love all loveliness, nor yearn
> With tyrannous longings; undisturbed might live
> Greeting the summer's and the spring's return
> Nor wailing that their bloom is fugitive."

BUDDHISM AND ASCETICISM.

THE religion of Ancient India was a form of natural religion in which sacrifice played an important part. In the beginning, probably sacrifices were offered with a view to avert the wrath of the gods whom men feared. But in later times sacrifice was regarded as a means of communication between men and gods. As fire is both celestial and terrestrial, Agni, the god of fire, which is kindled in every sacrifice, was supposed to act as the middleman between men and gods and bear the oblation to the gods. If sacrifice could be a means of communicating with the gods, it would not be impossible for man to enter into economic ralations with them. If man could offer the gods something that would please them, it should also be possible for the gods to give man in return what he might desire. Thus in due course sacrifice developed into a kind of bartering with the gods. "*Dehi me dadami te*—I give in order that you may give" is the burden of almost every Vedic hymn, and is the explicit or implied reason of every Vedic sacrifice. From the conception of sacrifice as a kind of barter easily arose the idea that sacrifices could not only buy the gods, but that the gods could, even against their will, be coerced by means of sacrifices to do what man desired. As Prof. Sylvain Levi* has pointed out, morality finds no place in this system. Sacrifice which regulates the relation of man to the divinities, is a mechanical act, operating by its own spontaneous energy, and the magic art of the priest brings out what is hidden in the bosom of nature. The gods are conquered and subjected by the same power that has given them their greatness. Whether the gods like or not, the sacrificer is elevated to the celestial sphere and assured there a definite place for the future.

Naturally the sacrificial arts rose in the estimation of the people, and eventually those that possessed the knowledge

* La doctrine du sacrifice dans les Brāhmṇas.

of the sacrificial arts succeeded in dominating the people of India. "*Devādhīnam jagat sarvam*," says a well-known Sanskrit verse, "*mantrādhīnam tadaivatam; tanmantrā brāhmaṇādhīnam, brāhmaṇā mamadevatā*." The universe is subject to the gods, and the gods are subject to the sacrificial *mantras*. But the *mantras* themselves are in the hands of the Brāhmans. Hence the Brāhmans are the real gods, though they live on this earth. The Brāhmans could make him a deity that was not a deity, and they could divest one that was a deity of his status as such. Thus, like the pontifices in Ancient Rome, the Brahmans became powerful and mighty in India.

Of all sacrifices the greatest is that in which a human being is offered to the gods. There can be no doubt that human sacrifices were once common in India. "Despite protestant legends, despite formal disclaimers," says Prof. E. W. Hopkins, "human sacrifices existed long after the period of the Rig Veda, where it is alluded to; a period when even old men were exposed to die." The ritual manuals and Brāhmanic texts prove that the *anādha-purusha* is not a fiction and that a real victim was offered. A human sacrifice was very expensive, for ordinarily it cost 'one thousand cattle' to buy a man to be sacrificed. It was indeed meritorious for one to put himself to this heavy expense, and offer a human victim to the gods, but it would be more meritorious for the very individual to whose benefit accrued the sacrifice to immolate himself. Thus was evolved the theory and practice of self-mortification as a means of coercing the gods to bestow gifts on man. The Hindu books are full of legendary accounts of the wonderful powers attained through self-mortification and austere penance. By self-mortification Rāvaṇa became invulnerable against gods and demons. By austere fervour Nahusha obtained the undisputed sovereignty of the three worlds. Visvāmitra, who was born a Kshatriya, raised himself by intense austerities to the Brāhman caste. In order to obtain elevation to the position of a Brāhman, Matanga, a Chandāla, went through such a course of austerities as alarmed the gods. Indra persistently refused such an impossible request. Nothing daunted Matanga balanced himself on his great toe till he was reduced to mere skin and bone, and was on the point of falling. Indra even came down to support him, but inexorably refused his request, and when further importuned, he granted him the power of moving about like a bird, and changing his shape at will, and of being honoured and renowned. Such was the deep belief of the people of Ancient India in the efficacy of asceticism and self mortification.

At the time of the rise of Buddhism the belief in the efficacy of self-mortification would appear to have reached its acme. Asceticism was regarded as identical with religiousness. In both Brāmanism and Jainism, which were in a flourishing condition in the time of Sākyamuni, great stress was laid on asceticism. The Jain religion teaches that twelve years of ascesticism of the severest type are necessary to salvation. The ideal life for a Jaina monk is described in the ***Ākārānga sutra*** as follows. "Giving up his robe, the Venerable One was a naked, world relinquishing, houseless sage. When spoken to or saluted, he gave no answer. For more than a couple of years he led a religious life, without using cold water; he realized singleness, guarded his body, had got intuition and was calm. For thirteen years he meditated day and night and was undisturbed in spirit. Practising the sinless abstinence from killing, he did no injurious acts; he consumed nothing that had been prepared for him; he consumed clean food. Always on his guard, he bore the pains caused by grass, cold, fire, flies, gnats, undisturbed. Whether wounded or unwounded, he desired not medical treatment. Medicines, anointing of the body and bathing, cleansing of the teeth, did not behove him after he had learned the path of deliverance. Sometimes the Venerable One did not drink for half a month or a month. Sometimes he ate only the sixth meal, or the eighth, or the twelfth. Without ceasing in his reflections the Venerable One wandered about, and killing no creatures he begged for his food: moist or dry or cold food, old beans, old pap, or bad grain—whether he did or did not get such food, he was rich in self-control." Logically self-mortification should lead to suicide. And in Jainism, while all other kinds of killing are strictly forbidden, suicide is highly praised. The proper method of committing suicide is to retire, after practising mendicancy and the approved austerities for twelve years, to a secluded spot, and having cleared it of all living creatures, starve one's self to death. "This method," says the *Ākārānga sutra*, "has been adopted by many who were free from delusion. It is good, wholesome, proper, beatifying, meritorious." Consistently with its asceticism Jainism abhors and despises womanhood. The *Yogasāstra* characterises women as "the lamps that burn on the road that leads to the gate of hell." In the *Uttarādhyayana sutra* women are called "female demons on whose breasts grow two lumps of flesh, who continually change their minds, who entice men and then make a sport of them as slaves." In the popular romances of the Jains the hero is the pious young man who, when going to his own wedding feast to be united to his bride, is smitten with remorse and pity for the numerous living beings that might be killed during the wedding festival, and so gives away his jewels in charity, plucks out his hair to its roots, and joins the order of ascetics. These austerities practised by the Jain monks form but a poor illustration of the extent to which self-torture and self-mortification had been pushed in the Buddha's time.

Gautama Siddārtha also fell into the trap of asceticism, but fortunately for the world he escaped from it. As was the fashion of his day Siddārtha also left his home and family, and retired to the forest to seek after truth. He placed himself under the guidance of the wisest hermits of his day. He studied all their teachings and endeavoured to follow their example. He tried to purify himself by ceremonies and sacrifices, by starvation and austerities, by nakedness and self-torture. He has himself desecribed how for six years in the jungle of Uruvilva he patiently tortured himself and suppressed all the wants of nature. He led the most rigorous ascetic life. He ate each day a single grain of rice. His body became emaciated and shrunken, so much that his arms and legs looked like withered reeds, his buttocks resembled the hump of a camel, and his ribs projected like the rafters of a house. The fame of his austerities spread in the neighbourhood, and crowds came to see him. He pushed his fast even to such an extreme that at last he fell into a swoon from sheer starvation and exhaustion. And when he came to himself, he found that no revelation had come to him in his senselessness. He once more began to eat and drink so that he recovered his strength. He pondered over the fruits of his self-mortification and found out that this was not the path to the wisdom he sought. Just as he realized in his palace that the way to salvation does not lie in the indulgence of worldly pleasures, so did he in the forest realise that fasts and penances do not advance people in their search for deliverance from misery.

In his sermon to the five bhikshus in the Deer Park at Benares the Tathāgata explained the Middle Path, the true means of attaining salvation, thus:

"Neither abstinence from fish or flesh, nor going naked, nor shaving the head, nor wearing matted hair, nor dressing in a rough garment, nor covering oneself with dirt, nor sacrificing to Agni, will cleanse a man whose mind is full of delusion.

"Neither reading the Vedas, nor sacrificing to the gods, nor fasting often, nor lying on the ground, nor keeping hard and strict vigils, nor repeating prayers will cleanse a man who is in error.

"Neither bestowing gifts on priests, nor self-mortification nor the performance of penances, nor the observance of rites can purify the man who has not overcome his passions.

"It is not the eating of flesh that constitutes uncleanness, but anger, drunkenness, obstinacy, bigotry, deception, envy, self-praise, disparagement of others, superciliousness and evil intentions—these cause uncleanness.

"Let me teach you, O bhikshus, the Middle Path, which keeps aloof from both extremes. By suffering the emaciated devotee produces confusion and sickly thoughts in his mind. Mortification is not conducive even to worldly knowledge; how much less to a triumph over the senses!

"He who fills his lamp with water will not dispel the darkness, and he who tries to light a fire with rotten wood will fail.

"Mortifications are painful, vain and profitless. And how can any one be free from self by leading a wretched life if he does not succeed in quenching the fires of lust?

"All mortification is vain so long as selfishness leads to lust after pleasures in this world or in another world. But he in whom egotism has become extinct is free from lust; he will desire neither worldly nor heavenly pleasures, and the satisfaction of his natural wants will not defile him. He may eat and drink to satisfy the needs of life.

"On the other hand, sensuality of every kind is enervating. The sensual man is a slave of his passions, and pleasure seeking is vulgar and degrading.

"But to satisfy the necessities of life is not evil. To shelter the body from the weather, to cover it decently and comfortably, to protect it against the numerous external causes of pain, to save it as far as possible from fatigue, to eliminate sensations that are disagreeable, in short, to keep the body in good health, is a duty, for otherwise we shall not be able to trim the lamp of wisdom and keep our minds strong and clear.

"This is the Middle Path, O bhikshus, that keeps aloof from both extremes."

Starting as it does from the first great truth that sorrow and suffering are concomitants of every conceivable form of egoism, the Dharma does not consign man to the sensualist's (*chārvāka*) "let us eat and drink for to-morrow we die." The Dharma spurns not only asceticism, but also all luxury. The aim of the Dharma is enlightenment and peace and not pleasure. Hence no mode of living, which is merely intended to increase pleasure without materially promoting health or efficiency, can be rational. On this ground all luxury, the mere increase of an individual's pleasure by superfluous consumption, is condemned. It cannot be doubted that luxury has in the long run a baneful effect on one's health. Who does not know the excesses in sensual indulgence committed by persons of wealth and leisure and the difficulty of avoiding them even by care and self-control? Luxurious habits make men disinclined for labour and incapable of sustained exertion and patient endurance, which are the powers needed for most kinds of strenuous work. Even if the prospect of luxury may act in some cases as an incentive to work, still from an ethical point of view it would seem base that one should not be able to do his duty without bribing himself by a larger share of consumable wealth than falls to the common lot. A man who lives in luxury consumes what, even from a purely utilitarian point of view, could have produced more happiness, if it had been left to be consumed by others. No body can eat his cake and also have it. It is an absurd fallacy to suppose that a man by living luxuriously provides work and therefore bread for the many. A man, properly speaking, benefits others by rendering service to them, and not by requiring them to render service to him. Luxury appears to receive some support from the Spencerian formula of "passage from indefinite homogeneity to definite heterogeneity," but really it finds no basis in the general law of evolution. Rather it has its origin in a conception of life which is opposed to the teachings of science. As Elie Metchnikoff says in his *Etudes sur la nature humaine*, "when the meaning and aim of life has become more precise, it will be found that true welfare does not consist in luxury, which is opposed to the normal cycle of human life."

Wealth is often supposed to procure ease of body and peace of mind, and give time for ideal ends and exercise for ideal energies. But it actually does so in very rare cases. As Adam Smith has rightly remarked in his *Theory of Morals*, "wealth and greatness are mere trinkets of frivolous utility no more adapted for procuring ease of body or tranquillity of mind than the tweezer-cases of the lover of toys ; and, like them too, more troublesome to the person who carries them about with him than all the advantages they can afford him are commodious.........In ease of body and peace of mind all the different ranks of life are nearly upon a level, and the beggar who suns himself by the side of the highway, possesses the security which kings are fighting for." Very few desire wealth for great purposes. Most covet large incomes for fine garments, handsome apartments, the theatre, public houses, horses and coaches, all for making a show of their money and never for increasing the sum of social benefits. The desire of gaining wealth and the fear of losing it generally breed cowardice and propagate corruption. In many circumstances the man in pursuit of wealth is a slave, whilst a man for whom poverty has no terrors is free.

Personal indifference to poverty gives the seeker after truth strength to devote himself to a noble but unpopular cause, and thus bear witness to the higher life. Small wonder, therefore, that the Buddhist bhikshu takes the vow of poverty!

The attainment of *bodhi* is much more than plain-living and high-thinking. It implies perfect sanity of life and perfect freedom from lust. Hence it involves the unusual sacrifice implied by a celibate life. The attainment of Nirvaṇa is an achievement so rare and grand that celibacy does not seem too great a sacrifice. Even in married life it may not be impossible to accomplish a good deal in the direction of the perfect life. Evolution would seem to indicate a necessary connection between celibacy and the higher life. Evolution points to a natural antagonism between individual perfection and race multiplication. While in the lower stages of animal life the race is everything and the individual nothing, in the higher types the reproductive function becomes subordinated, and the individual rises in importance. In the bacillus or the fish we see a prodigal fecundity, but the major portion of mankind has arrived at the stage of 'one at a birth.' The highest stage would, therefore, be that in which the individual is all to himself, no longer concerned with the propagation of the race. Hence the perfect individuality and the highest altruism demanded of the seeker after *bodhi* would seem to be impossible except at the cost of fitness for the multiplication of the species.

It is a charge frequently brought against the Buddhist bhikshu that he is a drone dependant on others for support. But this is an accusation not warranted by facts. No doubt there are black sheep in every fold. But Buddhism teaches that indolence is defilement and that strenuousness is the path of immortality. The Buddha never taught the doctrine of nonaction. To the Nirgrantha General-in-Chief, Simha, the Blessed One clearly pointed out that what he taught was the not doing of anything unrighteous either by word, by thought or by deed, and the doing of everything righteous by word, thought and deed. "O monks," says the Blessed One in the *Itivuttaka*, "be not afraid of good works: such is the name for happiness, for what is wished, desired, dear and delightful,—namely good works."

It may indeed be true that the Buddhist bhikshu does not take much interest in worldly matters, for he fears that they may lead him into wrong paths. But even from a worldly point of view he has rendered invaluable service to his country and his supporters. In all countries where Buddhism has flourished, the bhikshus have been the pioneers of civilization and the repositories of learning. In India, during the Middle Ages, no places were more famous for learning than Nālandā, Vallabhi, Odāntapuri and Vikramasīla. Nālandā was a seat of universal learning, where all the arts and sciences—*sabdavidya*, *silpasthāna-vidya*, *chikitsavidya*, *hetuvidya*, *adhyātmavidya*—were taught. "The monks of Nālandā to the number of several thousands," says Huen Thsang, "are men of the highest ability. Their conduct is pure and unblamable, although the rules of the monastery are severe. The day is not sufficient for asking and answering profound questions. From morning till night the monks engage in discussion, the old and the young mutually helping one another. Those who cannot answer questions out of the Tripiṭaka are little esteemed, and are obliged to hide themselves for shame. Hence, learned men from different cities come here in multitudes to settle their doubts and thence the streams of their fame spread far and wide. For this reason, some persons usurp the name of Nālandā students, and in going to and fro receive honour and consequence."

Speaking of the work done by the Buddhist bhikshus in Japan, Nobuta Kishimoto says: "It is often said against Buddhism that monks and priests are idle and unprofitable members of the community like drones living on the industry of others. This, in one sense, is true. But we must remember that, if Buddhism introduced into Japan certain numbers of these "drones" of society, it also introduced various arts, such as painting, sculpture and architecture. Most of the famous paintings, sculptures and buildings of the present Japan are religious, but principally Buddhistic. Moreover, the Buddhist monks and priests were not altogether idle and unprofitable. It is true that they were living on the gifts of the believers. But the Christian pastors, too, live on the gifts of the Christians, just as much as the Buddhist clergy do; yet no one calls them idle and unprofitable. Apart from their moral and religious functions it was mostly the monks who, in their pilgrimages in search of quiet spots, built roads and spanned bridges, thus making travelling and communication easy. It was often the monks who encouraged the people in the cultivation of the arts of peace and life. Often they themselves led the people in the transformation of waste land into rice fields." But, perhaps, the greatest value of Buddhism to Japan was educational. Going hand-in-hand with Chinese culture, Buddhism offered the boon of education to all. The Buddhist schools became centres of popular instruction. The village schools were all connected with Buddhist temples. The common people were taught the arts of reading and writing, ethics and philosophy for a nominal cost. The Buddhist bhikshu was the schoolmaster everywhere, and even the Imperial household employed Buddhist instructors. In Burma also every monastery is a school, and the bhikshus impart the elements of education to all, free of charge. No wonder that in Burma every man is able to read and write! Only in a Buddhist country such a simple solution of the problem of mass education would have been possible.

Some critics allege that the Buddha failed to inculcate the civic virtues comprehended in the idea of patriotism. This objection rests on ignorance. The Buddha actually taught the Vajji, a mighty people living in the neighbourhood of Magadha, the prime conditions of social welfare, the fundamental principles of that social order from which alone all civic virtues develop. Ajātasatru, the king of Magadha, once planned an attack upon the Vajji, and sent his prime-minister to inform the Buddha of his purpose. When the Blessed One received the message, he asked Ānanda if the Vajji held full and frequent assemblies. On Ānanda's answering in the affirmative, the Master said: "So long as the Vajji hold these full and frequent assemblies, they may be expected not to decline, but to prosper. So long as they meet in concord, so long as they honour their elders, so long as they respect womanhood, so long as they remain righteous, performing all proper duties, so long as they extend rightful protection, defence and support to the holy ones, the Vajji may be expected not to decline but to prosper." Then, turning to the king's messenger the Buddha said: "When I staid at Vaisālī, I taught the Vajji these conditions of welfare, that so long as they should remain well instructed, so long as they will continue in the right path, so long as they should live up to the precepts of righteousness, we could expect them not to decline, but to prosper." As soon as the prime-minister had gone, the Buddha called together the bhikshus and spoke to them on the conditions of the welfare of a community. "So long, O bhikshus, as the brethren hold full and frequent assemblies, meeting in concord, rising in concord, and attending in concord to the affairs of the Saṅgha; so long as they, O brethren, do not abrogate that which experience has proved to be good, and introduced nothing except such things as have been carefully tested; so long as their elders practise justice; so long as the brethren esteem, revere, and support their elders, and hearken unto their words; so long as the brethren are not under the influence of craving, but delight in the blessings of religion, so that good and holy men shall come to them and dwell among them in quiet; so long as the brethren shall not be addicted to sloth and idleness; so long as the brethren shall exercise themselves in the sevenfold higher wisdom of mental activity, search after truth, energy, joy, modesty, self-control, earnest contemplation, and equanimity of mind; so long the Saṅgha may be expected not to decline but to prosper. Therefore, O bhikshus, be full of faith, modest in heart, afraid of sin, anxious to learn, strong in energy, active in mind, and full of wisdom."

It is said in the *Mārasamyutta* (*Vagga* 2) that the Blessed One once asked himself if it would not be possible, following the teachings of the Dharma, to rule as a king who does not himself slaughter living beings, nor permits slaughter by others; who does not himself oppress people, nor sanctions oppression by others; who has himself no troubles and sorrows, nor causes trouble and sorrow to others. There can be no doubt that Emperor Asoka, the Dharmarāja of the Buddhist books,* sought to realise this ideal. By precept and example he tried to make his people better and happier. "In this way," says Asoka in his edicts, "acts of religion are promoted in the world, as well as the practice of religion. *viz.*, mercy and charity, truth and purity, kindness and goodness. The manifold acts of goodness which I accomplish serve as an example." "For me there cannot be too much activity in the administration of justice. It is my duty to procure by my instructions the good of the public; and in incessant activity and the proper administration of justice lies the root of public good, and nothing is more efficacious than this. All my endeavours have but this one object,—to pay this debt due to my people!" "All men (are like) my children. As I desire that (my) children should be safe now and hereafter, so do I desire (this) to all men." No sovereign ever rendered to his country a greater service than Asoka did to India. No wonder that his name is venerated from the Volga to Japan and from Siam to Lake Baikal! "If the greatness of a man," as Koeppen† says, "may be measured by the number of hearts that cherish his memory and by the number of lips that have uttered and still utter his name with reverence, then surely Asoka is greater than Cæsar or Charles the Great."

Spurning both sensuality and asceticism the Dharma urges a healthy simplification in living, discerning that the higher life must be rooted in hygiene, and not in hysteria. It therefore regards the mortification of all desire, the stultification of the will, as mere madness. Though it freely accepts the inevitable, it does not despair but diverts the mind from things that cannot satisfy—because they cannot endure—to aims intellectual and ethical. It is not the severing of the ties of life that constitutes renunciation, but the utter eradication of egoism. It is not the shaving of the head, nor the mowing of the chin, nor the donning of the yellow robe that constitutes *bhikshuta*, but it is the weeding of the heart from passion and pride, from lust and greed.

* See Divyāvadāna.

† Religion des Buddha.

"Restrained of hand, restrained of foot, restrained in speech, the best of the self-controlled, reflective, calm, content, alone, it is he that is a true bhikshu":* says the *Dhammapāda*. Still the bhikshu is no ascetic. He may not over-eat, but he eats enough to keep himself healthy and strong. He may not use garlands, scents, unguents, or ornaments, but he is clean and tidy. His yellow robes may not be fine and charming, but they are decent and comfortable. He may not live in a proud dwelling, but he always lives under a roof sheltered from the weather. He may not use a high or broad bed, but he sleeps on a soft couch. He may abstain from dancing, singing and stage plays, but he never cuts himself off from society. He may live a retired life, but he is freely accessible to men and women, with whom he talks on religious subjects. Not being a priest he may have no concern with births, deaths, or marriages, but he is devoted to spreading the knowledge of the Dharma. He may not beg his food, he may not speak of his wants to others, but he lives on their charity not because of indolence, but because it is a part of the discipline that trains his mind to humility. He struggles on the path of righteousness, not because he hopes to obtain heavenly gifts, but because in the fulness of gladness he will make an end of grief. He is honoured not for his learning or wisdom, but for the sanity and purity of his life, which serves as an example to others to

> "Dismiss their ideals of wealth and grandeur betimes,
> And heap up a store of that to which may never come
> Any prospect of perishing, nor danger of decay."

---

* The Buddhistic books speak of five classes of bhikshus: saṃjñābhikshu; pratijñābhikshu; bhikshaṇaçīlo bhikshu; jñāpti-chaturthakarmādyupasampanno bhikshu; and bhinnakleço bhikshu Of these the last is the highest, and the fourth respectable. The rest are disreputable.

BUDDHISM AND PESSIMISM.

IN his principal work, *The World as Will and Idea*, Schopenhauer declares : " If I were to take the result of my philosophy as the standard of truth, I would be obliged to concede to Buddhism the pre-eminence over the rest. In any case it must be a satisfaction to me to see my teaching in such close agreement with a religion which the majority of mankind upon the earth hold as their own." To Schopenhauer this avowal of a close agreement between his philosophy and Buddhism might have been a gratification, but for Buddhism it has certainly proved a misfortune. It has given rise to a serious misconception about Buddhism. The Buddhist ideal has been misjudged to be the result of a Schopenhauerian pessimism as to the worth and promise of life. Nothing can really be more untrue than the identification of Buddhism with any form of pessimism.

The keynote of Schopenhauer's philosophy is that inward discord is the very law of human nature. Consequently man, so long as he is conscious, must be an unhappy creature. " Painless the battle of life," says Schopenhauer, " cannot be, it may not end without bloodshed, and in any case man must mourn." On the contrary, the very aim of Buddhism is inward harmony, the Great Peace in which one can find refuge from the struggle and turmoil of life. " He whose delight is inward, who is tranquil and happy when alone—him they call a true bhikshu : " says the *Dhammapāda*. Not to despair, not to mourn is the burden of much of the teaching of the Buddha to his disciples. When Ānanda was mourning over Sāriputra's death, the Blessed One said :

" Ānanda, often and often have I sought to bring shelter to your mind from the misery caused by such grief as this. There are two things alone that can separate us from father and mother, from brother and sister, from all those who are most cherished by us, and those two things are distance and death. Think not that I, though the Buddha, have not felt all this even as any other of you ; was I not alone when I was seeking wisdom in the wilderness ?

"And yet what would I have gained by wailing and lamenting either for myself or for others? Would it have brought to me any solace from my loneliness? Would it have been any help to those whom I had lelt ? There is nothing that can happen to us, however terrible, however miserable, that can justify tears and lamentations and make them aught but a weakness."

It is indeed true that the Buddha recognises the existence of suffering and misery as honestly and fully as the deepest pessimist. It is also true that he insists strongly on the necessity of renouncing all sensuality, worldly ambitions, and feverish cravings, and the longing for mere life as such here or in another world. If he condemns as worthless what men generally consider natural and valuable, he does so because he finds them to be defilements (*ăcrava*) which stand as obstacles in the way of attaining perfect bliss. Worldly ambitions arise from a cleaving to things changeable, and as such cannot but prove dangerous. Life for its own sake is not worth living. If mere existence satisfied us, we should want for nothing. On the other hand, man finds delight only when he is struggling for the satisfaction of some want. When he has nothing to struggle for, man feels the emptiness of life in the form of boredom. Man's hankering for the strange and unusual proves beyond doubt how much he feels the tedium of ordinary life. Mere quantity of life, without quality, stands self-condemned. A life worth living is one that is full of active aspiration for something higher and nobler, a life full of culture and refinement, philosophic enthusiasm and earnest devotion to the good of others. And of such life the Dharma can never say we have enough. Often and often the Buddhistic books impress upon us the necessity of such life. Here is what the *Sutra of four perfections* says about the life worthy of an aspirant after *bodhi* :—

"What is the fruit of the thought of the bodhisatva? Answer:—Higher morality, higher perception of truth, great love, great pity. A spirit exempt from anger ; a spirit of compassion for the erring; a spirit which forbids falling away from wisdom: a spirit of perseverance to the end."

"What is his rule of duty?—To attach himself with high desire to all laws of virtue; not to despise the ignorant; to be a friend to all men; to expect no more from new births."

"What his bliss?—The joy of having seen a Buddha, of having heard the Dharma; of not repenting in giving; of having procured the good of all creatures."

"What his health?—The sound body, the mind not drawn to perishing things; bringing all beings into right and equal condition; freedom from doubt on every point relating to the Dharma."

"To what should he adhere?—To meditation; to beneficence; to compassionative love; to the discipline of wisdom."

"Since consciousness, body, life, self are impermanent, therefore, is there pefection in morality, in tranquillity, in wisdom, in release."

The Blessed One has nowhere condemned all life, because it results, and must inevitably result, in more pain than bliss. No doubt all life is a struggle of some sort, and struggle we must to live. Were this struggle, as Christianity teaches, the result of sin, and the misery accompanying it a punishment from heaven, this world would be the worst possible and we should be driven to pessimism. But the Dharma teaches that the painfulness of this struggle arises from our point of view. Life is so miserable, because we struggle in the interest of self, and not in the interest of truth and righteousness. How can he be happy who struggles in life with envy, hatred, and lust, so that he himself may be great or powerful, rich or famous? He that is anxious about his personal happiness must necessarily be full of fear. He may be indifferent to the misery of his fellow-beings, he may have his fill of the good things of the world, but he cannot be blind to the fact that the same end awaits us all. He alone can be truly happy who has realised that life and death are one. He who resigns to death that which belongs to death will be calm and self-possessed, whatever be his fate. Man may try to console himself with all sorts of chimeras and falsehoods, but experience shows how reluctant men are to die, whether they be pessimists or devout believers in a future life in a happy world. Just four days before his death, Charles Renouvier, a famous French philosopher, wrote:—"I have no illusions regarding my condition. I know that I am soon to die, in a week or, perhaps, two, and yet I have so many things to say about our doctrine. At my age one has no right to hope. One's days or one's hours are numbered. I must be resigned......I cannot die without regret that I can in no way foresee what will become of my ideas. Besides I am going before I have said my last word. One always has to leave before terminating one's task. This is one of the saddest of the sadnesses of life......This is not all. When one is old, very old, habituated to life, it is very difficult to die. I readily believe that young people accept the idea of death more easily than the old. When one is beyond eighty years, he becomes cowardly and does not wish to die, and when one knows beyond question that death is near, a feeling of melancholy pervades the soul......I have studied the question in all its aspects. I know that I am going to die. It is not the philosopher in me that protests. The philosopher in me does not believe in death, it is the old man who has not the courage to face the inevitable. However, one must be resigned." These words illustrate how men are blindly athirst for life. This thirst cannot be got rid of except by the complete liberation from the illusion of self. Hence, according to the Dharma, what we should strive for is not life but peace, the Great Peace of Nirvāṇa.

If the Buddha has taught us the vanity of grief and the selfishness of sorrow, if he has taught us to be resigned before the inevitable, he has also shown us the means of attaining true happiness. The Blessed One has fully recognised the fact that the world runs desperately after happiness in some form or other. But he has at the same time pointed out that happiness will not be found if it is directly sought, just as one aiming at the bull's eye of a target inevitably misses it. Nay more; the Dharma teaches that life would not be worth living, if its goal were the mere satisfaction of egoistic desires. If happiness in the eudœmonistic sense were the ideal of human life, it were better to return to the savage, if not the animal, state. Can it be denied that the animal and the savage are more happy than the civilized man of culture? No doubt civilization and culture have removed many evils and created many new comforts, but with them also have come into existence many new previously unknown sufferings, which are becoming keener and more intense with advancing refinement and increasing sensibility. While the animal suffers from actually existing pain, man's reason makes him multiply his afflictions by anticipation and rumination. As Kant has said, if the special purpose of a being endowed with reason and will were only its self-preservation and prosperity, or, in a word, its happiness as ordinarily understood, the creature has been badly equipped to secure the end in view. A pig with its instincts is perfectly happy, while a Socrates highly endowed with reason is always unhappy. Accordingly, the goal set before man by the Dharma is not happiness but perfection. "And who have perfection? Is it the pleasure-loving, or the painstaking? The right answer is: The painstaking, not the easy-going." But he who attains perfection also enjoys the bliss arising from the complete realization of his being. In one place the Buddha says: "Of those that live happily in this world am I also one." As the *Dhammapâda* says, he who attaches himself to the teaching of the Buddha lives happily free from ailments among the careworn, free from repining among men sick at heart, free from greed among men overpowered by greed, free from ill-will among the hating. He who has overcome all hindrances brightens the world like the moon free from clouds, and like the celestials feeds upon changeless bliss.

"Happy is the Buddhist's fate
For his heart knows not of hate.
Haters may be all around,
Yet in him no hate is found.

"Happy is the Buddhist's fate
He all pining makes abate.
Pining may seize all around,
Yet in him no pining's found.

"Happy is the Buddhist's fate
Him no greed will agitate
In the world may greed abound,
Yet in him no greed is found

> "Happily then let us live,
> Joyously our service give,
> Quench all pining, hate and greed:
> Happy is the life we lead."—*Dhammapāda*, 197—200.

A tree is judged by its fruit. Were Buddhism, as some writers try to make out, a dark and dreary creed characterised by a feeling of melancholy which bemoans the unreality of being, what should have been its effect upon the peoples professing it? They should be gloomy, cheerless, and entirely apathetic to all that interests man in life. But what is the reality? Has there been any people on the face of the earth more cheerful and happy than the Buddhists of Burma. Says Mr. Scott O'Connor in *The Silken East*: "Yet of all peoples of the earth the Burmese are probably the happiest. Most of the requisites of the modern Utopias they already possess: leisure, independence, absolute equality, the nearest approach to a perfect distribution of wealth; in addition a happy temper cheerful in all adversities. Who is there in the world who would not wish for some at least of these things for himself? And many, struggling with all the problems of modern life, of pauperism, of congestion in great cities, with social hatreds and the deep antagonism of classes, look in vain as for an unattainable thing for what the Burmese race, as a whole, has attained." Much the same can be said of the Siamese and the Japanese. There is nothing in the life of any people professing Buddhism which can give any room for characterising the faith which they profess as a 'religion of despair.' How dreary, on the contrary, must be a religion which makes its adherents bow down in submissive awe before a terrible monster who revels in preying over the weak? True religion is not that which turns man into a cur, but that which makes him more of a man and removes from him the feeling of dependence. The Dharma makes man free by raising him, through self-culture and self-control, to the supreme heights of perfection.

Man has furthered evolution unconsciously and for personal ends, but the Dharma teaches that it is his duty to do so deliberately and systematically for the attainment of perfection. For Buddhism life is "neither as pretty as rose pink nor as repulsive as dirty drab." It admits the plain fact that life is not worth its own troubles, if we live merely for the selfish enjoyment of life. It therefore places the value of life in ideals that transcend the narrow limits of individual existence. It aims not merely at the alleviation of present suffering, but also the creation of conditions under which no suffering can exist. As Aristotle says, "the wise man seeks after freedom from pain, not pleasure." So does the Buddhist direct his actions to the prevention and removal of suffering without caring for any pleasure which may thereby be attained or promoted. Still this does not imply the denial of the blessings of life. On the contrary, when the Blessed One was asked to declare what he regarded as the blessings of life, he did not like the pessimist say:

> "Count o'er the joys thine hours have seen,
> Count o'er thy days from anguish free;
> And know, whatever thou hast been,
> 'Tis something better—not to be."

But he replied:

> "The succouring of mother and father,
> The cherishing of child and wife,
> The following of a peaceful calling,
> This is the greatest blessing.
>
> "Acts of charity, a pious life,
> Aid rendered to your kin,
> And actions that are blameless,
> This is the greatest blessing.
>
> "Self-discipline and purity,
> The comprehension of the four Great Truths,
> And the attainment of Nirvana,
> This is the greatest blessing."—*Mangala Sutta.*

THE NOBLE EIGHTFOLD PATH.

"TWO extremes, there are," said the Blessed One in his first sermon at Benares, "which he who strives after holiness must avoid. Which two?—A life addicted to pleasure, for it is enervating, vulgar, mean and worthless—and a life given to self-mortification, for it is painful, vain and profitless. By avoiding both these extremes has the Tathagata arrived at the Middle Path (*Madhyama pratipada*), which leads to insight, to wisdom, to knowledge, to peace, to Nirvaṇa. But which is this Middle Path?—It is the Noble Eightfold Path."

No man can truly call himself a Buddhist, if he has not entered the Noble Eightfold Path. Mere study and investigation of the teachings of the Buddha do not qualify one to be a Buddhist, if he is not at the same time pursuing the Eightfold Path. The Eightfold Path represents the morality of Buddhism, and in Buddhism the moral life is no mere adjunct but its very core and essence. He who has merely understood the Dharma but has not shaped his life and thought in accordance with its spirit is like one who having read a book on cookery imagines that he has eaten the sweets described in the book.

Straight and broad indeed is the noble path that leads to blessedness, but no one can traverse it unless he is fully equipped with the eight essentials. The torch of right belief (*samyak drishti*) must light his way. Right aspiration (*samyak samkalpa*) must be his guide. Right speech (*samyak vāk*) must form his dwelling place on the road. Right action (*samyak karma*) must be his erect gait, and right living (*samyak ājīva*) must form his refreshments on the road. Right effort (*samyak vyayāma*) must be his steps, right thought (*samyak smriti*) his breath, and right tanquillity (*samyak samādhi*) his sleeping couch.*

The real history of the development of man consists in

* Asvagosha's Buddha-charitra.

the history of his beliefs. History, whether it be of the arts or of the sciences, or of society, or of religion, always involves an account of man's beliefs and their growth. Men's doings are largely a reflection of their beliefs. Consequently, all superstitious customs and practices are the result of an irrational state of mind issuing logically from wrong beliefs. It is therefore natural that right belief should form the first equipment for the pilgrimage on the noble path of purity. Again the spring of all action is motive, and the intellectual stimulus to motive is belief. Hence only right belief can lead man to right action.

Animistic and metaphysical beliefs have been the fruitful sources of religious error. The right starting point for religion can be nothing else than the universally recognised fact of the existence of sorrow and suffering, from which every religion proposes to save mankind. The right comprehension of the existence of misery and its cause, the illusion of a permanent self, will enable one to find easily the means of removing it. But the belief in a soul or the dependence on a supernatural being for one's salvation can only lead to error which would stultify one's efforts towards emancipation from misery.

It is the possession of the right belief that differentiates the educated from the uneducated, the thoughtful from the unreflecting. People come by their beliefs in four different ways. Some merely take refuge in the calm satisfaction of a faith that their view alone is the right one, and look with pity, contempt, or even horror on all other views. These men of tenacity are like the ostrich that buries its head in the sand as danger approaches and then feels satisfied that there is no danger. More often, imposed authority forms the expeditious means of producing a general belief. But this method, though lightly tolerated by the many, is not acceptable to the thoughtful few, who easily penetrate the mist of dogma, and, detecting the pretentiousness of all infallibility, look elsewhere for obtaining a sounder belief. Even when freed from the fetters of authority, men frequently fall victims to their hopes and wishes, and accept views which seem plausible, agreeable, or elevating. From this condition of mind no progress can result. Only when one scrutinises one's inclinations and wishes, and cares more for the validity of one's reasoning than for its agreeableness, would it be possible to find the truth. It is one of the glories of Buddhism that it appeals to reason and science, and not to blind faith and authority. Only he who has set aside vain hopes and wishes can perceive that the power with which he combats suffering and sorrow is natural and not supernatural. Only the sceptre of reason and science can safeguard to all the most cherished opportunities for right action, right thought, and right peace.

When an earnest intelligent man has gained right views concerning the existence of misery, its cause and its cessation, how could he find satisfaction in pleasure-seeking? He has found that to seek pleasure is to multiply pain. When one has begun to see things as they are, how could he be swayed by motives of dollars and cents, or of mere personal interest? When one has perceived that there is the infinite to traverse and the perfect to attain, how can he find happiness in repose? His mind will always be directed towards the attainment of *bodhi*. His aspiration will be to free his mind from doubts and contradictions as to the possibility of reaching the goal; to be paying homage to the Blessed One by investigating his Dharma and disciplining himself in accordance with its teaching; to abandon the idea of separateness; and to deliver himself and all beings drowned in the sea of misery by the employment of the various expedients which lead to the haven of the Great Peace. "What then, O friend, is right aspiration?" says the *Sacchavibhanga*: "It is the longing for renunciation; the hope to live in love with all; the aspiration after true humanity." With the firm resolve to attain *bodhi* the aspirant must enter on the prescribed course of self-culture and self-control.

Aspirations and resolutions will be of little avail, if they are not followed by practices which can secure the end in view. The inner life of the individual will become strengthened only when it energises into the external world as activity. Consequently right aspirations must find objective manifestation in right speech, right action and right living. "To abstain from falsehood, to abstain from back-biting, to abstain from harsh language, and to abstain from frivolous talk is called right speech." The words of one who aspires to the higher life must be kind, open, truthful, unequivocal; encouraging to others and helpful in improving them; and free from vanity and bitterness of feeling. He must not "gossip about great people;" he must not speak at all about "meats, drinks, clothes, perfumes, couches, equipages, women, warriors, demigods, fortune-telling, hidden treasures, ghost stories, nor about empty tales concerning things that are not." Whatever he speaks he must speak kindly and with a pure thought.

Hand-in-hand with the elimination of selfishness from one's speech must proceed the purification of one's acts from all egotistic taint. "*Atmabhāvān tathā bhogān sarvatrāvagatam subham nirapekshastyajām yesha sarvasatvārtha siddhaye*—I give up all my pleasures and enjoyments for the good and benefit of all beings." So says the *Bodhicharyāvatāra*. The aim of right action is not one's own happiness which may result from it. Right action consists in the avoidance of all that is subversive of the higher life and in the doing of all that is good and noble. Progress in the higher life cannot be effected by means of rituals, sacrifices, prayers and incantations, and these are therefore forbidden. But real merit (*punyam*) is acquired by the practice of morality (*çīla*) and charity (*dāna*). "Not superstitious rites," says Asoka in his edicts, "but kindness to servants and underlings, respect to those deserving of respect, self-control coupled with kindness in dealing with living creatures; these and virtuous deeds of like nature are verily the rites that ought everywhere to be performed."

The practice of morality (ç*īla*) consists in the observance of all moral precepts; in feeling fear, shame and remorse at the smallest violation of any of them; in not giving room for blame or disgust; in practising those deeds which lead to moderation and contentment, and in endeavouring to induce all human beings to abandon evil and practise virtue. He alone truly practises morality, who desists from evil-doing when the best opportunities present themselves for doing evil. In Buddhism the moral life is of fundamental importance. Of all the *pāramitās*, the excellences which form the means of arriving at Nirvaṇa, the *çīla pāramitā* is the foundation. Some of the other *pāramitās* may in some respects be higher than *çīla*, but they may be dispensed with, if necessary, for the sake of *çīla*, as the latter, owing to its being the basis of good acts, can on no account be neglected.

While morality is in some respects passive, charity is always active. Charity implies much more than the mere observance of certain rules, such as those of *ahimsa* and *adattadāna*. It implies not only some amount of self-sacrifice, but also the feeling of gladness arising from helping those in need of help. How charity is to be practised is clearly inculcated in the Dharma. When people ask one for something, one ought, as far as one's means permit, to supply it ungrudgingly and make them rejoice in it. "The giving of alms is a blessing to him who receives as well as to him who gives; but the receiver is inferior to the giver." If one finds people threatened with danger, one ought to try every means of rescuing them and impart to them a feeling of fearlessness. As far as one is acquainted with the Dharma, one ought to instruct others in it, for the gift of the Dharma, the Truth, exceeds all other gifts. "There is no such charity," says one of Asoka's edicts, "as the charitable gift of Dharma, no such friendship as the friendship in Dharma, no such distribution as the distribution of Dharma, no such kinship as kinship in Dharma." The *bodhisattva* is expected to be not only a donor but also one compassionate and forgiving. "Loving and compassionate," said the Blessed One to Anāthapindika, the supporter of the orphans, "he gives with reverence and banishes all hatred, envy and anger."

In performing acts of charity one's aim ought not to be either fame or any other advantage in this or another world. No doubt one thinks of benefiting others, but one's mind is set wholly on the attainment of Nirvāṇa. Even when there may be no one to profit by his acts, his disposition ought to be charitable. As the *Bodhicharyavatāra* says, "by the *dānapāramitā* we understand the disposition to live for the good and benefit of all beings."

It is the attitude of mind that measures the merit of a charitable act. A legend tells us that in Pushpapura there was the begging bowl of the Buddha, which would become full when the poor put in a single flower, but rarely showed signs of being filled when the rich put in thousands. Many of the Jātaka stories are also intended to illustrate the same point. These stories are not meant to be understood literally. They merely emphasise the ideal of charity. Though in them we often come across self-destruction, it must be remembered that the Dharma does not regard self-destruction as right. As the *Bodhicharyāvatāra* says, "this body that can do righteous deeds ought not be made to suffer for petty things even in the interest of others. How could it then serve to realise the hopes of all beings? Life should not be abandoned in an impure disposition of pity, but when the body can no longer be serviceable to others, it is time to abandon life in a spirit of pure disinterestedness, as then there can be no degradation attaching to it." He whose end is another world regards this life as comparatively worthless or immoral. Hence there is for him no limit whatever to the destruction or diminution of personal existence. But it is different with the Buddhist. For him birth as a human being is the highest of all births, as in it alone he can succeed in the struggle against ignorance, lust and hatred.

The logical outcome of right action is right living. No aspirant for the higher life can be without occupation. Mere going about bowing and scraping to patrons cannot inspire self-confidence and courage, or self-respect and dignity. Every one must take upon himself some duties that will exercise his abilities, and make himself useful to his fellowmen. But the occupation followed should bring no hurt or danger to any living being. Such occupations, as divination by dreams, prognostication of good or evil by omens, indulging in prophecies, discovering magical virtue in gems, boasting of supernatural powers, pretending to perform miracles and wonders, the employment of spells and supplications, which involve lying and deceit, are unworthy of the seeker after the higher life. Similarly he finds his way to all trades blocked with abuses. As a well-known writer says, "the ways of trade are grown selfish to the borders of theft and supple to the borders of fraud." "The general system of our trade is a system of selfishness; is not dictated by the high sentiments of human nature; is not measured by the exact law of reciprocity, much less by the sentiments of love and heroism, but is a system of distrust, of concealment, of superior keenness, not of giving but of taking advantage." All the lucrative professions are equally unsuited, for each has its own wrongs. "Each finds a tender and very intelligent conscience a disqualification for success. Each requires of the practitioner a certain shutting of the eyes, a certain dapperness, and compliance, an acceptance of customs, a sequestration from the sentiments of generosity and love, a compromise of private opinion and lofty integrity. Nay, the evil custom reaches into the whole institution of property, until our laws which establish it and protect it seem not to be the issue of love and reason, but of selfishness." Further, the moral worth of a profession depends upon what it can do for the needs of mankind and on what it can also do for the worker in the profession by reason of the moral influence it exerts. No wonder, therefore, that the Blessed One found it necessary to lead the life of a preacher of Truth!

The goal of the path of purity being nothing less than the destruction of all sorrows *(kleça)* and the removal of all perturbing causes *(āvaraṇa)*, mere change in external life and conduct cannot be productive of much benefit unless coupled with a thorough cleansing of the mind. This subjective purification is to be effected by right effort, right thought, and right tranquillity of mind. Right effort consists in practising what are called the *samyakprahāṇas* (*sammappadāna* in Pali), that is to say, in heroically mastering the passions so as to prevent bad qualities from arising; in suppressing sinful thoughts so as to put away bad qualities that have arisen; in producing goodness not previously existing; and in increasing the goodness which already exists by fixed attention and application. The chief aim of right effort is to cultivate a highly developed will as such, namely, the capacity of control. "Mature will," says Professor Sully, "implies the inhibition of certain nerve centres by others... a repression of action when conflicting motives arise...the maintaining of a definitive purpose beyond the movement and the persistent concentration of mind on this." Thus the Blessed One recommends the novice who is obsessed by some haunting idea of an undesirable character to try five methods in succession for expelling it. "(1) Attend to some good idea; (2) face the danger of the consequences of letting the bad idea develop into action; (3) become inattentive to the bad idea; (4) analyse its antecedents, and so paralyse the sequent impulse; (5) coerce the mind with the aid of bodily tension." These ought not to be confounded with any ascetic practices involving self-mortification. The method of pure asceticism is explicitly and deliberately rejected by the Blessed One. In the *Indriyabhāvanasutta* the Buddha asks a pupil of Parasarīya, a Brahman ascetic, how his master teaches the cultivation of the faculties of sense. The answer is that with the eye he sees no object and with the ear he hears no sound. On that system, rejoins the Blessed One, those who have their senses best cultivated would be the blind and the deaf. Finding the youth unable to reply, the Master explains to Ānanda the exact nature of the supreme sense-culture of the Noble Path. In this noble discipline the novice is taught to discriminate every sense-consciousness, whether it be pleasant or painful, and appraise it psychologically as a mode of feeling, as something that is changeable, and then view it ethically as inferior to disinterestedness (*upeksha*) which is the attitude of mind he is seeking to acquire or maintain. In this way the attitude of the mind towards sense impressions becomes cognitive and analytic of them as such. And the intellect then dictates by its regulative power how and how much shall really be enjoyed.*

It is only by the putting forth of effort and by persistence that one acquires self-control. As the *Bodicharyāvatāra* says, "*virye bodhir yata sthitā nahiviryam vinā puṇyam.*" Without strenuous effort there can be no *bodhi*; without strenuous effort there can be no merit. Without self-control and forbearance it is impossible to cleanse one's mind and develop holiness. Moral advice may be very helpful, moral convictions may direct one's will, but the vigour and per-

* Mrs. C. F. Rhys Davids:—*The Will in Buddhism.*

sistency with which one's will acts depends more on habit. It is therefore absolutely necessary to train the will, not by directing it by mere advice or reasonable suggestion, but by suitably changing the environment and regulating the motives.

The Dharma does not treat the will as an entity or faculty which is determined by nothing but itself. As the *Bodhicharyāvatāra* says, "*sarvam tat pratyaya balāt svatantrantu na vidyate*—nothing comes into existence of itself." Volition is a state of consciousness resulting from the more or less complex co-ordination of a number of states, psychical and physiological, which all united express themselves by an action or an inhibition. The chief factor in the co-ordination is the character, an extremely complex product formed by heredity, prenatal and postnatal physiological conditions, education and experience. Only a part of this psychological activity enters into consciousness in the form of a deliberation. The acts and movements which follow the deliberation result directly from the tendencies and feelings, images and ideas, which have become co-ordinated in the form of a choice. Choice is, therefore, not the cause of any thing, but is itself an effect. To suppose that choice is without cause would be to admit that the unaccountable and inconsistent actions of the insane form the normal type and standard of comparison. Besides, if choice were uncaused, every choice ought to lead to happiness. No one would of himself choose something miserable. As the *Bodhicharyāvatāra* says, "*yaditu svecchayā siddhihi sarvēshām ēva dēhinām na bhavet kasya chit dukkham na dukkham kaschid icchati*—if everything could be as one willed, there should be no misery at all in the world." Free will has, therefore, no existence except in the imagination of the theologian and the metaphysician. Were one's will free, it would not be possible to change one's character by education. But experience teaches that a man's character is composed of various qualities, and is changeable by certain lines of effort. Just because man's will obeys motives and is dependent on causes, he can be made to transform himself by changing the environment of his activities and by thoughtfully regulating the motives of his will.

A will trained in the right direction implies a necessary preparation of the heart by efforts of right desire (*bhāvanā*). A wish, which is attainable, is an act of will begun, and when it is strengthened, it makes the act of will complete. By the *asubhabhāvanā* one creates in himself a disgust for all that is corrupt by reflecting on its evil consequences. This gives the necessary strength and courage to practise the other *bhāvanās*. In the *maitri bhāvanā* one so adjusts his heart that he longs for the weal and welfare of all beings including the happiness even of his enemies. *Maitri*, as Emil Burnouf says, is nothing less than universal love. No one can cultivate *maitri*, unless his heart has been completely purified of all sensuality (*rāga*) and malevolence (*dvesha*). All means of acquiring religious merit, says the *Itivuttaka*, have not six tenths of the value of *maitri*, the purification of the heart. The might of *maitri* is beyond all measure. It alone can confer all possible benefits. There is no good of life which is not a shade flung from *maitri*. In the *karuṇabhāvanā* one thinks of all beings in distress, vividly representing in his imagination their sorrows and anxieties so as to arouse for them a deep compassion in his heart. In the *muditabhāvanā* one desires the prosperity of others and rejoices in their welfare and joy. Even under the most trying circumstances, even when the greatest mishaps may occur, one ought never to give up *mudita*, for it is the one great source of perennial consolation. When *mudita* blooms, it manifests itself as a rage to suffer for mankind. In the *upekshabhāvanā* the aspirant, freed from pride and selfishness, rises above all ideas of power and oppression, wealth and want, fame and contempt, youth and age, beauty and ugliness, disease and health, and views with disinterested calmness and equanimity whatever may happen to him,

> "As one, in suffering all, that suffers nothing;
> A man that fortune's buffets and rewards
> Hast ta'en with equal thanks."

It is only by efforts of this kind that man can acquire the capacity of determining himself in accordance with the laws of the good, instead of being the mere victim of external circumstances. Thus alone will he be able to annihilate all his evil dispositions and perturbations; to get rid of all idea of separateness and difference; to fill his mind with thoughts of universal compassion, friendliness and benevolence; and attain the sublime freedom characteristic of *bodhi*. In this atmosphere of true freedom he will work for the benefit of all beings with indefatigable zeal without the least thought of indolence, for, as the *Dharmasamgīti* says, the *bodhisattva* has no other concern than securing the happiness of all beings.

By right effort the will is trained and controlled. But, as there can be no isolated feeling, willing, or thinking, independent of one another, right effort must be coupled with right thought *(smriti)*. The mind must therefore be guided in the right direction. It is the mind that creates fears and sorrows, that develops good and bad *karma*. As the Blessed One has said, all penances and austerities will be of no avail even when practised for an extraordinarily long time, if the mind is not directed towards the right object. *Chittādhino dharma dharmādhino bodhihi.* On the mind depends the practice of dharma, and on the practice of dharma depends the attainment of *bodhi*. "The mind is the origin of all that is; the mind is the master; the mind is the cause. If in the mind there are evil thoughts, then the words are evil, the deeds are evil, and the sorrow which results from sin follows that man as the chariot wheel follows him who drags it. The mind is the origin of all that is; it is the mind that commands, it is the mind that contrives. If in the mind there are good thoughts, then the words are good and the deeds good, and the happiness which results from such conduct follows that man, as the shadow accompanies the substance. It is the mind that makes its own dwelling place; the mind reflecting on evil ways courts its own misery. It is the mind that creates its own sorrow. Not a father, not a mother can do so much; if only the thoughts be directed to that which is right, then happiness must necessarily follow. The wise man, who restrains his six appetites and guards his thoughts, shall certainly conquer in his struggle with evil, and free himself from all misery."

> "Mind is the master-power that moulds and makes,
> And man is mind, and evermore he takes
> The tool of thought, and, shaping what he wills,

> Brings forth a thousand joys, a thousand ills :—
> He thinks in secret, and it comes to pass;
> Environment is but his looking glass."

Hence, the mind must be guarded from being affected by bad thoughts. Man must always practise right thought. He must know what ought to be avoided and what ought to be done. He must always be mindful as to how his body and mind are engaged. The man devoid of thought is like an invalid incapable of doing work. The exercise of right thought can be possible only when one possesses intellectual insight and wisdom *(pragnā)*. "Wisdom," says Buddhagosha in his *Visuddhi-magga*, "is manifold and various, and an answer that attempted to be exhaustive would both fail of its purpose and tend to still greater confusion. Therefore, we will confine ourselves to the meaning here intended,—wisdom is knowledge consisting in insight and conjoined with meritorious thoughts." By wisdom is meant an adequate understanding of the law of cause and effect; of the real nature of body (*kāya*) and mind (*chitta*); of pleasure and pain (*vedana*); and of the true relations (*yathābhutam*) of all things (*dharma*) in the universe.* Wisdom will lead the *bodhisattva* to perceive that all things come into existence by a combination of various circumstances (*hetupratyaya*); that all things are subject to change (*anitya*); that there is neither a personal ego soul (*ātman*) nor an unconditioned unknowable substrate in things (*ding an sich*, *brahmam*, or *paramātman*); and that through their ignorance of the true nature of things (*avidya*) all beings are experiencing mental and physical sufferings in numberless ways. This knowledge will awaken in the *bodhisattva* the deepest compassion for all suffering beings and impel him to work with dauntless energy for their salvation.

It is a glory of Buddhism that it makes intellectual enlightenment an essential condition of salvation. In Buddhism morality and intellectual enlightenment are inseparable from one another. While morality forms the basis of the higher life, knowledge and wisdom complete it.

* *Kāya*, *chitta*, *vedana* and *dharma* are called the *smrtyupasthānas* (satipattana in Pali).

Without a perfect understanding of the law of causality and transformation (*pratītyasamutpāda*), no one can aspire to attain *bodhi*, however moral he may be. No one can even be said to be truly moral, if he does not possess the necessary insight and knowledge. In this respect Buddhism differs from all other religions. All monotheistic religions start with certain assumptions, and when these assumptions are contradicted by the growth of knowledge, they bewail that "he that increaseth knowledge increaseth sorrow." But Buddhism starts with no assumptions. It stands on the firm rock of facts, and can therefore never shun the dry light of knowledge. Some have attempted to place the *advaita* form of Vedanta on the same level with the Dharma, as in the *advaita* religion the chief means of salvation is what is called *gnānam*. But the *gnānam* of the Vedantin is entirely different from what the Buddhist understands by *pragnā*. *Pragnā* means ratiocination based on observation and experience, and as such has nothing to do with intuition or what is called superconsciousness. On the other hand, "the adherent of Brahmaṁ defines the nature of the cause and so on, on the basis of scripture, and is, therefore, not obliged to render his tenets throughout conformable to observation." It is only on the authority of the Veda that Brahmaṁ is taken as the cause of the origin of the world. In his *System des Vedānta* Dr. Deussen specially emphasises the fact that the so-called *gnānam* (*metaphysische Erkenntniss*) of the Vedantin is not different from the faith (*glaube*) of the Christian.

Though knowledge and insight are of the highest value, yet they must be prevented from leading to a fluctuating mood of mind. Hence, side by side with *pragnā*, the aspirant for bodhi must also practise *dhyāna* to attain tranquillity. Right peace (*samādhi*, *çamata*) alone will bring to a standstill all mental states which produce frivolous sophistries. *Dhyána*, as understood in Buddhism, is the contemplation of the facts of life from the highest point of view, and as such plays an important part. The Dharma discards prayer as a means of attaining salvation. How can the law of cause and effect be influenced by the supplications of defaulters? The consequences of a fault can only be removed by due repentance and reparation inspired, not by the selfish fear of punishment, but by the love of truth and righteousness. But contemplation, under the necessary moral conditions, coupled with sufficient knowledge for directing it to profit, will enable one to know himself better, to examine his conscience more minutely, and to illuminate his mind. *Dhyāna* comprises four stages : a stage of gladness and joy born of seclusion accompanied by investigation and reflection ; a state of elation and internal calm without reasoning, consequent on investigation and reflection ; the total absence of all passion and prejudice ; and, lastly, a state of self-possession and complete tranquillity. *Dhyāna* is therefore a discipline of the mind which leads finally to a state in which the mind is flooded by an illumination which reveals the universe in a new aspect absolutely free from all traces of interest, affection, or passion.

Dhyāna, as practised by the Buddhist, is not losing consciousness. It is, on the other hand, a self-possessed purposive eradication of egotism with a view to investigate all things dispassionately. It is a strenuous endeavour to bring the mind into perfect harmony with all that is righteous. *Sarva dharma sukhākranto nāma samādhi. Dhyāna* has, therefore, nothing in common with ecstasy or trance, which we find so largely associated with religious mysticism. "No member of our community," says the Blessed One, "may ever arrogate to himself extraordinary gifts or supernatural perfection, through vainglory give himself out to be a holy man ; such, for instance, as to withdraw into solitary places on pretence of enjoying ecstasies and afterwards presume to teach others the way to uncommon spiritual attainments. Sooner may the lofty palm-tree that has been cut down become green again, than an elect guilty of such pride be restored to his holy station. Take care for yourself that you do not give way to such an excess." Dreams and ecstasies, visions and trances, which are the very proof of holiness in other religions, are vain and foolish imaginings to the Buddhist.

The Buddhist *dhyāna*, sometimes called *anuttarayoga*, should not be confounded with the Brahmanical *yoga*. The latter is predominantly physical and hypnotic ; the former, though it may have its physical and hygienic side,* is predominantly intellectual and ethical, its chief purpose being to understand the true nature of consciousness and therefore of man. The *yogin par excellence* in Buddhism is the generous *bodisattva* who practises the six *pāramitās.* While the Brāhman *yogi* endeavours to become absorbed in the universal *Brahmaṁ*, the *bodhisattva* attempts to realise by contemplation the self-devoid character of all things (*sarvadharma anupalambha çunyata*). *Sunyatā karunayor abhinnam bodhichittam.* The mentality corresponding to *bodhi* is inseparable from universal compassion and the negation of a self. In his *Mahāyāna sraddhotpāda sutra* Asvaghosha specially warns the aspirant for bodhi against confounding the *samādhi* of the Buddhists with that of the *tīrthakās*, the heretics. All *samādhis* practised by the heretics are described as being "invariably the production of the egoistic conception and desire and self-assumption." And we may add that the most intense and so-called divine raptures are the results of the unconscious activity of at least some of the organs of the sexual life.

The practice of *dhyāna* uncoupled with *pragnā* cannot be productive of any good, but when the two go hand in hand, the mind is freed not only from disquietude by the removal of all inconsistencies, but also from *ātmamoha*, the lust of self, which is the mother of all egoism. The destruction of egoism enables the *bodhisattva* to get rid of all sorrows and all obstacles to progress, to acquire self-control and fortitude, to feel compassion for all beings and to rejoice in doing good acts. It is no wonder that the Buddhist *dhyāna* has been able to produce such remarkable results as we observe in the modern Japanese. Says Mr. Okakura Yoshisaburo in his *Japanese Spirit:* "The self-control that enables us not to betray our inner feeling through a change in our expression, the measured steps with which we are taught to walk into the hideous jaws

* He who would seek perfection must carefully observe all hygienic conditions. The rules of diet, the habit of deep breathing, and fresh air at all times, the wearing of proper clothing that does not impede the free passage of air over the body, the habit of frequent bathing, regular rest, and a sufficient amount of exercise—all are essential.

of death—in short, all those qualities which make a present Japanese of truly Japanese type look strange, if not queer, to your (*i.e.*, European) eyes, are in a most marked degree a product of that direct or indirect influence on our past mentality which was exercised by the Buddhist doctrine of *Dhyāna* as taught by the Zen priests."

In the way of those who traverse the Noble Path lie the ten impediments (*samyojana*) which must be overcome. The foremost among these is the delusion of a permanent self (*satkāyadrishti*). To one who considers himself a permanent immutable being, and does not realise that he is only a unity originating from an aggregation of *skandhas*, whose present condition has been determined by causes working in the past, and whose future will be determined by causes at work in the present, any progress in the direction of emancipation and enlightenment is impossible. But when once a man has realised that there is no permanent ego (*ātman*) which can gain an eternal paradise beyond the grave, the temptation is not far to run to the sensualist's extreme of "let us eat and drink, for to-morrow we die." Hence, it is necessary to have faith in the possibility of attaining perfection. Pyrrhonism (*vichikichcha*) is therefore the next obstacle in the path of the neophyte. With its shibboleths of *Ignorabimus* and *Unknowable*, phyrrhonism denies all possibility of solving the problem of existence, and thus becomes a mental and moral malady which can only stultify all endeavour towards progress. Scepticism is often nothing more than a cloak in which ignorance masquerades. Scepticism cannot regenerate men; it can only kill but not give life. Only faith in a new ideal will impel men to move forward in search of a new life.

The third obstacle is the belief in the efficacy of purificatory ceremonies and rites (*çīlavrata parāmarsha*). Rites and outward observances are mere sham supports, and can afford no emancipation from misery, even when there is the right spirit within. People who are punctilious in the observance of rites and ceremonies are not free from the *kleças* of lust, hatred and ignorance. If bathing in the Ganges could confer merit, then the fishermen should indeed be the most meritorious, not to speak of the fishes and other animals, which are day and night swimming in its waters. The conquest of these three obstacles forms the first stage (*srotāpanna*) of the Noble Path, whose fruit, as the *Dhammapāda* says, is "better than universal empire in this world, better than going to heaven, better than lordship over all worlds."

Success in the first stage is no guarantee of no lapse back into the old ways. The man who has overcome the delusion of self, doubt and ritualism has to a large extent rectified himself, but not till he has broken the next two fetters of sensuality (*kāma*) and malevolence (*pratigha*) are his chances of falling back reduced to a minimum. When he has overcome these two impediments to a great extent, he attains to the second stage and becomes *sakridāgāmin.* Only when all sensuality and malevolence are destroyed, there can no longer arise in his heart the least love of self or ill-feeling towards others, and then he becomes *anāgāmin.* But he is not yet free from all error. He has still to overcome the remaining impediments. He has to destroy all craving (*rāga*) for material (*rupa*) and immaterial (*arupa*) pleasures in this world or another world; he must overcome pride (*mana*), self-righteousness (*ouddatya*), and the ignorance of the true nature of things (*avidya*). When he has burst all these fetters and freely traversed the Noble Path, then all things appear to him in their true relations. Having no evil desires, he cherishes right desires for himself, and feels tender and disinterested love for all beings. Having traversed the path he reaches the goal; he becomes perfect, an *arhat*, and attains the blessedness of Nirvaṇa. He who has attained supreme enlightenment no longer looks upon the world (*prapancha*) with contempt, but sees that it is the land of bliss, where pervades the serene light of *bodhi.*

It is an accusation often made against Buddhism that, by placing the goal of life in the attainment of perfection through enlightenment, it tends to make the cultivation of the intellectual powers of greater importance than the acquirement of the ethical virtues. To one who has carefully considered the various qualifications needed for the pilgrimage on the path of purity nothing can be more baseless and absurd than this charge. Such a charge might hold good against the Vedānta, but not against the Dharma. In the Vedānta the perfected sage is subject to no moral law. Anandagiri tells us that Saṅkara drank toddy and projected his soul into the corpse of a king to learn the erotic arts. We are told in the *Bhāgavata purāṇa* that the transgressions of virtue observed in such superior beings as Krishna must not be regarded as faults, for they can have no moral restraints. On the other hand in Buddhism obedience to the laws of morality is the primary condition that must be fulfilled before the mind can become the fit receptacle of truth. The *Bodhicharyāvatāra* says: "The *pāramitās* of *dāna*, *çīla*, *kshānti*, *vīrya*, *pragnā* and *dhyāna* are in the ascending order of importance, so that one may neglect the lower *pāramitās* for the higher; but for the sake of *çīla* one may even forego the higher, as *çīla* forms the foundation of all good acts." In ultimate analysis the *bodhichitta*, the cast of mind of the man who has attained bodhi, resolves itself into two essential virtues, which are identical in aim, and whose acquisition forms the double duty of the *bodhisattva*. These virtues are *pragnāpāramitā*, knowledge and insight, and *çīlapāramitā*, morality. All the other *pāramitās* proceed from these two as their sources. At the commencement the one is complementary to the other, but in the last stage the two become identical. Till their unification morality is a means to attain enlightenment, but morality alone does not constitute enlightenment. To lead the higher life intellectual illumination is absolutely necessary, but it cannot be obtained except by a previous discipline in charity, morality, and forbearance. The acquisition of wisdom (*gnāna sambhāra*) necessarily presupposes the presence of compassion, devotion, and morality (*puṇya sambhāra*). The Blessed One has said:

> "Virtue is the base on which the man who is wise,
> Can train his mind and make his wisdom grow.
> Thus shall the strenuous *bhikshu* undeceived,
> Unravel the tangled skein of life."

> "This is the base like great earth to man
> And this is the root of all increase in goodness,
> The starting point of all the Buddha's teaching
> Virtue, to wit, on which true bliss depends."

THE RIDDLE OF THE WORLD.

"KARMAJAM *loka vaichitryam.*" All things are born of activities. Everything is in a state of continual transformation. "*Na cha nirodhosti na cha bhāvosti sarvadā ; ajātam aniruddham cha tasmād sarvam idam jagat.*" There is neither creation nor destruction ; there is neither beginning nor end. "*Vichāreṇa nāsti kim chid ahetutah.*" Yet nothing happens without cause and reason.

Every change is determined by a number of conditions. The most striking of these conditions is ordinarily called its cause, and the change itself is said to be the eflect of that cause. Strictly speaking the cause (*pratyaya*) of any change is the totality of all the conditions needed for its occurrence. That in the cause which makes the effect possible is spoken of as the reason (*hētu*) of the change. When a seed changes into a plant, that in the seed which makes it become a plant of a particular kind is the reason of the change, while the totality of conditions, such as the soil, water, light, air, space, needed for its germination and growth, constitutes the cause. Similarly sentiency, the germ of consciousness (*vignāna bījam*), is the reason for the development of individuality (*nāma rupa*), while the union of parents, the womb of the mother, the potentialities derived from parents, vegetative and animal activities, and the environment constitute the causes that produce a particular individuality.

No change occurs by itself. Every change stands in the relation of cause to some other change, and in the relation of an effect to a third change. All changes in the world depend more or less upon one another. This causal nexus, which is found everywhere in experience, is called in the Dharma by the technical name of *pratītya samutpāda.* A correct understanding of this dependent origination, of the conditioned nature of all existence which has neither beginning nor end, is of the greatest importance in Buddhism. "*Pratītya samutpādam paçyanti te dharmam paçyanti ; yo dharmam paçyati sa buddham paçyati.*" He who has understood the chain of causation has understood the inner meaning of the Dharma, and he that has grasped the Dharma has perceived the essence of Buddhahood.

If every change has a cause, and that cause again a cause, is there then no ultimate unchangeable or first cause? Replies the Blessed One in *Samyuttaka Nikāyo*: "If a man should gather all the grasses and herbs, twigs and leaves of this vast continent of India, and arrange them in heaps, saying: This is my mother, this is the mother of my mother, and so on, there would be no end seen to the mother of mother of this man, even though he might reach the end of all the grasses and herbs, twigs and leaves of this continent of India. What is the reason of this? Without beginning and end is this world-process (*samsāro*)." There can be no first cause. In experience we find no absolute beginning. We come across no change instituting a series of changes, which has not itself been preceded by some other change. The question of cause never even arises except where there is change, and the cause demanded is always another change. Hence, it is meaningless to speak of a first cause. Science knows nothing of first causes. There is no branch of rational investigation from which they can be inferred. Wherever we find the existence of a first cause asserted, we find we have reached a temporary limit to knowledge, or that we are inferring something outside the limits of sense experience, where knowledge and inference are meaningless. As Prof. A. Riehl says in his *Philophische Kriticismus*, "a first cause with which as a creative act the series of changes should have begun originally, would be an uncaused change. The necessity of conceiving every change as effect which has its cause in a preceding change makes such an uncaused change absolutely unthinkable."

Is there then no I'svara? In a conversation with Anātha-pindika the Blessed One argued the matter as follows. "If the world had been made by I'svara, there should be no change nor destruction, there should be no such a thing as sorrow or calamity, as right or wrong, as all things, pure and impure, must come from him. If sorrow and joy, love and hate, which spring up in all conscious beings, be the work of

I'svara, he himself must be capable of sorrow and joy, love and hatred, and if he has these, how can he be said to be perfect? If I'svara be the maker, and if all beings have to submit silently to their maker's power, what would be the utility of practising virtue? The doing of right or wrong would be the same, as all deeds are his making and must be the same with their maker. But if sorrow and suffering are attributed to another cause, then there would be something of which I'svara is not the cause. Why, then, should not all that exists be uncaused too? Again, if I'svara be the maker, he acts with or without a purpose. If he acts with a purpose, he cannot be said to be all perfect, for a purpose necessarily implies the satisfaction of a want. If he acts without a purpose, he must be like the lunatic or suckling babe. Besides, if I'svara be the maker, why should not people reverently submit to him, why should they offer supplications to him when sorely pressed by necessity? And why should people adore more gods than one? Thus the idea of I'svara is proved false by rational argument, and all such contradictory assertions should be exposed." (Asvaghosha's *Buddhacharitra.*)

Is not the world in which we live, it is asked, an orderly world where everything is governed by law? Do not laws imply a law-giver? All the order which exists in the world arises from the simple fact that, when there are no disturbing causes, things remain the same. The observed grouping of things and sequence of events we speak of as the order of the world, and this is the same as saying that the world is as it is and no more. No natural law is the cause of the observed sequence in nature. Every natural law merely describes the conditions on which a particular change is dependent. A body falls to the ground not in consequence of the law of gravitation, but the law of gravitation is the precise statement of what happens when a body is left unsupported. A law of nature does not command that something shall take place, but it merely states how something happens. While a civil law is a prescription involving a command and a duty, a natural law is simply a description, in which is formulated the repeated sequence of perceptions. As Karl Pearson says, "law in the scientific sense is essentially a product of the human mind and has no meaning apart from man. There is more meaning in the statement that man gives laws to nature than in its converse that nature gives laws to man." When a law has been found to be true in all known cases, we naturally expect that it would apply to cases that might hereafter come to our knowledge. The greater the number of cases in which a law has been observed to hold good, the greater is the probability that it is universally true. If the sun has risen daily without fail during the last 5,000 years (= 1,826,213 days), the odds in favour of its rising to-morrow are 1,826,214 to 1, and this amounts to saying that the rising of the sun to-morrow is pratically certain. Thus every natural law represents a limitation of our thoughts, of our expectations. The more closely our thoughts are adapted to the sense-given facts, the greater are the restraints to the possibilities of our thinking, and stronger is the instinctive tendency to expect an event to happen in exactly the same manner as before. It is only in this sense that we speak of the uniformity of nature. We can only say that the laws of nature are practically universal, but not theoretically so. This practical certainty is all that man is capable of obtaining, and this is enough to serve him as a guide in life. Theoretical certainty would imply perfect and infinite knowledge, but this evidently is beyond man's capacities. All attempts to go far beyond the region of experience, whether it be in time or in space, must be affected with the greatest insecurity, because the probability of the results is nil.

This so-called teleological argument for the existence of I'svara often takes another form. From certain relations observed between the parts of organisms, it is inferred that they have been designed to serve a definite purpose. The eye, it is imagined, has been made for the purpose of seeing, just as a watch is constructed to show the hour. But in drawing this inference they are applying analogy to a region far beyond the limits of experience, and the conclusion must accordingly be "infinitely precarious," that is to say, can have no element of probability connected with it. Further, the idea of purpose, as has been pointed out by Kant, is not a principle of the knowledge of nature, but a mode in which the human mind judges of certain organic forms. Just as man gives laws to nature, so man thinks the organising character of nature as analogous to causality aiming at ends. But this cannot be presumed to offer an explanation, just as no scientific law can account for any natural phenomenon. Just as law in the scientific sense is a product of the human mind and has no meaning apart from man, so the end is merely a point of view which arises from man's reflection about organic forms, and not a principle according to which they have been created. Properly speaking, teleology belongs only to the description of nature, and can give no valid conclusion as to the origin and inner possibility of organic forms. If one should ask whether material bodies could apply geometrical calculations to themselves, if material bodies could be the joint artists of their own combinations, we can only answer that under such and such conditions they do behave in such and such a way. Beyond this we know nothing. If we could penetrate into the intimate nature of bodies, we might clearly see that natural beings could not admit of any other disposition than what they possess at present. Because the facts of this world can be conveniently described in some special fashion, does it follow that the world has been designed by I'svara? Because one finds a wound on one's body, does it follow that it has been inflicted by Hotchli Potchli with a Rimbo Rambo? All that we could infer from the condition of the world is that there must be a cause. But the necessity of thought which compels us to affirm that the world had a cause compels us to postulate a cause of that cause, and so on *ad infinitum*, a first cause being, as we have already seen, even unthinkable.

If the heavens above do not declare the glory of I'svara, does not the moral law within derive its sanction from the belief that I'svara has ordained it, and that he will distribute to men, according to their deeds, rewards and punishments in a life beyond the grave? No doubt the observance of the laws of morality is of supreme importance to mankind, but it has nothing to do with the belief either in a future life or in I'svara. He who thinks that this world would be a worthless place without immortality is on the same level as the child who thinks that "grown up" life to be worth having must be a life of continual play and no work. Nor can one be called truly moral who does not think it worth his while to be virtuous, unless he can look forward to remuneration hereafter for not having lived like a beast. Again, what connection can morality have with the belief in I'svara? Morality finds its authority and sanction not in illusions, threats, or hypothetical promises, but in the realities of life. 'It has sprung from those human relationships in which the individual finds himself compelled to live and act. It has its roots in the individual's needs, both physical and mental, which other human beings can satisfy, and in the sympathies which answer to those needs. Candid observation proves that man is fundamentally an emotional and volitional being, whose instinctive feelings and actions, originally sense-aroused and sense-guided, have become gradually enlightened and directed by developing reason. And it seems pretty clear that the emotional and volitional root (*kusala mūla*) of what we hold to be most precious in life is to be found in those instinctive affections that bind together the lives of kindred beings. "Even in their purely instinctive origin these affections are fundamentally and essentially altruistic. However ravenous and lustful, even to revelling in hot blood and the tearing of palpitating flesh, tiger-like voluptuousness may dwell in beast and man; surely the affectionate solicitude of the tigress for her cubs is essentially devoted to their well-being, and not a mere pleasurable gratification of her own appetites. Nor are the caresses of the mates mere expressions of self-regarding passions. They unmistakably betoken affectionate consideration for each other; a sympathetic community of needs, grounded in the fact that, though different individuals, they are in verity bearers of complemental lives."

That man should be truthful, just, merciful, loving and kind to his neighbours, that he should avoid vice and practise virtue, are injunctions that obtain their validity, not because there is I'svara, but because human society would become impossible if they were set at nought. Good action, as W. K. Clifford says, is that which makes the organic more organic. Virtue possesses a self-propagating power. Vice and wrong are ever destroying themselves. The more single-eyed selfishness is, the more it destroys itself. By a necessary contradiction egoism which aims at the destruction of others leads to the unconscious destruction of self. In seeking to increase life, make it richer and more happy, egoism really diminishes, impoverishes and annihilates it. Sympathy and love are rooted in the same natural bonds which have conditioned the very continuance of the race on the faithful discharge of their duties to others besides themselves. It is an assumption not warranted by history and psychology that man, so far as he acts rationally, has his own individual pleasure as his conscious aim to the exclusion of what is for the interest of others. As far as we are able to penetrate into pre-historic times, man has been found to be a gregarious being, who could not have maintained himself except by the instincts of sympathy, the feeling of solidarity, and a certain degree of unselfishness, which are all presupposed in life in a community. As Aristotle has said, the man who could live without society must either be a beast or a god. Only as a member of society and by the observance of ethical laws can man enjoy the highest and most durable bliss. He must be a monster or a savage who will dare to say that, if there be no I'svara, it is right or permissible for any man, apart from the terrors of civil or criminal law, to commit murder, theft and adultery as freely as he pleases. On the other hand, the moral character of I'svara varies with the ethical standards of his worshippers. As man advances to higher stages of morality, his earlier conceptions of the moral character of I'svara no longer satisfy him, and are accordingly criticised and reconstructed to meet the demand of his new ideals. The religious mind is incapable of expressing its relations to I'svara in any other way than by attributing to him a nature similar to its own. The history of religious thought amply proves this. Hence, instead of saying that I'svara is the creator of the world, we ought to say that man has created his idea of I'svara including all its moral elements. As Xenophanes said, if lions could picture a god, they would picture him in the form of a lion ; the horses like a horse ; the oxen like an ox.

"In all ages and climes man creates his gods,
And makes them utter such revelations
As bespeak his growth and mental vision.
As the germs of goodness and love unfold,
Man's noblest fancy, a loving deity,
Takes shape, and sways his life for right and wrong."

How can we deny the existence of I'svara, when most people who have existed heretofore have believed in a god of some sort? When we examine this argument *ex consensu gentium*, we easily see its hollowness. Granting that the existence of I'svara is a matter of general belief, does it establish any probability that I'svara exists? It cannot, for many things, now admitted to be errors, have in the past been matters of general belief. Such, for example, is the belief that the sun went round the earth. Ignorance of science and fallacious reasoning have in the past been the main props of the belief in I'svara. With the growth of scientific knowledge and the recognition of the fallacies underlying natural theology, the belief in I'svara is becoming less general. Again, though there may be a widespread belief in I'svara, I'svara does not mean the same thing for all. Just consider the phases through which the idea of God has passed in the developmental history of such a small people as the Jews. The God of Samuel orders the slaughter of infants, but the tender mercies of the God of the Psalmist are over all his works. The God of the Patriarchs is always repenting, while the God of the Apostles is the same yesterday, to-day and for ever without any variableness or shadow of turning. The God of the Old Testament walks in the garden in the cool of the day, but the God of the New Testament cannot be seen by man. The God of Leviticus is punctilious about the sacrificial furniture and utensils, but the God of the Acts cannot dwell in temples. The God of Exodus is merciful only to those who love him, whereas the God of Jesus is kind unto the unthankful and the evil. Not only has the idea of God been different at different times with one and the same people, but it has never been the same for any two persons. No wonder that Wesley told Whitefield: "Your God is my devil!" Temperament, training, surroundings are determinative factors in an individual's idea of God. At best the argument from general belief can only prove that in worshipping I'svara a man only yearns towards his utmost possible conception as regards the unknown. This is well illustrated by the fact that the most ignorant of mankind have the most concrete idea of God, who is to them one like themselves, with immensely magnified powers, whereas the more cultured a man is and the more facts he knows, the less definite is his idea of God. While the savage sees his gods in stocks and stones, the philosopher considers a god comprehended as no God.

> "There is in God, the seer feels,
> A deep but dazzling darkness."

The so-called historical proofs for the existence of I'svara are from their nature fallacious. What they attempt to establish is the existence of miracles. If by a miracle is meant an event which had no natural cause, history cannot accept such events. For all historical evidence rests on inferences from effect to cause, and we can infer from effect to cause only on the assumption that we can find the complete causes of events in nature itself. If miracles were possible, we should never be able to say that a particular event was the cause of any other. Hence no historical proofs can ever establish that an event, which happened, was in reality a miracle. But if by miracle is meant only a great and wonderful work, then a man's ability to perform astonishing feats does not prove that he knows the truth, or tells it. Apart from miracles historical proofs can only show that somebody said something, but they cannot establish the truth of his statements, which has to be tested on quite other grounds. Hence, neither history nor science can apodeictically establish the existence of I'svara. As Prof. W. James says in his *Varieties of Religious Experience*, "all arguments for God but follow the combined suggestions of the facts and of our feelings. They prove nothing rigorously. They only corroborate our pre-existent partialities. ... ... If you have a god already whom you believe in, these arguments confirm you. If you are atheistic, they fail to set you right."

If the world has not been created by I'svara, may not all existence be a manifestation of the Absolute, the Unconditioned, the Unknowable behind all appearances? Said the

Blessed One to Anāthapindika: "If by the Absolute is meant something out of relation to all known things, its existence cannot be established by any reasoning* (*hetuvidyasāstra*). How can we know that any thing unrelated to other things exists at all? The whole universe, as we know it, is a system of relations; we know nothing that is, or can be, unrelated. How can that which depends on nothing and is related to nothing, produce things which are related to one another and depend for their existence upon one another? Again, the Absolute is one or many. If it be only one, how can it be the cause of the different things which originate, as we know, from different causes? If there be as many different Absolutes as there are things, how can the latter be related to one another? If the Absolute pervades all things and fills all space, then it can not also make them, for there is nothing to make. Further, if the Absolute is devoid of all qualities (*nirguṇa*), all things arising from it ought likewise to be devoid of qualities. But in reality all things in the world are circumscribed throughout by qualities. Hence the Absolute cannot be their cause. If the Absolute be considered to be different from the qualities, how does it continually create the things possessing such qualities and manifest itself in them? Again, if the Absolute be unchangeable, all things should be unchangeable too, for the effect cannot differ in nature from the cause. But all things in the world undergo change and decay. How then can the Absolute be unchangeable? Moreover, if the Absolute which pervades all is the cause of everything, why should we seek liberation? For we ourselves possess this Absolute and must patiently endure every suffering and sorrow incessantly created by the Absolute." (Asvaghosha's *Buddhacharitra.*)

The Absolute owes its origin to the erroneous assumption that every concept has a distinct counterpart in reality, and that the higher or more comprehensive concepts exist prior to the lower or less comprehensive ones, and contain the latter by implication. A simple reference to the process of

* "Through scripture only as a means of knowledge Brahmaṁ is known to be the cause of the origin, &c. of the world." "Nor finally can the authoritativeness of the Veda be proved by inferential reasoning."—Saṁkara's Commentary on the Vedānta Sutras.

formation of concepts reveals the absurdity of this assumption. In our experience there is nothing more original than sensation. What we speak of as reality is connected with sensation. We know that sensations arise, but we can form no idea of how they arise, as every idea has sensations for its content and its presupposition. A primary datum of sensation is the consciousness of difference. Without this no act of sensation would even be possible. The recognition of identity amidst difference is the basis of all ratiocinative or discursive thought. While we perceive objects as different, we conceive them as identical by directing our attention to their points of agreement. Thus objects are classified into groups, those attributes which belong to the objects in common serving as the basis of classification. When the number of objects to be classified is large, and some of them have more attributes in common than others, they are arranged in a number of groups. First, all those objects which have the greatest number of attributes in common, are grouped so as to form what is called a species; the different species are then grouped together in a higher class or genus, which has only a small number of common attributes, and so forth. The totality of attributes pertaining to a class is called a *concept.* Thus out of complexes of sensations which constitute reality we build up in thought our concepts. By the omission or rejection of the differentiating attributes, and by the ideal conjunction of the common characters, we form the higher, or more comprehensive concepts from the lower, or less comprehensive ones. In this process of abstraction we find nothing from which we may infer that the rejected attributes are contained or implied in those that are retained and combined to form the higher concepts. It is this error of regarding the higher concepts as giving birth to the lower concepts, coupled with the fancy that the highest concepts, such as being, existence, substance, matter, energy, consciousness, which represent the attributes common to all things, form the invariable substrata of the variable characters by which things are distinguished from one another, that has been the prolific mother of metaphysical speculation concerning the unknown. For subjective reasons man is often inclined to overestimate the value of the unknown and prefer it to the known. His practical dissatisfaction with the reality, that is to say, the sense-world, has inspired him to seek satisfaction in a metaphysical, supersensible phantasm. Out of what is abstracted from sense experience, by a fanciful concatenation of words, the metaphysician constructs what he fancies to be a transcendental existence. And feeling himself unable to clutch his fanciful creation, the metaphysician employs fantastic means to realise his vain hopes.

In different ages and climes different methods have been employed to get into touch with what is called the transcendental or supernatural. These methods may be roughly grouped into three principal classes. The first class comprises all those cases in which some supernatural being, whether it be I'svara, his messenger, or some angel, or demon, appears before the favoured person, and reveals directly by visible signs or articulate sounds, what he was elected to reveal. In the second are included those cases in which an individual is mysteriously possessed and overpowered by some supernatural agent, who makes revelations through the obsessed individual. The chief feature of the third class is the condition of trance or ecstasy in which the subject, withdrawn from things of sense, enters into direct connection with the deity, or other spiritual agencies, or the Absolute, and discerns the truths of a transcendental world which is inaccessible to the ordinary means of apprehension by the senses and the understanding. For the cultured man of modern civilised countries the first two methods appear too crude for acceptance. But the third method, that of ecstatic intuition, still finds favour with many, and in recent times attempts have even been made to prop it up by some new psychological discoveries, and as such it deserves greater consideration. However, before entering on an examination of the nature of ecstatic intuition, we shall just repeat the general warning of John Stuart Mill concerning the possibility of discerning truths by abnormal methods. "The notion that truths external to the mind," says J. S. Mill, "may be known by intuition or consciousness, independently of observation and experience is, I am persuaded, in these times the great intellectual support of false doctrines and bad institutions. By the aid of this theory every inveterate belief and every intense feeling, of which the origin is not remembered, is enabled to dispense with the obligation of justifying itself by reason, and is erected into its own all-efficient voucher and justification. There never was a better instrument devised for consecrating all deep-seated prejudices."

In ecstatic intuition there is an abstraction of the mind from the body in order to enter into direct communication with I'svara, or to overcome the limitations of individuality to become one with the Brahmam or Absolute. The method ordinarily employed is as follows: By means of prolonged and intense concentration, often assisted by fixing the gaze on a particular object, thought is made to flow along one definite channel *(ekāgrata)*, and the mind is thus thrown into a condition in which, sense and reason being suspended, the loss of individual consciousness is felt as an absorption into the infinite, and truths, unattainable by discursive reason, are perceived by immediate intuition. The condition of the organism in this case does not essentially differ from what it is in morbid states, such as drunkenness. In both cases the subject is beside himself, and the outward and visible characters are the same. If a naturalistic explanation is sufficient for morbid states, it must be equally suitable for ecstatic intuition. Nevertheless, ecstatic intuition is ascribed to the entrance of higher spiritual agencies into a "subliminal self," while the morbid states are regarded as the result of the play of secondary consciousness. Of the existence of secondary consciousness, that is, of an organised system of conditions formed in and through bygone conscious experience, which, though not themselves present to consciousness, determine the onward flow of thought in every moment of its course, there need be no doubt. It is but a stream of mental process of the same order as that of our normal conscious life, but separated from, and more or less independent of it. It pre-supposes no other source of material for psychic evolution than earthly experience, and no laws of mental process other than those recognised by ordinary psychology. But what warrant is there for believing in a "subliminal self," which exists independently of psychical phenomena and serves as the medium of communication with spiritual agencies? Granted that telepathy, clairvoyance and so forth do really occur, does it follow that the mental life in each one of us can be split into two primarily distinct and discontinuous streams of personal consciousness, one mainly connected with a mundane, and the other with an extramundane, environment? As Prof. Hugo Munsterberg says, "metaphysical dreams and doubtful speculations cannot help us, when we seek convictions on which we are to base all that is valuable in our life. The more we separate our life of idealistic belief from the practical reality between morning and evening, the more do we deprive our daily life of its inner dignity and force it to the superficial hopes of an external hereafter."

It is claimed that ecstasy and other so-called mystical states of consciousness possess "the right to be absolutely authoritative over the individuals to whom they come," and that as such they not only "break down the authority of the rationalistic consciousness" based solely upon the understanding of the senses, but also show the latter to be only one kind of consciousness, opening out the possibility of other orders of truth. No one will deny the absolute authority over the subject of what is merely given, namely, visions, voices, entrancing feelings, and volitional attitudes. Nor need we contradict the mystic when he speaks of elation, of freedom, of illumination, of union, or of the increased moral courage and vigour resulting from the so-called higher mystical states. On the merely subjective side these experiences of the mystic are invulnerable and absolute, and as such they are not amenable to any criticism. But considered from the point of view of causal relations the matter becomes different. When the ecstatic ascribes his experiences to the descent of a deity into him, or to the existence of a world of spiritual beings, he is going beyond what is merely felt into the field of rationalistic elaboration. He is no longer in the region of the mystic consciousness, but has trespassed into the domain of rational consciousness, and therefore becomes amenable to the criticism of the latter. Moreover, the subjective character of the experiences of all mystics inevitably vitiates them. No one can feel sure, not even the participant himself, that the transcendental or supernatural element in it is objective reality and not subjective illusion. Nor can the mystic demand from others an absolute and unwavering faith in the intuition of his ecstatic feeling. Besides, in all kinds of ecstasy there is a withdrawal of the individual entirely as a conscious, and, to a large extent, as an active being, from his external life of relation. His consciousness is absorbed, so to speak, in a purely internal strain of activity, which is comparable to nothing in normal experience, and is therefore incapable of being recalled to memory when he returns to his life of relation. It is no wonder that he regards what appears so much outside the range of normal experience as beyond the compass of thought and speech (*avāṇg mānasa gocharam*). No wonder, too, that its rapture seems to him a foretaste of that final beatitude which consists in the absorption of self in the Absolute! But what can be the logical outcome of this? In plain language the so-called consciousness or superconsciousness (*sakshātkāra or samyagdarsana*) appertaining to the supreme goal of all mystics can be nothing else than absolute unconsciousness.

If the world is neither the creation of I'svara nor the manifestation of the Absolute (*brahmaṁ*), may it not be a product of the individual self? Without entering on the question of the reality of the self, the Blessed One has shown the absurdity of regarding the self as the maker of the world as follows. "If you say that the self is the maker, then the self should make all things pleasant. But there are many things in this world not pleasing to one's self; how then could it be asserted that the self is the maker? If it be said that the self does not wish to make things pleasant, then he who wishes for things pleasant is opposed to his self, the maker. Sorrow and joy are not self-existing. How could it be said that they are made by the self? If we admit that the self is the maker, there should, at least, be no evil *karma*, but, as is well known, our deeds produce good and evil results. Hence the self can not be the maker. Perhaps it might be said that the self is the maker according to the occasion, but then the occasion ought to be for good alone. Still, as good and evil both result from cause, it cannot be that the self has made it so." (Asvaghosha's *Buddhacharitra*).

The view here refuted has its origin in the fact that the appearance of things is influenced by the condition of the sensory organs of the percipient. To the jaundiced eye everything looks yellow. This fact is well known to the naive man, but it never occurs to him to regard the whole world as a creation of his senses. Even the metaphysician, who believes himself a solipsist, is never such in practical life. He does not attempt to cloy the hungry edge of his appetite by the bare imagination of a feast. Why should the mind be unable to unmake what it made? If things were really made by the mind, there could not be this divergence between theory and practice. Indeed there ought to be no misery at all in this world. Rightly has the Blessed One laid stress on this point in discarding the absurd view of the idealist.

From these negative criticisms we may now turn to consider the exact position of the Blessed One in relation to the fundamental problems of philosophy. As the Blessed One incessantly laid stress on the ethical life, it is generally supposed that he was indifferent to all epistemological questions. It is indeed true that the Buddha has propounded no hypothesis concerning the origin and end of things; nor has he given a systematic shape to his views. But, from what we find in the Sutrapiṭaka and the Abhidharma piṭaka, it is not difficult to see clearly his exact position. The Blessed One always spoke in a manner suited to the capacities of his hearers. In his discourses to ordinary men he naturally appears to be a realist (*sarvāstivādin*). On the basis of such discourses the Vaibhāshikās and the Sautrāntikās have erected a materialistic system of their own. Both these schools accept the existence of an extrapsychic outside world; the former maintaining that things in themselves are as they are perceived, and the latter that our perceptions are only reflections of the things in the mind. On the other hand, the Yogachārās, the followers of Asangha, form a class of subjective idealists (*vigjnānāstimātravādin*), denying altogether the reality of the external world and regarding it as the creation of a self-subsisting consciousness (*ālaya vignāna*). The Blessed One might indeed have given some room for the development of these schools of thought, but he himself never propounded these views. He was neither a materialist who tried to evolve consciousness out of the motions of self-existing physical atoms, nor was he a solipsist who regarded the world as the product of the activity of self-subsisting spirits. He was a *māthyamika* in thought as well as in life. He steered a middle course. He denied the reality neither of the mind nor of the external world. But he denied the existence of all transcendental substrata, all things in themselves, both *jivātma* and *paramātma*. He was therefore generally called a *çunyavādin*. But he never denied the phenomenal world (*prapancha*) nor the empirical ego (*nāmarupa*). He taught a consistent incontrovertible phenomenalism.

One of the few points on which all philosophers of the present day are agreed is that all that one experiences is given to him only as a content of his consciousness. What is not presented as a content of one's consciousness is entirely outside the range of his knowledge. Though the content of one's consciousness varies from moment to moment, the certainty of the momentary content is so direct that it cannot with any reason be called in question. Though the content of one's consciousness may be valid only for one and only at the moment when it is present, still it may be rendered serviceable for all time and also to others by making known the conditions in which its validity holds. But it must never be forgotten that all that one can know is psychic. Psychic, being conscious, existing—all mean one and the same thing. *Esse* is *percipi*. There can be no such thing as extrapsychic or metapsychic. The neglect of this fundamental fact has given rise to all sorts of supposititious problems about self-subsisting unknowable things, foreign to one's consciousness but working on it.

Every content of consciousness of whatever kind it may be has the character of uniqueness. No two contents of consciousness are exactly alike. But memory, which forms a fundamental phenomenon of consciousness, enables us to place these diverse contents in relation to one another, and note their similarities and differences. We are thus able to analyse the contents of conciousness into certain elements out of which all experience may be regarded as built up. But what is primarily given in consciousness at any moment is the whole content and not these elements. We obtain these elements by a process of abstraction. These elements are the sense impressions and their memory images. As empirical psychology teaches, all other psychical contents may be built up out of them.

The ordinary man believes that sense impressions are produced by a real thing outside consciousness, and that an internal "I" has these sense impressions. The "thing" and the "I" are both inferences and are not originally given. In so far as they are evolved out of the memory images of many different sense impressions, they may be spoken of as complex ideas, and as such they are certainly real. But as substrates, the former external to consciousness and the latter as the vehicle or bearer of consciousness, they have no existence. If all that we experience consists exclusively of processes that occur in our consciousness, is there then no essential difference between outer and inner? Yes; as contents of consciousness there is no intrinsic difference between them.* As the Sutta Nipāta says, "*nātthi ajjhātañ cha bahiddhā cha kinchīti passato.* For him who has understood the truth there is neither external nor internal."

The distinction between inside and outside, between the "I" and "the external world" has a practical origin. To understand clearly the practical difference between inner

* "My feelings arrange and order themselves in two distinct ways. There is the internal or subjective order, in which sorrow succeeds the hearing of bad news, or the abstraction "dog" symbolizes the perception of many different dogs. And there is the external or objective order, in which the sensation of letting go is followed by the sight of a falling object and the sound of its fall. The objective order, *qua* order is treated by physical science, which investigates the uniform relations of objects in time and space. Here the word *object* (or *phenomenon*) is taken merely to mean a group of my feelings, which persists as a group in a certain manner; for I am at present considering only the objective order of my feelings. The object, then, is a set of changes in my consciousness, and not anything out of it......The inferences of physical science are all inferences of my real or possible feelings, inferences of something actually or potentially in my consciousness, not anything outside it."—*W. K. Clifford.*

experience and outer experience, let us consider an example. For instance, we take a needle. Certain sense impressions relating to colour and form associated with images of past sense impressions constitute for us the reality of the needle. Ordinarily we suppose these to reside in a thing outside. But when our finger is pricked by the needle and an unpleasant sense impression is produced, the pain is supposed to be inside. Yet the colour and form of the needle are as much contents of consciousness as the pain produced by the prick. To what then is this difference due? The experience of pleasure and pain (*vedana*) gives birth to a cleaving (*upādāna*), and this leads to the formation (*bhava*) of the idea of a centre of consciousness, an ego, to whose enjoyment all experience is directed. Thus arises the difference between one part of the content of consciousness as the enjoyer and the rest as being outside him and ministering to his pleasure. But when one pursues the Noble Eightfold Path and his prejudiced attachment to pleasure is destroyed, he understands the true nature of all things, and enters the blissful temple of Nirvāṇa,

> "A temple neither Pagod, Mosque, nor Church,
> But loftier, simpler, always opendoored,
> To every breath from heaven, where Truth and Peace,
> And Love and Pity dwell for ever and aye."

PERSONALITY.

VARIOUS have been the views propounded concerning human personality, its nature and destiny. Brahmanism, Jainism, Christianity and Islam, which are the leading animistic faiths of the world, teach that a man's personality or self is his soul (*ātman, pudgala, pneuma, psyche*), which enters the body at birth and quits it at death. The soul, it is said, forms the invisible, immaterial ego, which, knowing itself as 'I,' remains the same amidst all that is changeable. It is the recipient of knowledge through the five gate-ways of sight, hearing, smell, taste and touch. It is the agent that is active in the movements of the various motor organs. It is the lord not only of the body but also of the mind. Though it may not be seen by the eye, nor reached by speech, nor apprehended by the mind, its existence has to be perceived by faith. "Not by speech, not by thought," says the *Kāthaka* Upanishad, "not by sight is he apprehended; "he is," by this word, alone and in no other way is he comprehended. Only by him whom he chooses is he comprehended; to him the *ātman* reveals his nature." Without a soul there could be no immortality, and without immortality life would not be worth living. The existence of a soul alone could ensure to each individual the fruit of his actions; without a soul there could be no rewards in heaven nor punishments in hell. Without a soul there could be no recompense for one's deeds by metempsychosis; and without transmigration how would it be possible to account for the differences between man and man in endowments, character, position and fate?

The Dharma of the Blessed One teaches that this animistic view, this belief in a permanent self or soul, is the most pernicious of errors, the most deceitful of illusions, which will irretrievably mislead its victims into the deepest pit of sorrow and suffering. *Satkāyadrishti*, the belief in a transcendental self, is the very first fetter which one has to cast off before he can set his foot on the threshold of the Noble

Eightfold Path. The belief in a permanent self must naturally produce attachment to it, and attachment to it must necessarily breed egotism, and craving for pleasure here on earth and then beyond in heaven. Therefore the discernment of a permanent self can not be the condition of emancipation from sorrow. The very search for *ātman* is wrong, and like every other wrong start it must lead in a false direction. As Asvagosha says in his *Sraddhotpāda Sutra,* "all false doctrines invariably arise out of the *ātman* conception. If we were liberated from it, the existence of false doctrines would be impossible." Said the Blessed One to King Bimbisāra: "He who knows the nature of his self and understands how his senses act, finds no room for the "I" nor even any ground for its supposition. The world holds to the idea of "I" and from this arises false apprehension. Some say that the "I" endures after death, others say it perishes. Both have fallen into a grievous error. For if the "I" be perishable, the fruit people strive for will perish too, and then deliverance will be without merit. If, as others say, the "I" does not perish, it must be always identical and unchanging. Then moral aims and salvation would be unnecessary, for there would be no use in attempting to change the unchangeable. But as there are marks of joy and sorrow everywhere, how can we speak of any constant being?"

The false belief in a permanent self, which is so widespread, has its origin in a wrong conception of the unity of compound things. A thing *(guṇi)* can be separated from its qualities (*guṇa*) only in thought, but not in reality. Can the properties of a thing be actually removed and the thing still left intact? If heat be romoved from fire, would there be any such thing as fire? No doubt we can separate heat from fire in thought and argue about it, but can we actually do so? Suppose the walls, roof and foundation stones of a house were removed, would there be any self or soul of the house left behind? Just as a house is the result of the special combination of all its parts, so the personality is that peculiar activity which manifests itself as a combination of sensory and motor organs, perceptions, ideas and volitions. "Just as the word chariot," says Buddhagosha in his *Visuddhi magga*, "is but a mode of expression for axle, wheels, pole, and other constituent parts, placed in a certain relation to each other, but when we come to examine the members one by one, we discover in the absolute sense there is no chariot...in exactly the same way the words "living entity" and "I" are but a mode of expression for the five attachment groups (*skandhas*), but when we come to examine the elements of being, one by one, we discover in the absolute sense there is no living being there to form a basis for such figments as "I am" or "I"; in other words, that in the absolute sense there is only name (*nāma*) and form (*rupa*)." In another place the same author writes: "They say it is a living entity that walks, it is a living entity that stands; but is there any living entity to walk or to stand? There is not. But even as people speak of a cart's going, though there is nothing corresponding to the word cart to go or to stand, yet when the driver has yoked up four oxen and drives them, we then, by a mere convention of speech, talk of the cart's going or of the cart's standing; in exactly the same way the body on account of its lack of intelligence resembles the cart, the impulsions of the thoughts resemble the oxen, the thought resembles the driver, and when the thought of walking or of standing arises, the windy element (= nervous impulse) arises and shows itself in the actions, and walking etc., are brought about by this action of the mind and permeation by the windy element. Accordingly, to say: 'It is a living entity that walks, it is a living entity that stands; I walk, I stand,' is but a mere convention of speech." Similarly says Nāgasena in the *Milindapanha:* "Just as it is by the condition precedent of the co-existence of its various parts that the word "chariot" is used, just so is it that where the *skandhas* are there we talk of being." "In relation to the eye and form arises visual consciousness, and simultaneously with it contact (*sparsa*), emotion (*vedana*), idea, thought, subsumption, perception of reality and attention—these processes (*dharma*) arise in dependence on one another, but there is perceived no cognising subject."

As Buddhism resolves the whole phenomenal universe (*prapancha*), outside which nothing exists, into pure psychic processes (*dharma*), it is but natural that it should categorically reject the existence of an *ātman*, a transcendental subject outside consciousness. But it does not deny the existence of a personality, an empirical ego, an "I" built up out of the elements of experience and reacting on the elements themselves. "Personality, personality, they say; what has the Blessed One said that this personality is?" So asks a bhikshu of the bhikshuni Dhammadinna. And she answers: "The Blessed One has said that personality consists of the five elements of life-impulse." Man is an organism built up of the five *skandhas*, namely, *rupa*, *vedana*, *vignāna*, *samjna*, and *samskāra*. Each of these *skandhas* is a group of psychical processes. *Rupa* represents the totality of sensations and ideas pertaining to one's body; *vedana* the momentary emotional states; *vignāna* the thoughts; *samjna* the memories and fancies; and *samskāra* the dispositions or inclinations. "Whatever is gross, that is form (*rupa*);" says the *Milindapanha*, "whatever is subtle, mental, that is name (*nama*). Name and form are connected one with the other, and spring into being together. This is their nature through time immemorial." This view* is *mutatis mutandis* precisely the same as that of modern psychology, which also regards the "I" as nothing more than the complex collective idea of one's body (= *rupa*) and one's momentary dispositions (= *saṁskāra*) and perceptions (= *vedana*, *samjna*, *vignāna*). "We should say to-day," says Prof. Titchener in his *Outlines of Psychology*, "that life is the general name for a number of complicated physical and chemical processes; not an added principle, a mysterious something over and above them. Similarly, we no longer think of mind as something apart from mental processes, and of intellect, feeling and will as faculties with which this something is endowed. Mind is a sum of mental processes, and intellect, feeling and will are sub-divisions of mind, special groups of the processes contained in the sum." All that we know consists of colours, sounds, spaces, pressures, temperatures and so forth bound up together in manifold ways, and with these are also found associated ideas,

* See Max Walleser: Die philosophische Grundlage des älteren Buddhismus, pp. 119-120.

emotions, desires, memories and so forth. Out of this complex texture rises into prominence that which is relatively more fixed and permanent and impresses itself on the memory, and finds expression in language. Certain of these complexes of relatively greater permanency are called things. But none of these complexes is absolutely permanent. A thing is regarded as one and unchangeable, only so long as there is no necessity to consider details. Thus we speak of the earth as a sphere when great precision is not necessary. But if we are engaged in an orographical investigation, we can not overlook the earth's deviation from the spherical form and can no longer treat it as a sphere. Similarly the personality of a man is a complex of certain sensations (= *rupa*) and certain ideas, emotions, volitions, &c. (= *nāma*). As Prof. Charles Richet says, human personality "arises first and principally from the memory of our past existence, then it emanates from all the sensations which come to us, sensations of our internal organs, sensations of the outside world, consciousness of effort and of muscular movement." The personality of a man is as little absolutely permanent as are other things. Its apparent permanence consists in the slowness of its changes and in the fact of its continuity.

Modern psychology considers the substantial soul, *ātman*, as an outbirth of that sort of ratiocination whose guiding principle is: Whatever you are ignorant of is the explanation of what you know. The assumption of a soul, independent of the body, might be difficult to disprove, as in experience we always find a residuum of unexplained facts. But it is not a scientific hypothesis, and even any attempt to investigate it, as Prof. E. Mach* says, is a methodological perversity. To formulate and describe all the facts of experience, all that psychology need admit is the existence of a stream of conscious processes, each substantially different from, but cognitive of, the rest, and appropriative of each other's contents. There is not the smallest reason for supposing the existence of an experiencing self altogether outside this series. The unity which constitutes conscious

* Erkenntnis und Irrthum.

selfhood needs for its growth no absolutely permanent elements. It only needs the presence of some relatively permanent elements which change at a much less rapid rate than others. And such relatively permanent elements we find in the "organic" sensations and the habitual emotional tone which characterises them and in the predispositions (*samskāra*) which have been inherited or acquired in the earliest period of psychic life. Strictly speaking, none of these can be said to be really permanent and unchanging. The organic sensations of a man in the prime of life are not the same as those of childhood or of dotage. No psychical process (*dharma*), whether it be organic sensation or feeling tone, remains permanently the same from the beginning to the end of life. But, as compared with the sensations and ideas which from time to time form the content of consciousness, the changes in the organic sensations and the emotional tone are so slow within long periods of life that this relative permanency gives rise to the growth of a distinction between the permanent self and its incessantly changing sensations and ideas, an illusion, so to say, which it is the purpose of the science of psychology to dispel. To quote the words of Prof. James,* no mean authority on modern psychology, "the consciousness of self involves a stream of thought each part of which as 'I' can remember those which went before and know the things they knew; and emphasise and care paramountly for certain ones among them as '*me*' and *appropriate to these* the rest. The nucleus of the '*me*' is always the bodily existence felt to be present at the time. Whatever remembered past feelings *resemble* this present feeling are deemed to belong to the same *me* with it. Whatever other things are perceived to be associated with this feeling are deemed to form part of that me's experience; and of them certain ones (which fluctuate more or less) are reckoned to be themselves constituents of the *me* in a larger sense,—such are the clothes, the material possessions, the friends, the honors and esteem which the person receives or may receive. This *me* is an empirical aggregate of things objectively known. The "I" which knows them cannot itself be

* **Principles of Psychology.**

an aggregate, neither for psychological purposes need it be considered to be an unchanging metaphysical entity like the soul, or a principle like the pure ego viewed as out of time. It is a thought, at each moment different from that of the last moment, but appropriative of the latter called its own. All the experiential facts find their place in this description unencumbered with any hypothesis save that of the existence of passing thoughts or states of mind." Again in another place the same writer says: "If the passing thought be the directly verifiable existent which no school has hitherto doubted it to be, then that thought is itself the thinker." Similarly says Buddhagosha in his *Visuddhimagga*: "Strictly speaking the duration of the life of a conscious being is exceedingly brief (*kshanika*), lasting only while a thought lasts. Just as a chariot wheel rolls only at one point of the tire, and in resting rests only at one point; in exactly the same way, the life of a living being lasts only for the period of one thought. As soon as the thought has ceased, the being is said to have ceased. As it has been said:—The being of a past moment of thought has lived, but does not live, nor will it live. The being of a future moment of thought will live, but has not lived nor does it live. The being of the present moment of thought does live, but has not lived, nor will it live."

Those that see something inscrutable in psychical processes often compare the soul to a piano. "Ideas," says Herbert Spencer, "are like the successive chords and cadences brought out from a piano, which successively die away as other ones are sounded. And it would be as proper to say that these passing chords and cadences thereafter exist in the piano as it is proper to say that passing ideas thereafter exist in the brain. In the one case, as in the other, the acual existence is the structure which, under like conditions, evolves like combinations." But the inappropriateness of this analogy has been pointed out by Dr. H. Maudsley. Says the latter in his *Physiology of Mind*: "This analogy, when we look into it, seems more captivating than it is complete. What about the performer in the case of the piano and in the case of the brain, respectively. Is not the performer a not unimportant element, and necessary to the completeness of the analogy? The passing chords and cadences would have small chance of being brought out by the piano if they were not previously in his mind. Where, then, in the brain is the equivalent of the harmonic conceptions in the performer's mind? If Mr. Spencer supposes that the individual's mind, his spiritual entity, is detached from the brain, and plays upon its nervous plexuses, as the performer plays upon the piano, his analogy is complete; but if not, then he has furnished an analogy which those who do take that view may well thank him for. There is this difference between the passing chords and cadences in the brain—and it is of the essence of the matter—that, in the former case, the chords and cadences do pass and leave no trace of themselves behind in the structure of the piano; while in the latter case they do not pass or die away without leaving most important after-effects in the structure of the brain; whence does arrive in due time a considerable difference between a cultivated piano and a cultivated human brain, and whence, probably, have arisen, in the progress of development through the ages, the differences between the brain of a primeval savage and the brain of Mr. Spencer......With the brain function makes faculty, not so with the piano."

Cogito ergo sum—I think, therefore I exist: say Descartes and his followers. Yes; but the *I think* is merely the expression of my existence. By it I know only that I am, not what I am, and therefore not that I am a thinking soul or spirit. What is orginally given is not one's *self*-consciousness, but merely one's consciousness. "As for me," says Kant, "whenever I contemplate what is inmost in what I call myself, I always come in contact with such or such special perception as of cold, heat, light or shadow, love or hate, pleasure or pain. I never come unawares on my mind existing in a state void of perceptions. I never observe aught save perception......If any one after serious reflection without prejudices, thinks he has any other idea of himself, I confess I can no longer reason with him. The best I can say for him is that, perhaps, he is right no less than I, and that on this point our natures are essentially different. It is possible that he may perceive something simple and permanent which he calls himself, but as for me, I am quite sure I possess no such principle." The experience *I am* is not simple. In becoming conscious of myself I at the same time become conscious of something not myself. No inner perception is apprehended as such without distinguishing it from a simultaneous outer perception and setting it in antithesis to this. No inner experience is possible without the simultaneous construction of outer experience. Neither inner experience nor outer experience is directly given, but only the consciousness which includes inner and outer experience in constant interdependence. It is the reciprocity of ego and not-ego that is originally given. The ego and not-ego mutually condition each other; the one is not even thinkable without the other; for their special features lie in the feeling of contrast between them. The idea of "I" cannot even originate without the idea of "not-I", for children first speak of themselves in the third person. Were it possible for any one through mere accident to grow up away from the society of all fellow beings, he would not be able to distinguish between sensations and ideas nor succeed in forming an idea of "I" and setting it against the world. For him all experience would be of only one kind. When the "not-I" is completely effaced, as in narcosis and sleep, the "I" also disappears. Only an *advaita* Vedantin who prefers the absence of consciousness to consciousness will imagine the self as perceiving itself in dreamless sleep.

That which is called the ego, which says 'I am,' is merely an aggregate of *skandhas*, a complex of sensations, ideas, thoughts, emotions and volitions. It is not an eternal immutable entity behind these. The word 'I' remains the same, but its significance continually changes. It originates in the child with the development of self-consciousness (*svasamvédanam*), and denotes first a boy, then a youth, after that a man, and, finally a dotard. There is an identity in a certain sense only. As the Blessed One says in the *Kuṭadanta Sutra*, the sameness is constituted by continuity, just as we speak of the identity of a river or a fountain, though the water is continually changing; or of the identity between the flame of a lamp at one moment and that at another moment, although different particles of the wick and oil are consumed in succession, and the flame itself might have been put out for some time in the interim. What characterises the apparent sameness of the "I" is the cohesion and co-ordination of a certain number of very frequently recurring sensations and ideas, which therefore come to be regarded as a permanent stock. These are primarily the sensations of one's own body, but they also include the daily recurring sensations of our environment. "Even the speculative philosopher," says Prof. Wundt, "is incapable of severing his self-consciousness from the feelings and sensations, which form the sensory background of his 'I.' This itself is, therefore, in essence a collective feeling (*totalgefuhl*), of which the feelings of apperception form the dominant elements, and the special feelings and sensations bound up with one's own self form the variable secondary constituents."* In short, the "I" represents one's customary sensations and ideas. The unity of the ego has accordingly nothing to do with the single entity of the spiritualists. We might as well speak of the kernel of a water-bubble as of the self which is supposed to be the lord of one's body, of one's mind, and of one's character. As Prof. Alois Riehl puts it, the "I" is the summary expression, grasped from within, of that unity of the individual life, which appears to external sense as an organism with interacting parts and functions.

It is urged that personality is a cause, that every psychic process is essentially one of effort or conation, that every thought is a function of the will; in short, the "I" is characterised by spontaneity. By the spontaneity or self-activity of the "I" is meant nothing more than the fact that each of us is in a position to manipulate with the contents of his consciousness, to observe them carefully or overlook them, to analyse them and compare their parts with one another, and so on. This is supposed to prove the simplicity of consciousness. But how? May not a subject built up out of the elements (sensations, ideas, &c.) be capable of reacting on the elements themselves? Of the

* Wundt: Grundzuge der phys. Psychologie, III, p. 375.

complex of *skandhas* the *samskāras*, the volitions, form, so to speak, a supporting backbone. They represent a continuum of such presentations of consciousness as are essentially alike, and are therefore conceived as the proper core of one's own personality, and set in opposition to the continually varying sensory presentations, among which those that constitute the idea of one's body occupy a special place. For, strictly speaking, the sensory impressions do not become one's own till they are apperceived, that is to say, till they have been placed by the will in relation to one another. Only in this sense can we say that what a man can truly call his own is his will.

It is said that the will is free. Yes; the will is free in so far as it is self-determined. Only when one is restrained by causes that lie entirely outside him, can his will be said to be not free. But, so long as one's resolutions and actions are determined solely by what he knows, thinks and feels, that is to say, by what forms a part of his own nature, so long is his will also actually free. Yet his will is not free in the sense that it is free from the law of causality. Every act of will is causally determined, but not every one of the causes determining an act of will may be known to us. Modern psychology has shown that what comes within the sphere of distinct consciousness does not comprise every portion of the appetitive, remembering, thinking and reasoning self. Each of us is as ignorant of the larger part of himself as he is of what may be happening in the most distant celestial body. While consciousness is of the individual, the substratum on which it is developed is of the race. Out of *avidya*, the nebulous undifferentiated racial life, are born predispositions, *samskāras*, which form the roots of volition and the basis of character. Volition, considered as a mere state of consciousness, is nothing more than an affirmation or a negation, and as such has no efficacy to produce an act. The acts and movements which accompany a volition result directly from the dispositions, feelings, perceptions and ideas which have become co-ordinated in the form of a choice. Only a part of the psychological activity involved in a choice enters into consciousness, and the subconscious processes escape notice. The surface phenomena of one's consciousness may lead to the misconstruction of one's acts of will as uncaused, for the chain of causation is often obscure. But deeper reflection always reveals that every act of will is necessarily caused. Nor is it necessary to make the ego a transcendental entity in order to recognise in it a true causality.

The activity of the "I," above referred to, manipulates with extant elements of consciousness, and produces by its manipulations new contents of consciousness. In this way we come to divide the contents of consciousness into two classes: those that are simply given, and those which we ourselves create, that is, those which we are able to call forth at will. When a content of consciousness appears to us as simply given, we are not in a position to efface it or even modify it at will; if I stand before a green tree, I *see* the green tree, whether I will or not. On the other hand it is entirely different with the idea of a tree, a *remembered* tree. The representation of a tree is completely at my command, and I can at will modify it, or replace it by another. Phenomena of consciousness of the first kind form the material for the building up of the external world; those of the second kind are generally called the constructions of one's mind, the creations of one's fancy. The difference between *seeing* a green tree and *remembering* a green tree is so clear; that there can be no question about it. We note that the two are situate in different spheres. The elements which constitute the two and their connection are not the same. But the fundamental nature of the elements of both is the same, and is not different from the elements which build up the "I." The elements are always sensations, ideas, &c. When one finds that the phenomena of consciousness of the second kind are the products of an activity which is at work in his own consciousness, the temptation is not far to regard the phenomena of consciousness of the first kind also as the similar creations of an unknown activity. This is the error of the followers of Berkeley and of the solipsist in general. Further if one has fancied the "I" to be a spiritual entity, he naturally constructs similar ideas in explanation of the whole world. Thus have come into being the ideas of spirits and demons, gods and demigods, God and Nature, and other similar creations of mythology. Such transcendental hypothetical entities have proved the greatest obstacles to the advance of reason. As Kant says, transcendental hypotheses render fruitless the exertions of reason in its own sphere, which is that of experience. "For when the explanation of natural phenomena happens to be difficult, we have constantly at hand a transcendental ground of explanation which lifts us above the necessity of investigating nature."

Human personality is a compound of body and mind. Disembodied personality is no personality in the real sense of the term.* Poverty of language and practical sufficiency permit the use of such expressions as a truncated cone, a cube with bevelled edges, disembodied personality, which involve contradictions. Personality or the ego is, as has been so often repeated, really a complex of sensations, ideas, &c. But because it is possible to take away constituent parts in thought without destroying the capacity of the residual image to stand for the whole, we give the same name to the residuum. Thus has arisen the practice of regarding the ego as being made up of volitions, emotions, ideas, &c., only of a *nama* without a *rupa*. Even then what is of importance in personality is not the "I" but the elements which constitute it and the manner in which they are connected. If this does not satisfy us, and we ask, Who or What has these volitions, emotions, &c.?, and then assume the existence of a transcendental or noumenal self, an *ātman*, we have only succumbed to the primitive habit of treating an unanalysed complex as an indivisible unity, like the Fiji islander who ascribes a soul to a cocoanut. This primitive habit of treating the unanalysed complex of personality as an indivisible unity has manifested itself in remarkable ways in psychology. From the body the nervous system is first isolated as the seat of psychical activity. In the nervous system again the brain is chosen as the part best suited to be the organ of the mind,

* "If the immortal life," says a recent writer on immortality, "is to be more than a name for a shadow, it must be a life where men are members one of another, not less, but more than they are here. We desire an immortality which shall signify a personal life in the full sense of these words, not the existence of a 'disembodied spirit,' or a 'pure indivisible, immaterial substance,' and a personal life must be an embodied life."

and finally to preserve the supposed psychical unity—imagined to be like the mathematician's point without parts or magnitude—some small part of the brain, such as the pineal-gland, is chosen as the seat of the soul. The crudity of such conceptions is made clear by the following analysis taken from Avenarius's *Menschliche Weltbegriffe*. "Let an individual M denote a definite whole of 'perceived things' (trunk, arms, hands, legs, feet, speech, movements, &c.) and of 'presented thoughts' as I,......then when M says 'I have a brain,' this means that a brain belongs as a part to the whole of perceived things and presented thoughts denoted as I. And when M says 'I have thoughts,' this means that the thoughts themselves belong as a part to the whole of perceived things and presented thoughts denoted as I. But, though thorough analysis of the denotation of I leads to the result that we *have* a brain and thoughts, it never leads to the result that the brain has the thoughts. The thought is, no doubt, a thought of 'my ego,' but not a thought of 'my brain' any more than my brain is the brain of 'my thought.' That is to say, the brain is no habitation, seat, generator, instrument or organ, no support or substratum of *thought*. *Thought* is no indweller or commander, no other half or side, and also no product, indeed not even a physiological function, or so much as a state of the brain."

So long as one regards the "I" as a real mysterious entity behind the elements which alone are accessible, he must puzzle himself with all sorts of contradictions and perplexities. But if we regard the ego as a more strongly linked group of elements, which are themselves less strongly linked to other groups, we no longer meet with difficulties and absurdities. We then clearly perceive how the subjective feeling of unity has been generated by the ease with which the imagination runs along those of our ideas which are closely knitted with one another through the bonds of association, and what purpose this assumed unity of the ego serves. This suppositious unity serves to delimit the ego, and thus discharges a valuable function in practical life. Just as caste bias, race prejudice, national pride, narrow patriotism may have a high value for certain purposes, so the narrowing of the limits of the ego is highly serviceable to the intellect in the work it does for the pain-avoiding, pleasure-seeking will. Nevertheless, this practical unity of the ego has neither sharply defined limits nor is it unalterable. Each one of us knows how he is striving to alter the content of his ego. Is it not a change in this content that is sought after in every attempt to alter the character of a person? If the world consists of the same elements as one's ego, and if every element in the world can become a constituent of that ego, why should not that ego be so extended as ultimately to embrace the entire world? Because the elements which constitute an individual are more strongly and closely knitted among themselves than with those which constitute other individuals, he imagines himself to be an indissoluble unity independent of others. But the life of the individual has no meaning apart from collective life. That which is truly human in each one of us, the true, the beautiful, the good, has something of the universal, and is created and realised only through the communion of minds. Moreover, when the content of an ego is sufficiently wide, it generally breaks through the shackles of individuality, engrafts itself in others, and pursues an over-individual life. It is the dissolution of individuality which contributes to the greatest happiness of the artist, the discoverer, the social reformer, and all others who co-operate in the welfare of the many, and live, as Schiller says, in the whole. Says the Blessed One in the *Mālunkya-putta Sutta:* "The man whose heart is set on the dissolution of individuality feels cheerful, happy, and elated, like the mighty man who has swum unhurt across the swollen Ganges from the one bank to the other."

The denial of a separate self, an *ātman*, does not obliterate the personality of a man, but liberates the individual from an error that is liable to stunt his intellectual and ethical development and hinder his attainment of perfection. The Dharma removes from life the vanity of self, which is the result of an erroneous belief in the existence of *ātman* and *karma* as separate entities. As what constitutes a man's personality is his own deeds and aspirations, he that holds his person dear should keep himself free from wickedness. The Blessed One has said:

"Let any one who holds self dear,
That self keep free from wickedness;
For happiness can never be found
By any one of evil deeds.

"Assailed by death, in life's last throes,
At quitting of this human state,
What is it one can call his own?
What is it follows after him?

"Nought follows him who quits this life;
For all things must be left behind:
Wife, daughters, sons, one's kin, and friends,
Gold, grain and wealth of every kind.

"But what a mortal does while here,
With body, or with voice, or mind,
'Tis this that he can call his own,
This is what follows after him.

"Deeds, like a shadow, ne'er depart:
Bad deeds can never be concealed;
Good deeds cannot be lost and will
In all their glory be revealed.

"Let all, then, noble deeds perform,
A treasure store for future weal;
For merit gained this life within
Will yield a blessing in the next."—*Samyutta-Nikāya.*

DEATH AND AFTER.

IN his complete nature man is a complex of *skandhas.* Only in thought can we separate him into body (*rupa*) and mind (*nāma*). Language reveals to us the true nature of personality. One speaks not only of one's body but also of one's mind. Who then is the possessor of both body and mind, if it is not the complete man, the complex? Just as we are in the habit of saying 'the wind blows,' as if there were the wind existing apart from the act of blowing, so also do we say, by a license of speech, that a person owns body and soul, performs actions, directs the emotions, controls the impulses, and so forth. But in reality the totality of all these constitutes the person. Whatsoever a man does with his body, with his voice, with his mind, it is that that constitutes his person. "I am," says Professor Josiah Royce, "what on the whole I am conscious of having done, and what I propose to do." On one occasion the Blessed One was asked by some disciples: "What are old age and death? And what is it that has old age and death?" The Blessed One replied: "The question is not rightly put. To say: 'What are old age and death? And what is it has old age and death?' and to say: 'Old age and death are one thing, but it is another thing that has old age and death,' is to say the same thing in different ways. If the dogma obtain that soul and body are identical, then there is no holy life (for the soul would perish with the body); or, if the dogma obtain that the soul is one thing and the body another, then also there is no holy life (for, if the soul were a distinct entity, an immutable *ātman*, it would not be influenced by conduct and become better, and then there would be no use in leading a holy life). . Both these extremes have been avoided by the Tathāgata, and it is a middle doctrine he teaches: On birth depend old age and death."

So long as the *skandhas* are united, we have being; when the *skandhas* dissolve, the being disappears and we have death. Just as fire, though not lying hidden in the two sticks rubbed against each other, originates through friction, in the same way, says the Blessed One, appears consciousness (*vignāna*) under certain conditions, and disappears when these conditions cease to exist. When the wood is burnt, the fire disappears. Just so, when the conditions of consciousness cease, consciousness disappears. Consciousness is known to us only as a phenomenon of life connected with an organism. Psychical processes are only known to us as dependent on organic processes. Changes in the brain and the nervous system are essential conditions for all phenomena of consciousness. Nor is the connection between psychic processes and organic processes as great as the connection between purely organic processes. Organic processes continue as long as there is life, but psychic processes are intermittent even during life. While organic life has no break in an individual's existence, conscious life performs its functions only from time to time, needs the refreshment of sleep, and varies in activity even when awake. The anaesthetised body lies pumping the blood through the vessels, and maintains the physical interchanges between the tissues, but contains no spark or vestige of consciousness. When the brain is injured or diseased, the loss of consciousness may last for an interminable period. Hence we should say that consciousness exists for the sake of life, and not life for consciousness. Rightly did the Buddha teach in plain language to his disciples: "It were better if the ignorant regarded the body, composed of the four elements, as the "I" instead of mind. And why do I say so? Because this body may endure for a year, ten years, hundred years and more. But what is called mind, cognition, cousciousness, is found to be day and night in restless change."

Normal psychology proves that consciousness can have no existence independent of the organism. This conclusion is strongly supported by mental pathology. Within the life history of a single individual various selves appear and disappear in a manner which shows that they cannot be regarded as connected by any felt continuity of interest with the rest of life. Cases of multiple personality and alternating personality prove that a plurality of selves might alternate regularly or even coexist in connection with the same body. Such abnormal psychic phenomena force on us the conclusion that the origination and the disappearance of selves in the course of psychical events is a fact of constant occurrence. There are no known facts that imply the existence of a soul separable from the body. The progress of psychology during the last thirty years has been great, but it has produced nothing that would strengthen the popular faith in extra-human spirit agencies influencing human destinies. On the other hand, it has made intelligible, conformably to the rest of our knowledge, all such phenomena as anaesthesias, analgesias, hallucinations, monitions, &c., which have always been the props of the ignorant belief in spirits. The endeavours of the innumerable spiritualistic and theosophical bodies have not brought to light any scrap of scientific proof of the continuance of human personality beyond the grave. Can any proof be expected from "a method of inquiry which is not repelled by the grotesquery of the 'spirits,' and which accepts balderdash as the poetry of Shakespere, twaddle as the philosophy of Bacon, and the medium's thinly disguised person as the reincarnation of Socrates, the Virgin Mary, or the repentant pirate John King?" Scientific investigation of spiritualistic phenomena has shown that fraud, unconscious suggestion, and co-operation form sufficient explanations of what are presented.

Even the researches of the Society for Psychical Research have not been able to demonstrate the existence of spirits, but have only helped to strengthen the intra-human explanation of many phenomena previously not well understood. "Facts, I think," says Professor W. James in his *Varieties of Religious Experience*, "are yet lacking to prove 'spirit return,' though I have the highest respect for the patient labours of Messrs. Myers, Hodgson, and Hyslop." Although the sole interest of these psychologists and philosophers of the highest academic rank has been, as Dr. Stanley Hall points out, to establish the existence of a land of disembodied spirits and to demonstrate the possibility of a communication between them and this world, yet every fact and group of facts on which they rely point for their explanation to the past of the individual and the race and not to the future, to the subnormal rather than to the supernormal, more to the body than to any disembodied spirit. Just as the alchemists in their search after the elixir of life neglected chemistry, just as astrologers in quest of the influence of the stars on human life overlooked astronomy, so have the leaders of the Psychical Research Movement in their zeal to find an answer to what is called the most insistent question of the human heart,—If a man die, shall he live again? —completely lost sight of the true import of the facts they have collected. They think and speak of the soul only in the future tense, and little does that word suggest to them any connection with the past. On the contrary, as the philosophic Roman poet has put it,—

> "Not from the blank inane emerged the soul:
> A sacred treasury it is of dreams
> And deeds that built the present from the past
> Adding thereto its own experiences.
> Ancestral lives are seeing in mine eyes
> Their hearing listeneth within my ears,
> And in my hand their strength is plied again.
> Speech came a rich consignment from the past,
> Each word aglow with wondrous spirit life
> Thus building up my soul of myriad souls."

Science affords no evidence of the continuance of the conscious person after death, but, on the whole, it suggests that the conscious person has ended too. Death, says the modern physiologist, consists in the dissolution of the combination of the various anatomical organs and in the dissolution of the consciousness which the individual possesses of himself, that is to say, of the existence of this combination. Similarly, it is said in the *Bhārahāra Sutra* that the laying down of the bearer (*hāranikkhepana*) is identical and simultaneous with the laying down of the burden (*bhāranikkhēpana*), that is, of the *skandhas.** More clearly is this truth brought out in the funeral elegy of the Buddhists: "Salutation to the Blessed One, the Holy

* It is interesting to note that in the *Brihadāraṇyaka Upanishad* Yāgnavalkya tells his wife Maitreyi: "A man comes out of these elements, and passes back into them as they pass away, and, after he has passed away, there is no more consciousness."

One, the Enlightened One. All sentient beings are doomed to die, for life indeed must terminate in death; even after reaching old age there comes death; such is the nature of sentient beings. Whether young or old, whether ignorant or wise, all fall under the hand of death, all are subject to death. Just as the seed in the field germinates and grows on account of the moisture in the soil as well as the vitality of the embryo, so do the elementary and composite forms of the organised being and the six organs of sense arise from a cause, and from a cause become disintegrated and perish. As the union of the constituent parts forms what is called a "chariot," so does the union of the *skandhas*, the attributes of being, form what is called a "sentient being." As soon as vitality, warmth and consciousness forsake the body, then the body is inanimate and useless. The deeper one reflects and meditates upon this body, the more he becomes convinced that it is but an empty and vain thing. For, indeed, in it does suffering originate, and in it does suffering perdure and perish; nothing else but suffering is produced, and nothing else but suffering perishes with it. All compound things are *anitya*: he who knows and comprehends this becomes freed from suffering; this is the way that leads to purity. All compound things are *duhkha*: he who knows and comprehends this becomes freed from suffering; this is the path that leads to purity. All existing things are *anātman*: he who knows and comprehends this becomes freed from suffering; this is the path that leads to purity. Therefore, let every one, after hearing the words of the Holy One, restrain his tears; let him, on seeing that one has passed away and is dead, conclude: 'Never more will he be found by me.'"

"How transient are things mortal!
How restless is man's life!
But Peace stands at the portal
Of death, and ends all strife.

"Life is a constant parting—
One more the stream has crossed;
But think ye who stand smarting
Of that which ne'er is lost.

"All rivers flowing, flowing,
Must reach the distant main;
The seeds which are sowing
Will ripen into grain."*

Though death is the dissolution of body and mind, yet it does not end all. The Blessed One has declared that he is neither a *sāsvatavādin* like the Brahmans, nor an *uccheda-vādin* like the Charvākās and the Lokāyatās. While the Dharma discards the existence of a permanent self, an *ātman* which transmigrates from birth to birth, it at the same time upholds the persistence of *karma*. Man is nothing more than the temporary union of the five *skandhas;* the beginning of this union is birth, and its end is death. But as long the union lasts, the ego manifests itself at every moment as an active, pain-avoiding, pleasure-seeking will, having relations to other individuals. From this point of view each individual existence is spoken of as a complex of *karmas.* But the content of one's ego, as we have already seen, is never confined wholly to himself; it passes on to others and remains preserved in them even after his death. So man dies, but his *karma* is reborn in other individuals. Just as when a man has written a letter, the writing has ceased, but the letter remains, so when the *skandhas* dissolve, the deeds remain to bear fruit in the future. When a lamp is lit at a burning lamp, there is a kindling of the wick, but no transmigration of the flame. The mango that is planted rots in the ground, but it is reborn in the mangoes of the tree that grows from its seed. From the seed to the fruit there is no transmigration of a mango soul, but there is a reconstruction of its form, and the type in all its individual features is preserved in the new mangoes. Thus man reincarnates, though there is no transmigration. One man dies, and it is another that is reborn. "What is reborn," says the *Milindapanha*, "is name and form. But it is not the same name and form. By one name and form deeds are done, and by these deeds another name and form is reborn. One name and form finds its end in death, another that is reborn. But that other is the result of the first, and is therefore not thereby released from its evil deeds." As Buddha-

* Translated by Dr. P. Carus. Gems of Buddhist poetry.

gosha says in his *Visuddhimagga*, "those groups which came into being in the past existence in dependence on *karma*, perished then and there. But in dependence on the *karma* of that existence other groups have come into being in this existence. Not a single element of being has come into this existence from a previous one. The groups which have come into being in this existence in dependence on *karma* will perish, and others will come into being in the next existence, but not a single element of being will go from this existence into the next. Moreover, just as the words of the teacher do not pass into the mouth of the pupil, who nevertheless repeats them; and just as the features of the face do not pass to the reflection in mirrors and the like, and nevertheless in dependence on them does the image appear; and just as the flame does not pass over from the wick of one lamp to that of another, and nevertheless the flame of the second lamp exists in dependence on that of the former; in exactly the same way not a single element of being passes over from a previous existence into the present existence, nor hence into the next existence; and yet in dependence on the groups, organs of sense, objects of sense, and sense consciousness of the last existence were born those of this one, and from the present groups, organs of sense, objects of sense, and self-consciousness will be born the groups, organs of sense, objects of sense, and sense consciousness of the next existence."

Here and there in the Piṭakas may be found passages which appear to suggest that the Buddha admitted the transmigration of an actual entity from one birth to another. But the fact that such statements occur in the popular discourses and the parables, the so-called *Jātaka* stories, shows that the Blessed One was speaking in a manner suited to the capacity of the ordinary man (*prthagjana*). In these parables the aim of the Master was to teach the common people in a simple way the truth of the relation between action and its fruit. But the Blessed One never wanted to imply that one and the same person is reborn. Once a bhikshu, named Sāti, disputed with the other bhikshus that consciousness (*vignāna*) persisted unchanged in the cycle of rebirths. The Blessed One sent for him and asked him: "What is it you regard as consciousness, Sāti?" The latter answered: "That which as self, O Master, enjoys again and again the fruits of good and bad actions." The Buddha then admonished him thus: "From whom hast thou, deluded man, heard that I have taught such a doctrine? Have I not in many ways explained the conditioned nature of consciousness? Without sufficient cause arises no consciousness." The teaching of the Dharma concerning *karma* cannot be clearly understood except in the light of what the Blessed One has taught as to the nature of personality. What is essential in personality is not the "I" but the content. This content is never for two moments the same. What serves to conserve this content is continuity, and it is this that gives rise to the illusory idea of identity. As the *Bodicharyāvatāra* says, "*aham eva tadāpīti mithyāyām parikalpana*, that I am one and the same person is the result of an illusion." Strictly speaking, man is dying every moment. But so long as the mode of association of the elements which constitute the ego remains largely the same, we speak of the ego as the same. But really at one moment it is one ego, and at the next moment it is a different ego, though connected with the former by certain links. It is the continuity of thought that gives rise to the oneness. What determines the connection between the doer of a deed and the enjoyer of its fruit is also this continuity of thought (*chittasamtāna*). As the *Bodhicharyāvatāra* says, "*hetumān phalayogīti driçyate naisha sambhavah, samtānasyaikyamāçritya kartā bhoktēty dēçitam.* If a person is changing from moment to moment, there is evidently no reason for supposing that the doer of a deed necessarily enjoys its fruit. Only the oneness arising from the continuity of thought determines the connection between the doer of a deed and the enjoyer of its fruit." Similarly, when a person dies, that is to say, when an ego ceases to have sensations, volitions &c., the elements no longer occur in their customary mode of association, but the content of the ego is not lost. Barring a few worthless personal reminiscences the content of an ego remains preserved in others. Thus the individual is preserved in new forms. *Anyaeva mrito, anyaeva prajāyate.* It is one that dies, and it is another that is reborn.

Na cha so, na cha anno—It is not he, and yet it is not another. As the poet says,

> "I call that something "I" which seems my soul;
> Yet more the spirit is than ego holds.
> For lo! this ego, where shall it be sought?
> I'm wont to say "I see", yet 'tis the eye
> That sees, and seeing, kindleth in the thought
> The beaming image of memory.
> "I hear" we say: Hearing is of the ear,
> And where the caught word stirs, there cords resound
> Of slumbering sentiment; and echoes wake
> Of sounds that long ago to silence lapsed.
> Not dead, perfected only, is the past;
> And ever from the darkness of the grave,
> It rises to rejuvenated life.
> The 'I' is but a name to clothe withal
> The clustered mass that now my being forms.
> Take not the symbol for reality—
> The transient for th' eterne. Mine ego, lo!
> 'Tis but my spirits scintillating play.
> This fluctuant moment of eternities
> That now are crossing where my heart's blood beats.
> I was not, am, and soon will pass. But never
> My soul shall cease; the breeding ages aye
> Shall know its life. All that the past bequeathed,
> All that life hath added unto me,
> This shall endure in immortality."

As science teaches, a particular person is not a discrete individual, but a focus to which converge and from which again diverge many physical and psychical activities. In him have been impressed *samskāras* by heredity, example and education. Only by a process of evolution do *samskāras* come into being. No *samskāra* ever comes into being without a gradual becoming. The whole history of the development of an individual, as observed in a higher organised animal, is a continuous chain of reminiscences of the evolution of all those beings which form the ancestral series of that particular animal. The history of no individual begins with his birth, but has been endless ages in the making. The assumption that each human being starts life for himself and commences a development of his own, as if the thousands of generations before him had been in existence in vain, is in striking discord with the facts of daily life. No human being can be regarded as something supernaturally added to the stock of nature; on the contrary, he must be treated as a new segregation of what already existed. No individual can wholly detach himself from his parent source. "Each one of us bears upon him," as Huxley says, "obvious marks of his parentage, perhaps of remote relationship. More particularly the sum of tendencies to act in a certain way, which we call 'character,' is often to be traced through a long series of progenitors and collaterals. So we may justly say that this 'character'—this moral and intellectual essence of a man—does veritably pass over from one fleshy tabernacle to another, and does really transmigrate from generation to generation. In the new born infant the character of the stock lies latent, and the ego is little more than a bundle of potentialities. But, very early, these become actualities; from childhood to age they manifest themselves in idleness or brightness, weakness or strength, viciousness or uprightness, and with each feature modified by confluence with another character, if by nothing else, character passes on to its incarnation in new bodies."

No human being can completely sever himself from other human beings. Human beings form constituent units of society, not only by reason of the inter-dependence of their divers external functions, but by reason of their mental inter-dependence. Man cannot isolate his mental life from that of his fellowmen. He is ever subject to the influence of the community of which he is a member. He can sever his connection with one circle of men only by joining another. Even a hermit is not alone. He lives psychically in a union conceived in his mind, but none the less real, with an ideal society (of his gods, of his saints) which is formed after the model of real society. It is indeed exclusively through psychical inter-dependence that human existence as such has been possible. It is through the mutual dependence of their minds upon one another that men are civilized, social, and ethical beings. A correct understanding of mental life is not possible with the belief in a substantial soul. He who regards physical separateness as a barrier between centres of psychic life can never understand the possibility of a mental life reaching beyond the individual, although its results are obvious in all that man does in his association with his fellowmen—in language, science, art, religion, and morality. Since men are physically independent of one another, it does not follow that they are also psychically separate from one another. The psychical life continues beyond each individual, because its real subjects are not individuals as such but the bonds uniting individuals. Every deed, every word, every thought is a part of our psychic life, and our psychic life remains unbroken, like an extinct flame that has kindled another.

> "Say not 'I am,' 'I was,' or 'I shall be;'
> Think not ye pass from house to house of flesh.
> Like travellers who remember and forget
> Ill lodged or well lodged. Fresh
> Issues upon the Universe that sum
> Which is the lattermost of lives."

"Do we then live after death?" asks a well-known living writer, and answers as follows: "Of course we do. We *live*. Our bodies dissolve, but our lives continue. What is *we*? And what is to *live*? If to live is to eat and drink, to feel joy and pain, to be conscious of action and thought, we cannot affirm about a state, which, so far as we can see, supposes the absence of a nervous system. For my part, I do not pretend to know what consciousness can be in the absence of a nervous system, for I mean by consciousness an organic state relative to a nervous system. And so far as *we* means this state of consciousness, I have no means of forming a rational opinion on the question.

"Happily we are not nervous systems. Life is not an agitation of the nervous system. We act, we work, we teach, we inspire love in places where we are not, where we have never been, and in souls which we have not seen in the body. We are not as the beasts that perish. And the social nature of man is not bestial. The soul of man has a subtle faculty of incorporating itself with the souls of our fellowmen. We are immortal by virtue of the intricate organism of which we are part. Nervous system, digestive apparatus, and locomotive organs are essential as a basis of life, but in due course that life can be practically continued by the agency of other bodies than those in which it begins. It cannot be continued, so far as we can see, without other like bodies, natures and souls, such as ours, and, therefore, not in Dante's and Milton's Paradise. The organism, man and woman, is mortal truly; but the organism, humanity, is immortal. We know of nothing that can destroy it within the conditions of our solar sphere.

"A good life in the flesh becomes thus incorporated with the mighty organism, and becomes immortal with it. Not an act of ours, not a look, nor a thought, is utterly lost and wasted in space. For good or for evil it forms us, and our character and our work. It forms some other brother or sister near us for good or for bad. If it be strong and noble, it shapes many. If it be weak and evil, it is gradually expunged. It may not be remembered, not recorded and not distinguished. But it continues, eternally pulsating unknown through generations of Humanity. It may be a drop in the ocean of human life. But as surely as every drop which falls on an Alp will pass on ultimately into the ocean, so every human life, every act of life, every kind word, every good deed, every clear thought, lives in the life to come. We live, and we live for ever, the greatest and the feeblest. We do not continue to have nervous sensations; we do not eat and drink; we do not think or act, it may be, and we do not add to our work on earth; but we *live*. Our lives remain here and continue our work. The humanity which nursed us as infants, trained us as children, and shaped our lives as men, prolongs that life in a collective eternity, when it has closed our eyes with reverent sorrow, and said in hope and love the last words over our bones. And it makes us as immortal as itself."

All creatures are such as they are through past *samskāras*, and when they die their lives shape new beings. In the slow process of evolution activities shape new personalities. What is called the person is but the living embodiment of past activities, physical and psychical. Past activities impress upon creatures the nature of their present existence. This is the law of *karma* as understood in Buddhism. No other interpretation of the doctrine of *karma* can be consistent with the teaching of the Blessed One as to the momentaneity (*kshaṇikatva*) and the unsubstantiality (*nairātmya*) of all existing things. That in the personal development of each individual every thought, or feeling, or volition counts for something is not difficult to perceive, but that there is a retribution upon wrong and selfishness after death, when there is no transmigrating *ātman*, can have no meaning and validity apart from the individual's relation to mankind as a whole. Physiologically considered, an individual reincarnates in his progeny, and his physical *karma* is transmitted to them. Ethically considered, the psychic life of an individual cannot be separated from the psychic life of the community of which he is a member. Duty and responsibility have no meaning apart from society. How, then, can a man have *karma* apart from other human beings? The enjoyments and sufferings of an individual are not always the result of his special *karma*. The *Milindapanha* tells us that it is an erroneous extension of the truth when the ignorant declare that "every pain is the fruit of (individual) *karma*." Yet no Buddhist will deny that everything is under the sway of causality. Unless we regard all mankind as linked together as parts of one universal whole, we cannot perceive the full significance of the doctrine of *karma*. Not only are the murderer and the thief responsible to society, but society is equally responsible for breeding such characters. The life of the individual has no other possible measure than that of its significance, its influence, and its value to other individuals. If he demands and hopes more than this, a continuance after death of his own particular life, he merely denies the meaning of his particular individuality. Rightly did Galileo say that those who desired perpetual life deserved to be transformed into mountains. True continuance of life consists in its perfect newness and freshness. But this is possible only through alternations of life and death.

Our view of reincarnation may not be acceptable to those Buddhists, who believe that an unexplained mystery underlies the transmigration of *karma*. Though these do not admit the existence of a transmigrating *ātman*, yet they suppose that a kind of *vignāna*, called the *prati saṁdhi vignāna*, serves in some incognisable manner as a connecting link between a dying man and an infant born just at the moment of his death. "Somewhere, at the moment of a man's death," says a partisan of this school, "there is being born a child of parentage such that the little brain can respond to and absorb the character of the dying man;—a brain that, without just that sort of stimulus, will never be galvanised into individual life. The man dies, and his death perturbs the Æther in the very complex way characteristic of that man;—and at the same instant, almost, a newborn child, hovering then very near to death, receives the impact of the death wave, and its brain thrills to a new life; the heart and respiratory centres are galvanised into action,—the newborn child draws breath and lives, or as our Buddhist scriptures put it, 'the new lamp is lighted from the dying flame.'" Here is a fine example of the fact that materialism and mysticism are twin-sisters. Where mysticism finds no possible hold on perception, it attempts to walk by the crutches of a materialistic imagination. If *prati saṁdhi vignāna* is really a *vignāna*, it is a *dharma*, a *skandha*, and as such it can not pass from one place to another. "*Na kinchi ito paralokam gacchati*:" say the Pali books. What, then, is it that passes from one life to the next? It looks as if *prati saṁdhi vignāna* was originally introduced to explain the phenomena of memory, and then unhappily extended to serve as a connecting link between one life and another in the transmigration of *karma*. Every *vignāna* leaves its impression (*vāsana*) on the subsequent *vignānas*. Though *vignānas* are momentary, they reproduce themselves in a connected series (*pratītyasamutpāda*). As the present *vignāna* of a living person is closely connected with the *vignāna* immediately anterior to it, it is supposed that the *vignāna* at the time of birth (*aupapattyaṁçika*) of one individual must be similarly connected with the *vignāna* which disappears at the time of death (*māraṇāntika*) of another individual. But such a supposition is not warranted by facts. As the Blessed One has said, "*dharma* is the refuge, and not *pudgala* (soul); the spirit is the refuge, and not the letter; the completed meaning of a *sutra* is the refuge, and not its provisional sense; *gnāna* is the refuge, and not *vignāna*."

It is said that in Buddhist countries children sometimes claim to have had such-and-such a name and to have lived in such-and-such a place, in their previous lives; and that occcasionally their claims are in a way substantiated. But does this fact prove that there necessarily exists a sort of syntony between a dying man's consciousness and the brain of an infant born just at the moment of his death? Should we not rather look for the explanation of these Burmese *Winzas* to subconscious processes? "By their brooding and incubation," says Dr. Stanley Hall, "the conscious person communes with the species, and perhaps even the genus to which he belongs; receives messages from and perchance occasionally gives them to it, appeals to mighty soul powers not his own, but which are so wise, benignant, and energetic that he is perhaps prone to the pathetic fallacy of interpreting the subhuman as superhuman, if, like the English Psychic Researchers, he has no intimation of the wisdom, depth below depth, that has been organised into our bodies, brains, automatisms, and instincts, which is vastly and incomparably greater than all that is in the consciousness of all men now living combined, and if he deems the surface phenomena in his own sapient soul to be its essential experience. This is the larger self, if such an anthropomorphizing, self-idolatrous term may be used, with which we are continuous. It is beneath, and not above us, immanent and not transcendent, and if only rightly interpreted it is veridicial in a sense and degree our voluble ratiocination knows not of."*

The Buddhist doctrine of *karma* is very wide in its scope. *Karma* operates not only in the sphere of sentient life, but extends over the whole of phenomenal existence *(prapancha)*. *Karmajam lokavaichitryam iti siddhatvāt.* In his *Outlines of Mahāyāna* Mr. Kuroda explains the scope of the Buddhist doctrine of *karma* as follows: "There are neither creators nor created; nor are men real beings. It is actions and causes that, under favourable conditions, give birth to them. For men are nothing more than the temporary combination of the five *skandhas*, or constituents. The beginning of this combination is their birth; its decomposition their death. During the continuation of the combined state, good and bad actions are done, seeds of future happi-

* Adolescence, Vol. II., p. 342.

ness and pain are sown, and thus the alternation of birth and death goes on without end. Men are no real beings that wander between birth and death by themselves, nor is there any ruler that makes them do this, but it is their own actions that bring about these results. The aggregate actions of all sentient beings give birth to the varieties of mountains, rivers, countries, &c. They are caused by aggregate actions, and so they are called *adhipatiphala* (aggregate fruits). As those who are virtuous at heart are never wicked in their countenance, and as in the countries where good customs prevail, good omens appear and where people are wicked, calamities arise, so men's aggregate actions bring forth their aggregate fruits. By the particular actions of individuals, each man receives mind and body corresponding to the causes at work, internal causes of actions being favoured by external conditions. And as these good and bad actions yield fruits, not when they are produced, but at some future time, they are called *vipākaphala* (fruits that ripen at some future time). The period from birth to death in which the body continues, is the life of man; and that from formation to destruction in which they assume similar forms, is the duration of countries, mountains, rivers, etc. The death of sentient beings as well as the formation and destruction of countries, mountains, rivers, etc., are endless in their operation. Like the circle which has no end, they also have neither beginning nor end. Though there exist neither real (substantial) men nor real things, yet effects appear and disappear where actions are accompanied with conditions, just as the echo follows the sound; and all things, rough or fine, large or small, come and go every moment without any fixed forms. Men and things, therefore, are mere names for durations in which similar forms continue. Our present life is the reflection of past actions. Men consider these reflections as their real selves. Their eyes, noses, ears, tongues, and bodies, as well as their gardens, woods, farms, residences, servants, and maids, men imagine to be their own possessions, but in fact they are but results endlessly produced by innumerable actions."

The Buddhistic doctrine of *karma* differs totally from

the Brahmanic theory of transmigration. Brahmanism teaches the transmigration of a real soul, an *ātman*, but the Dharma inculcates a mere succession of *karmas*. According to the Brahmanic conceptions the soul migrates from man to one or other of the so-called six kingdoms *(shadgatis)*, from man to animal, from animal to hell, from hell to heaven and so forth, just as a man migrates from one house to another according to his necessities. It may indeed be true that in the Buddhist sutras also there are references to a transmigration to one or other of the 'ten worlds'—heaven and hell,* gods and demons, men and animals, *sravakas* and *pratyekabuddhas*, *bodhisatvas* and *buddhas*, but this does not mean that any being passes from one world to another. "*Na kas chid dharmo asmāl lokāt paralokam gacchati*": says a Buddhist Sutra. In the Buddhistic sense transmigration is only a manifestation of cause and effect. Only by virtue of causes and conditions are produced mental phenomena accompanied by bodily forms, and thus results life after life, the nature and character of the successive lives being determined by the goodness or badness of the mental phenomena. It is to explain and illustrate the transmigration of *karma* to the ordinary man that the Blessed One employed the expression 'ten worlds,' while really he meant by the 'ten worlds' nothing more than the ten mental states typified by the beings and places referred to.

While the Dharma lays stress upon *karma* as the effect of past deeds, good or bad, it must not be forgotten that it also lays equal stress on the liberating power of education, on the perfectability of human nature by means of self-culture and self-control. Buddhism is no fatalism. Fatalism teaches that everything, including also the human will, has been predetermined. It pre-supposes the existence of a person whose will is constrained by an external power. Hence a man's character cannot be improved by education. On the other hand, Buddhism teaches that man himself is a product of causes. Hence his will cannot exist previous

* For the true Buddhist heaven and hell are not realities (*svabhāvasambhūta*). They are fanciful creations of the ignorant (*bālapṛthag-anair asadviparyūsavirachitaḥ svavikalpasambhutaḥ*.)

to his formation by these causes. Instead of being constrained by them, his will is made by them. Accordingly, the will can be made to acquire, by proper training, the power to repress the evil impulses. As fatalism regards a man's character as compelled, it can furnish no motive for action, and personal responsibility is out of the question. For the Buddhist, on the other hand, the innate character is caused, and therefore furnishes the strongest motive for action. The Buddhist knows exactly what is meant by the reign of law in the universe. There are not first laws, and then things and phenomena subject to them. Laws represent the forms in which the relations of things are conceived by the human mind under generalised or simplified circumstances. The human mind is, therefore, the proper lawgiver to the universe. Hence, the submission to *karma*, which Buddhism ascribes to action, is not a blind, but a discriminating submission. *Karma* is in form a creation of the mind, which makes action (*mano vāk kāya karma*) itself a *smṛtyupasthāna*, an object of meditation. Accordingly a man is responsible for his actions, though his volitions are determined by causes. By the avoidance of all evil and the practice of the *pāramitās*, it is possible to attain

> "that realm on earth,
> Where one may stand and be free from an evil deed absolved."

Death is the dissolution of mind and body. Yet the person that dies continues to live in his deeds. One's deeds are like the children born to him; they live and act apart from his will. Nay, children may be strangled, but deeds never. Wherever a man's words, thoughts, deeds have impressed themselves in other minds, there he has reincarnated. He that has no clear idea of death, and does not master the fact that death everywhere consists in the dissolution of the groups (*skandhas*), comes, as Buddhagosha says, to a variety of conclusions, such as 'A living entity dies and transmigrates into another's body'; and similarly, he that has no clear idea of rebirth and does not master the fact that the appearance of the groups (*skandhas*) everywhere constitutes birth, he comes to a variety of conclusions, such as 'A living entity is born and has obtained a new body.' There is not a being that is born, or acts and enjoys itself, or suffers and dies, or is reborn to die again, but simply birth, action, enjoyment, suffering and death take place. The life activities, the deeds alone are real, and these are preserved and nothing else. Therefore, has it been said :—

"No doer is there does the deed,
Nor is there one who feels the fruit;
Constituent parts alone roll on;
This view alone is orthodox.

"And thus the deed, and thus the fruit
Roll on and on, each from its cause;
As of the round of tree and seed,
No one can tell when they began.

"Nor is the time to be perceived
In future births when they shall cease,
The heretics perceive not this
And fail of mastery o'er themselves.

"'An ego,' say they, 'doth exist,
Eternal, or that soon will cease;'
Thus two and sixty heresies
They amongst themselves discordant hold.

"Bound in the bonds of heresy
By passion's flood they're borne along;
And borne along by passion's flood
From misery find they no release.

"If once these facts he but perceive,
A man whose faith on Buddha rests
The subtle, deep, and self-devoid
Dependence will then penetrate.

"Not in its fruit is found the deed,
Nor in the deed finds one the fruit;
Of each the other is devoid,
Yet there is no fruit without the deed.

"Just as no store of fire is found
In jewel, cow-dung, or the sun
Nor separate from these exists,
Yet short of fuel no fire is known.

"Even so we ne'er within the deed
Can retribution's fruit descry,
Nor yet in any place without;
Nor can in fruit the deed be found.

"Deeds separate from their fruits exist
And fruits are separate from the deeds;
But consequent upon the deed
The fruit doth into being come.

"No god of Heaven or Brahma world
Doth cause the endless round of birth;
Constituent parts alone roll on
From cause and material sprung."—*Visuddhi-Magga.**

---

* Warren's Buddhism in translations.

THE SUMMUM BONUM.

ANITYA, *anātman* and *nirvāṇa* have been rightly called the three corner-stones of Buddhism. They form the three cardinal principles of the Dharma. Any system of thought which accepts these three fundamental tenets may properly claim identity with Buddhism, whatever may be the adventitious beliefs and practices which hide them. But no system of thought, that does not recognise these three principles, can lay any claim to kinship with the Dharma.

What, then, is the meaning of these three principles? *Anitya* means impermanence. It signifies that all things are in a perpetual flux. All things lived through, all *erlebnisse*, as the Germans call them, are transient and impermanent. Nothing is permanent in the universe but change. Mutability is the very characteristic of all existence (*visvam kshaṇabhanguram*). Only non-existence, *çunyata*, can claim to be immutable. Permanent unchanging substances exist in our thought, but not in reality. Whatsoever exists is made up of colours, sounds, temperatures, spaces, times, pressures, ideas, emotions, volitions, and so forth, connected with one another in manifold ways. And these are continually changing. Everything is therefore momentary (*kshanika*). Some things may be relatively more permanent than others, but nothing is absolutely permanent. It is the mistaking of what is impermanent for something permanent that makes *anitya* the source of sorrow (*duhkha*).

What is *anitya* is not necessarily *mithya* or illusory, as some have supposed. That which is momentary might prove deceptive, and thus become a source of sorrow, when mistaken for something *nitya* or permanent, for no deliverance of consciousness is in itself complete. The fragmentary character of a single deliverance of consciousness will naturally mislead, if it is not controlled and rectified by other deliverances of consciousness. When the traveller in the desert sees before him a large expanse of water, which continually recedes and finally disappears, proving to be the effect of mirage, it is not the deliverance of consciousness that is deceptive. The characters that suggest the sheet of water are really present, but the deception arises from the failure to take into account all the facts. Similarly, when a man mistakes a rope for a snake, it is not the deliverance of consciousness that is at fault. The characters that suggest the snake are really there in the rope, but the failure to interrogate consciousness exhaustively gives rise to the deception. Were all experience deceptive, how could we know it to be deceptive? The fact that we are able to distinguish between deception and truth shows that all experience is not illusory. Nor can dreams cast doubt on the experiences of the waking state. The difference of conditions in the two states is so evident that the ordinary man finds no reason for confounding the one with the other. Even the Vedāntin, who would reduce everything to mere illusion (*māya*), regards the creations of the dreaming state to be refuted by the waking state.

The logical consequence of the doctrine of *anitya* is the principle of *anātmata*. This principle lays down that nowhere in the universe, neither in the macrocosm nor in the microcosm, there is an unconditioned, absolute, transcendent entity or substratum. All that we know consists of a flux of sensations, ideas, emotions, volitions, and so forth, associated with one another in various ways. Out of this fleeting complex texture rises into prominence that which is relatively more fixed and permanent, and impresses itself on the memory, and finds expression in language. Certain of these complexes of relatively greater permanency are called bodies, and special names are given to them. Hence colours, sounds, tastes,and other sensations are not produced by bodies, but complexes of these sensations make up bodies. Sensations are not signs by which we recognise things, but a thing is a mental construct or symbol of a relatively fixed complex of sensations. Such complexes are never absolutely permanent. Nor is there behind and beyond these sensations, these elements of experience, any *prakriti*, *pradhāna*, or *ding an sich.* Still this does not imply that things are illusory or unreal. They are at least as real as the minds that perceive them.

Among the many comparatively permanent complexes we find a complex of memories, volitions, emotions, ideas, aspirations, linked to a particular body, which is called the ego or "I." But even the ego, as we have already seen, is only relatively permanent. If the ego appears to be permanent, it is because the changes that occur in the elements, or the *skandhas*, which constitute the "I," are comparatively slow. The mere fact that there is a consciousness of identity does not prove the existence of an *ātman*, which is the witness or possessor of sensations, ideas, &c. When a man says that he has the sensation hot, it only means that the element of experience called hot occurs in a given group of other elements, such as sensations, memories, ideas, &c., (*rupa, vedana, vignāna, samgnā, samskāra*). When he ceases to have any sensation, that is to say, when he dies, then the groups, the *skandhās*, are dissolved, the elements no longer occur in their ordinary accustomed grouping or association. That is all. What has really ceased to exist is a unity constructed, as already pointed out, for economical and practical purposes (*samvriti* or *vyavahārika*), not a transcendental (*pāramārthika*) unity. The ego is not a mysterious, unchangeable unity. Each individual knows what changes his ego is undergoing. Knowing the mutability of the ego each one of us is striving to alter its attributes and improve it.

The unity of consciousness cannot be explained by the numerical unity of an underlying *ātman*. As Hermann Lotze has pointed out in his *Metaphysic*, the attempt to explain the unity of consciousness by the unity of an underlying substance is a process of reasoning, which not only fails to reach an admissible aim, but also has no aim at all. The ego is simply a group of elements, such as sensations, ideas, memories, emotions, volitions, &c., more strongly connected with one another among themselves, and less strongly knitted to the elements of other groups of the same kind, that is to say, to other individuals. But if we regard the ego as a numerical unity, which has volitions, ideas, sensations, &c., as a mysterious entity behind the *skandhas*, we must necessarily involve ourselves in a dilemma. Either one must set over against one's ego a world of unknowable entities, or one must regard the whole world, together with the egos of all other individuals, as products of one's own ego. The former procedure would serve no purpose but writing the unknowables with a capital U to terrify ignorant folk, and the latter is not followed by the solipsist himself in practical life.

There is nothing permanent in the ego, and it is therefore incapable of being saved. Partly the intuitive knowledge of this fact and partly the fear of it have been the prolific mother of the many optimistic, religious, and philosophical aberrations and absurdities. After deep thought and psychological analysis (*vibhajja sāstra*) the Blessed One recognised that all false doctrines invariably have their source in the *ātman* conception, whether it be a belief in the existence of a *jīvātman* (ego-soul), or a belief in the existence of an impersonal *brahman* (*or paramātman*) in things. It is the *ātman* conception that makes the ordinary man (*prthakjana*) regard the impermanent as permanent, and thus gives birth to all the sorrows of this world. As the *Bodhicharyāvatāra* says, " *ātmānam aparityajya duhkham tyaktum na çakyate.*" Without renouncing the *ātman* we cannot get rid of sorrow. Only when the craving for individual immortality is destroyed, will one be able to arrive at a freer and more enlightened view of life, which will not permit of the over-estimation of one's own ego in utter disregard of other egos.

This brief discussion of the principles of *anitya* and *anātmata* would have prepared the reader for a better understanding of the true import of *Nirvāṇa.* There are in vogue two false views concerning Nirvāṇa, which have first to be combated. Some think that Nirvāṇa is a state in which the individual soul is completely absorbed in the universal soul, just in the same way as the Vedanta philosophy of the Brahmans understands it. By others it is regarded as the annihilation of all activities (*chittavrittinirodha,* *nichtergendetwasheit*), in which love, life, and everything become extinct. As regards the first view we need only say that it is radically different from the true conception of Nirvāṇa. Buddhism denies a soul as well as an Absolute. How could it teach communion with, or absorption in, such a mysterious being as Brahman? In the *Tevigga Sutta* the Blessed One likens those who believe in Brahman, and seek a union with it to a man, who builds a staircase at the junction of four roads to mount up to a high mansion, which he can neither see nor know where it is, how it is, what it is built of, nor whether it exists at all. The Brāhmans base their authority on the Vedas, and the Vedas rest on the authority of their composers, and these authors rely on the authority of Brahma Prajāpati. They are like a string of blind men clinging to one another and leading one another, and their method of salvation is nothing but adoration, worship, and prayer. The Vedantic doctrine is clothed in high sounding words, but it contains no truth. The follower of the Vedanta, says the Blessed One, is like the monkey at the lake which tries to catch the moon in the water mistaking the reflection for the reality.

The second view may seem to accord better with the literal meaning of the word *Nirvāṇa*. Nirvaṇa is derived from *nir*, absence, and *vāta*, wind. The suffix *ta* is changed into *na*, if the word is not meant to apply to *vāta*, wind. Though references to *Nirvāṇa* may not be wanting in Brahmanical works, the technical sense in which the term is employed is undoubtedly due to the Buddha and his followers. In the Upanishads and the philosophical works of the Brāhmans we come across such terms as *amrita*, *moksha*, *mukti*, *nihçreyasa*, *kaivalya*, *apavarga* as Sanskrit equivalents for salvation, but it is only in the ancient Pāli and Sanskrit works on Buddhism that the word Nirvāṇa is frequently employed to mean salvation. The meaning of Nirvāṇa as employed by the Buddha would seem to be connected with the state of a flame that has been blown out. Whatever may be the literal meaning of the term Nirvāṇa, the life of the Blessed One gives the lie direct to the view that Nirvaṇa is the annihilation of all activities. Sākyasimha attained *bodhi* at the age of thirty-five, and he spent the remaining forty-five years of his life in active preaching and doing good. Nirvāṇa cannot therefore mean the annihilation of all activities. On the one side it is the destruction of the three fires of lust, hatred and ignorance; and on the other side it is the perfection of all human excellences. If it is annihilation, it is annihilation through growth. Just as the seed becomes annihilated by its growth into the tree, so does egoism become extinguished by its development into altruism. If Nirvāṇa meant nothing more than the annihilation of all activities, suicide would be the best and quickest means of making an end of suffering and sorrow. But to one who has understood the true nature of the ego and *karma*, the absurdity of this conclusion is obvious. Suicide sets an example which will bear evil fruit in the hearts of others. Being a cause of consternation and unrest, how could suicide lead to the cessation of suffering? Suicide is the result either of madness, or of egotism. It is due either to some temporary aberration of the intellect, or to a strong desire to protect one's life against certain dangers that threaten it. The suicide throws himself into the arms of death, because he fears some impending emotional or physical disturbance. Under no circumstances, therefore, could suicide conduce to the attainment of Nirvāṇa, though there might be nothing objectionable in a holy man who has attained Nirvāṇa voluntarily giving up his life, when he finds it no longer useful to others.

In its negative aspect Nirvāṇa is the extinction of the three fires of lust, hatred, and ignorance. The commentator on the *Jātakas* says: "By what can every heart attain to lasting happiness? And to him whose heart was estranged from sin the answer came: 'When the fire of lust is gone out, peace (*nibbuta*) is gained; when the fires of hatred and ignorance are gone out, then peace is gained; when the troubles of mind arising from pride, credulity and all other sins have ceased, then peace is gained.'" On the extinction of these three fires there result the perfect sinless peace of purity, good will, and wisdom. As Asvagosha says, "when in this wise the principle and the condition of defilement, their products and the mental disturbances are all annihilated, it is said that we attain to *Nirvāṇa*, and that various spontaneous displays of activity are accomplished." The evil inclinations cannot be annihilated without the simultaneous development of the moral and intellectual powers. How could all evil be destroyed without acquiring the supreme virtues which characterise Buddhahood? When all thought of self is annihilated, the holy man becomes the very embodiment of the virtues of generosity, kindliness, morality, renunciation, wisdom, forbearance, truthfulness, fortitude, resoluteness and equanimity. The man who has attained Nirvāṇa represents the perfect embodiment of Truth, not so much in respect of the scientific knowledge of things, but in its realization in a moral and virtuous life. "Just as a lotus flower of glorious, pure, and high descent and origin," says Nāgasena in the *Milindapanha*, "is glossy, soft, desirable, sweet-smelling, longed-for, loved, and praised, untarnished by the water or the mud, crossed with tiny petals and filaments and pericarps, the resort of many bees, a child of the clear cold stream, just so, is that disciple of the Noble One ....endowed with the thirty graces." "And if you ask, how is Nibbaṇa to be known? It is by freedom from distress and danger, by confidence, by peace, by calm, by bliss, by happiness, by delicacy, by purity, by freshness......"

Though Nirvā*n*a is the annihilation of all egotism, it does not imply the annihilation of personality. Annihilation of personality can occur in life only with the cessation of all consciousness, as in a swoon or in dreamless sleep. It is the Vedānta doctrine that teaches that "at the time of deep sleep the soul becomes one with the highest Brahman," and that "the state of senselessness (in swooning, &c.) is a half union with Brahman." The Dharma, on the contrary, gives no room for such a view, but distinctly declares such ideas to be mere madness. Bodhi, which is but another name for Nirvāṇa, is characterized by the seven qualities of zeal, wisdom, reflection, investigation, joy, peace, and serenity. Can these qualities be present where there is no consciousness? The very first of the thirty graces with which the perfect man is endowed is a heart full of affectionate, soft and tender love. The holy man who has attained Nirvāna lives and works, not for himself, but for others. Instead of being the absolute non-existence as some people think Nirvāṇa to be, it is really a life of perpetual fellowship in the pure atmosphere of truth, goodness, freedom and enlightenment. While Nirvāṇa is the annihilation of all thought of self, it is at the same time the complete attainment of perfect love and righteousness. In short, it is the realization in the thought and life of man of those necessary conditions which constitute perfect humanity.

It is often supposed that the man who has attained Nirvāṇa or Buddhahood is not bound by the law of *karma*. This is a mistake having its source in a confusion between the Buddhist ideal of an Arahat and the Hindu ideal of a Jīvanmukta. The Hindus think that the perfect sage is subject to no moral law. As Ānandagiri says, he may do good and evil for the rest of his days as he pleases, and incur no stain. Ānandagiri's view is supported by such texts as the following: "He that knows the truth is sullied neither by good actions nor by evil actions." "If he sees the unity of all things, he is unaffected alike whether he offers a hundred horse sacrifices or kill hundreds of holy Brahmans." "He whom nobody knows either as noble or ignoble, as ignorant or learned, as well-conducted or ill-conducted, he is a Brāhmaṇa. Quietly devoted to his duty, let the wise man pass through life unknown; let him step on this earth as if he were blind, unconscious, deaf." Such views are the logical outcome of the pantheistic doctrines of the Vedanta philosophy. If everything in the universe is nothing but a manifestation of the universal soul, how can anything or act be unclean or immoral? This is how the Hindu Aghorpanthi defends his disgustingly repulsive acts. But the Buddhist is no Vedantin. The Buddhist Arahat sees danger in the smallest offence. If he is to remain on the heights to which he has climbed, he cannot afford to neglect the steps by which he has risen. "In brief, the welfare of all beings at all times, pious and unworldly gifts, the mind characterized by true enlightenment—these increase one's holiness. Perfection lies in self-denial; it comes by never leaving watchfulness, by full understanding, by mindfulness, and deepest thought."* Hence the Arahat must always

"...... make virtue his only store,
And restless appetite restrain,
Beat meditation's drum, and sore
His watch against each sense maintain."

* Kārikās of the S'ikshāsamuchchaya.

All that man aspires and desires to attain through religion might in its essentials be reduced to three points : peace and tranquillity of mind ; fortitude and consolation in adversity ; hope in death. In Buddhism all these are attained through Nirvāṇa. The ordinary man seeks his rest and peace in God. For him all questions find their answer in God. But it is entirely different with the Buddhist. Buddhism denies an Isvara, and the latter cannot, therefore, be its goal and resting point. The Buddhist's goal is Buddhahood, and the essence of Buddhahood is Dharmakāya, the totality of all those laws which pervade the facts of life, and whose living recognition constitutes enlightenment. Dharmakāya is the most comprehensive name with which the Buddhist sums up his understanding and also his feeling about the universe. Dharmakāya signifies that the universe does not appear to the Buddhist as a mere mechanism, but as pulsating with life. Further, it means that the most striking fact about the universe is its intellectual aspect and its ethical order, specially in its higher reaches. Nay more, it implies that the universe is one in essence, and nowhere chaotic or dualistic.

> "Before beginning, and without end
> As space eternal and as surety sure,
> Is fixed a power divine which moves to good,
> Only its laws endure" :—*Light of Asia*, Book VIII.

Dharmakāya is no pitiable abstraction, but that aspect of existence which makes the world intelligible, which shows itself in cause and effect, in the blessedness that follows righteousness, and in the cursedness that comes from evil-doing. Dharmakāya is that presence which is forming the world in every detail, revealing itself most completely in man's rational will and moral aspirations. Though not an individual person like man, though not a limited being of a particular cast of mind, Dharmakāya is the condition of all personality. Without Dharmakāya there would be nothing that constitutes personality, no reason, no science, no moral aspiration, no ideal, no aim and purpose in man's life. In short, Dharmakāya is

> "The warp and woof of all that lives and moves ;
> The light whose smile kindles the universe ;

> The beauty which pervades all things and beings;
> The germ of goodness which, dwelling in all,
> From life's minute beginnings up at last
> To man, unfolds itself in loving deeds;
> Nay, the spirit of truth which inspires all
> With courage and hope in the fight for right."

Dharmakāya is the norm of all existence, the standard of truth, the measure of righteousness, the good law. Owing to the limitations of our knowledge and the imperfection of our goodness we may not yet know all about Dharmakāya. But we know enough about it to make it our guide in life. Like a cloud shedding its waters without distinction, Dharmakāya encompasses all with the light of comprehension. Though the great cloud full of rain comes up in this wide world covering all lands and seas, and pours down its rain everywhere, over all grasses, shrubs, herbs, trees of various species, families of plants of different names growing on the earth, on the hills, on the mountains, or in the valleys, yet the grasses, shrubs, herbs, and wild trees, though sucking the same water, all of one essence, poured down abundantly by the same great cloud, grow according to their karma, and acquire a proportionate development and bigness, shooting up and producing blossoms and fruits in their season. Similarly, though Dharmakāya is the same for all, different creatures appropriate in different ways the norms of truth and follow differently the light of Dharmakaya. Each creature has originated from unconscious potentialities through its own blind impulses; each one, in its own field of experience, has learned the lesson of life in its own way. Each one is responsible to itself, and no one can blame another for what he is and has become.

Dharmakāya is not a god who asserts himself, and calls sin what is contrary to his will. Dharmakāya does not say to man: "I am the almighty ruler of the universe; you are my special favourite, I have given you the highest place of all in the universe, and you can get still further privileges if you obey my commands and pay me tithes." Dharmakāya neither loves to be addressed in prayer nor delights in listening to the praises of worshippers. Dharmakāya is not a self-conscious individual whose creatures we are. We are largely creatures of our own making. Pondering on the problems of life and death the Blessed One recognised that life starts in unknown non-conscious potentialities with blind impulses, and that life's start is its own doing. It is this unconscious potency from which life starts, not knowing its whither, that is at the bottom of all evil. In his formula of *ādhyātmika pratītya samutpāda* the Blessed One has succinctly expounded the various links (*nidānās*) in the chain of causation that leads to the full development of life as manifested in human beings. In the beginning there is unconscious potentiality (*avidya*); and in this nebulosity of undefined life the formative and organising propensities (*samskāras*) shape crude formless aggregates. From the materials thus produced originate organisms possessing awareness, sensibility and irritability (*vignāna*). From these develops self-consciousness, the unity which differentiates self from not-self, and makes organisms live as individual beings (*nāma rupa*). With self-consciousness begins the exploration of the six fields of experience (*shadāyatanas*), belonging to the five senses and the mind. The exploration of the six fields brings about the contact (*sparsa*) with the external world. The perception of the external world and the exercise of the senses and the mind thereon leads to the experience of different kinds of pleasure and pain (*vēdana*). The experience of pleasure and pain generates in the individualised being, through not knowing its own nature, a grasping desire (*trishnā*) for its own individual satisfaction. The thirst for obtaining egoistic satisfaction induces a cleaving (*upādāna*) to worldly pleasures. The indulgence in worldly pleasures produces the growth and continuation of self-hood (*bhava*). Self-assertion manifests itself in incessant changes or births (*jāti*), and these incessant changes, looked at selfishly, become the sources of sorrow connected with sickness, old age and death (*jarāmaraṇa*). These give birth to lamentation, anxiety and despair.

Thus, the cause of all sorrow lies at the very source; it lies in the unconscious blind impulses with which life starts. When these blind impulses are checked and controlled, the wrong appetences born of them will no longer have sway;

with the removal of these wrong appetences the wrong perception begotten by them will be wiped out. When the wrong understanding of the world is wiped out, the egoistic errors peculiar to individualization will cease, and with the cessation of these the illusions of the six fields will disappear. If the illusions of the six fields disappear, sense experience will no longer produce misconception. When no misconceptions arise in the mind, all grasping desires will cease, and with the disappearance of these will arise freedom from morbid cleaving and indulgence. When morbid cleaving and indulgence do not exist, the selfishness of selfhood disppears. When this selfishness is annihilated, there will be Nirvāṇa, the complete escape from all sorrow arising from birth, disease, old age, and death and ignorance and evil desires.

It is therefore clear that the fate of each one of us rests in his own hands. If life is associated with suffering, no being has a right to blame another, much less Dharmakāya. It is not Dharmakāya that permits beings to suffer innocently for conditions which they did not create themselves. Life's suffering is life's own doing. He who knows the nature of life must not be afraid of suffering; he must bear its ills nobly. If he avails himself of the light of Dharmakāya, the essence of Buddhahood, and follows the Noble Eightfold Path, he can escape the suffering that is associated with life, and arrive at the blissful haven of Nirvāṇa.

He who has attained Nirvāṇa cannot live a life of selfhood, confined to the attainment of individual satisfaction. As the *Bodhicharyāvatāra* says, it is with the desire to make all beings happy that one desires to attain bodhi. Not only does the white-souled tranquil Arahat shrink from sin, but he is always devoted to the doing of good. Not only does he "exhale the most excellent and unequalled scented savour of the righteousness of life," but his heart is full of affectionate, soft and tender love. He may have no desires for himself, but he works for the good of all beings. His moral consciousness is wholly objectified, and is free from all subjective taints. He identifies himself with all that is good and noble. He extends his kindness to all beings. His sympathies are universal. His compassion is so far-reaching that it excludes none, not even those who hate and despise him. Just as a mother, at the risk of her own life, protects her only child, so does he who has attained Nirvāṇa cultivate good will beyond measure among all beings, toward the whole world, unstinted and unmixed with any feeling of making distinctions or showing preferences. The removal of the infinite pain of the world is his highest felicity. He remains steadfastly in this state of mind, "the best in the world," as the *Metta Sutta* says, all the while he is awake, whether he be standing, waking, sitting, or lying down. He is always in

> "That state of peace wherein the roots
> Of ever fresh rebirths are all destroyed, and greed
> And hatred and delusion all have ceased;
> That state from lust for future life set free
> That changeth not, can ne'er be led to change."

This is the *Sukhavaṭi*, where dwell boundless light (*Amitābha*) and infinite life (*Amitāyus*). When the Arahat dies, the skandhas which constitute his individuality dissolve, but he still lives. In the Nirvāṇa of life he may not be free from the ills naturally concomitant to a bodily life, but in *parinirvaṇa*, the Nirvāṇa of death, he has gone to a realm free from such ills. He has attained to "a state which is unborn, unoriginated, uncreated, and unformed, a state where there is neither earth nor water, nor heat nor air, neither infinity of space nor infinity of consciousness, nor nothingness, nor perception nor non-perception, neither this world nor another world." He has become one with those eternal verities of which he was an embodiment in life. *Le Bouddha "vide de natur proper" est eternite, amour et misericorde.* We may not look for him in any material form, or seek him in any audible sound. But whosoever sees the Dharma sees the Buddha. He is ever in the Dharmakāya, the womb of all Tathāgatas, that divine spirit of universal compassion and wisdom which carries humanity in its onward and upward march to truth and moral loveliness.

> "All mankind is his shrine.
> Seek him henceforward in the good and wise,
> In happy thoughts and blissful emotions,
> In kind words and sublime serenity,
> And in the rapture of the loving deed.

There seek him if you would not seek in vain,
There in the struggle for justice and right,
In the sacrifice of self for the all,
In the joy and calm repose of the heart,
Yea and for ever in the human mind
Made better and more beauteous by his word."